Richard Brown

EXPLORATIONS IN SOCIOLOGY

BSA Conference Volumes Series

Series Standing Order

If you would like to receive future titles in this series as they are published, you can make use of our standing order facility. To place a standing order please contact your bookseller or, in case of difficulty, write to us at the address below with your name and address and the name of the series. Please state with which title you wish to begin your standing order. (If you live outside the UK we may not have the rights for your area, in which case we will forward your order to the publisher concerned.)

Standing Order Service, Macmillan Distribution Ltd, Houndmills, Basingstoke, Hampshire, RG21 2XS, England.

THE EXPERIENCE OF UNEMPLOYMENT

Edited by Sheila Allen,
Alan Waton, Kate Purcell and Stephen Wood

First published 1986

Published by
THE MACMILLAN PRESS LTD
Houndmills, Basingstoke, Hampshire RG21 2XS
and London
Companies and representatives
throughout the world

Printed in Hong Kong

British Library Cataloguing in Publication Data
The Experience of unemployment.—
(Explorations in sociology)
1. Unemployment—Great Britain
I. Allen, Sheila   II. British Sociological
Association   III. Series
331.13'7941   HD5765.A6
ISBN 0-333-39693-6
ISBN 0-333-39694-4 Pbk

Contents

List of Tables

List of Figures

Acknowledgements

Earlier drafts of the chapters in this and the companion volume, *The Changing Experience of Employment: Restructuring and Recession* (Purcell *et al.*, 1986), with the exception of the editors' introductions, were originally presented at the British Sociological Association's annual conference on *Work, Employment and Unemployment* held at the University of Bradford in April 1984. The numbers who attended, the quantity and variety of papers given and the quality of debate all testified to the importance with which social scientists treat this issue. The material in this book and its sister volume was selected to produce two thematic collections, representative of the conference and of ongoing sociological research on work, employment and unemployment and we regret that the demands of thematic coherence forced us to exclude several excellent contributions. The editors would like to thank the authors for the time and effort that they have spent revising their papers for publication. Finally, we are grateful for the help, unfailing good humour and efficiency of Win Healy and Judith Hammond of the University of Bradford, who transformed successive, much-annotated drafts into elegant and accurate typescript.

The editors and publishers would like to thank Tieto Ltd for permission to publish Table 3.1 'Rates of unemployment of males and females' from *Economica*, 3 (1936).

Notes on the Contributors

Sheila Allen is Professor of Sociology at the University of Bradford. She has published extensively in the areas of ethnic relations, gender and work and is currently researching homeworking and social change in coal-mining areas.

Patricia Allatt is a Research Fellow in the School of Education, University of Durham. Formerly a teacher, she studied sociology at University College, Cardiff and the University of Keele, where she was employed as a Research Fellow then Lecturer. She has published on the youth service, crime prevention and family ideology. Her current research is on attitudes to the police and children's perceptions of other cultures.

Colin Bell has held the post of Social Scientist in the University of Leicester Medical School since 1985 and is working on social gerontology projects. During the previous ten years he was Professor of Sociology at the Universities of Aston and New South Wales and held visiting chairs at Madison: Wisconsin and La Trobe.

Avtar Brah is a Lecturer at the University of London. She has worked with the Greater London Council and has been a Lecturer at the Open University. She has also held research posts at the Universities of Leicester and Bristol.

Sarah Buckland is currently working as a Social Researcher in the Department of Sociology, University of Surrey, on a large collaborative project involving Universities and Industry. The project is funded by the Science and Engineering Research Council and the Alvey Directorate of the Department of Trade and Industry, and is concerned with developing a computer system that would enable potential claimants to obtain advice and assistance in claiming welfare benefits.

Bob Coles is a Lecturer in Sociology at the University of York. Since 1982 he has been engaged in a research project on young people in local labour markets in collaboration with a County Council in rural England. His other interests include the sociology of leisure, especially youth culture, and methodology for social research.

Jennifer Hurstfield is a Senior Lecturer in Sociology at the City of London Polytechnic where she teaches women's studies and social policy. She has done research on part-time employment and low pay, and is currently researching women's employment in Britain since the First World War.

Susanne MacGregor is Senior Lecturer in Political Sociology, Birkbeck College, University of London. Author of *The Politics of Poverty*, Longman, 1981 and joint author of *Dealing with Drug Misuse: Crisis Intervention in the City*, Tavistock, 1984. Current work focuses on the politics of social reform, comparative urban studies and 'the underclass' in contemporary London.

Lorna McKee is District Health Education Officer for Kidderminster and District Health Authority. Previously she has held research posts at Aston and York Universities and has undertaken research on aspects of family life and parenthood with a particular interest in gender divisions. Recent publications include work on fathers and childbirth, paternity leave and research methodology. Her current interests include women's health and mental health promotion.

Ray Pahl is Research Professor in Sociology at the University of Kent at Canterbury. He has considerable experience of empirical research in a variety of contexts from commuter villages to the Boards of major British companies. More recently his work has focused on a range of working-class categories including the long-term unemployed. His books include *Urbs in Rure* (1965), *Whose City?* (1975) and *Divisions of Labour* (1984).

Stephen Platt is a Research Sociologist and member of the nonclinical scientific staff at the MRC Unit for Epidemiological Studies in Psychiatry in Edinburgh. Recent research interests include sociocultural and epidemiological aspects of suicidal behaviour (suicide and parasuicide), and the impact of economic recession upon health.

Kate Purcell has carried out research on manual workers' employment experiences and attitudes to work, with a particular interest in the sexual division of labour and the relationship between class and gender. She has been a part-time Tutor of Open and Oxford University students, and is currently a Research Fellow at Warwick University.

David Raffe is Reader in Education and Deputy Director of the Centre for Educational Sociology at Edinburgh University. His current research projects include studies of trends in the youth labour market, intra-urban variations in youth unemployment, education and training initiatives for 14–18 year olds, and the origins and development of the Youth Training Scheme.

Jean Seaton teaches Sociology at the Polytechnic of the South Bank. The second edition of *Power Without Responsibility: the Press and Broadcasting in Britain* was published in 1985 and she is editing (with Ben Pimlott) a book *Politics and the Media in Britain* due to be published in 1986.

Claire Wallace is a Lecturer in Sociology at Plymouth Polytechnic. She worked as a Research Fellow at the University of Kent on an ESRC project with R. E. Pahl on the Isle of Sheppey. Currently she is writing a book about unemployment amongst young people based upon research for the Joseph Rowntree Memorial Trust.

Alan Waton has been a Lecturer in Sociology at the University of Bradford since 1973. He is particularly interested in problems of analysing power in industrial societies, and is currently engaged in research on ethnic minority use of the media.

Stephen Wood has lectured in Industrial Relations at the London School of Economics since 1974. He has written and edited several studies of work and unemployment, and is currently engaged in Anglo-American research on recent changes in the motor industry.

Susan Yeandle studied at the Universities of Bradford and Kent and is currently doing research on women in later working life at University College, Swansea. Previously she worked on a study of youth unemployment and family life at Durham University, and her publications include *Women's Working Lives: Patterns and Strategies* (Tavistock, 1985).

1 The Effects of Unemployment: Experience and Response

SHEILA ALLEN AND ALAN WATON

One of the most important relations in Western societies is that between capital and labour. Though it is increasingly recognized that this may take many forms, its major manifestation is the phenomenon of the wage. Those with no other source of livelihood, the vast majority of the population at any one time, sell their labour-power in return for monetary reward (with or without non monetary prerequisites). In this way they provide for and reproduce their material existence, a crucial part of all social existence. Not only those who sell their ability to work directly, but all those economically dependent on them are enmeshed in the structures of the wage-relationship. Earning one's living is more than an economic matter, for it pervades a whole range of cultural and political relationships. These become visible when individuals are no longer able to earn their own living. Their immediate loss of income is accompanied by loss of status, identity and rights through the multiplicity of rules and regulations to which the unemployed and their families are subjected. Additionally those without jobs are frequently denigrated and their abilities and motivation openly questioned. The wage-relationship, previously a main source of integration into wider structures of the society, is for more and more individuals and families severed.

Even in times of 'full employment' many of working age in Britain did not have a full-time, regular job with negotiated wage-rates and conditions of work. Integration into the labour market was differentially experienced according to gender, age and race as well as region and through education linked to class origin. None the less

1

for almost two decades after the Beveridge Report (1944) there remained a political consensus on the need for full employment, a consensus which involved government planning, not only for economic reasons, but as the underpinnings of the social security system, health service and education provisions. During the 1960s educational reforms designed to broaden access to higher education were introduced and the necessity for nursery education was seriously discussed, both issues being frequently linked politically to the requirements of an educated workforce. The elderly were encouraged to remain in employment, married women increasingly took up jobs (though these were largely poorly paid and part-time) and some of the physically disabled found work. There was much to criticize during this period, for many inequalities remained, but the tone of the debates was about how improvements could be made in working lives and elsewhere in society. Complementary discussions centred on economic growth and the increased leisure to be achieved by the application of new technologies which would bring high productivity, reductions in working hours and a shortening of number of years spent in employment, through sabbaticals for all workers and an increase in opportunities for full-time and continuing education. Any return to mass unemployment was unthinkable.

The reality of the 1980s poses a stark contrast in both material and ideological terms. Those still in employment have, in general, had no increase in 'leisure' time or improvement in the quality of their working lives. More often they have been subjected, directly or indirectly, to various forms of pressure, to work harder, faster, longer, to take early retirement or voluntary redundancy, to relinquish hard-won rights in areas such as health and safety or maternity leave. In the context of high unemployment such pressures are reinforced by the fear of losing a job. They may engender feelings of guilt or good fortune at having a job at all.

The papers brought together here are mainly concerned with sociological studies of unemployment. They illustrate the effects on men and women who lose their jobs, or those who have never (or only briefly) experienced paid employment and on their families, friends and communities. These studies are of a variety of groups, located in different geographical regions of Great Britain. They do not give comprehensive coverage of what is, in the 1980s, a widespread phenomenon involving, albeit differentially, most sectors of the population of working age. Much previous work on unemployment deals only with men and for the most part it comes to be seen as a problem, by academics, politicians and others, only when able-bodied, adult men cannot find or lose full-time jobs in large numbers. It is one of the aims of this volume to go beyond this narrow view, and its chapters indicate a range of issues which demand more serious attention.

The view that, in the future, not everyone can expect to hold, or even to find, employment has gained increasingly wide currency in political and academic circles in recent years, among both supporters and opponents of the present high levels of unemployment and the economic policies of the conservative administration since 1979. According to this view, there is an imbalance between the number of people of working age and the number of profitable jobs in British industry, public and private. The creation of such a 'surplus population', due in part to technological innovations, in part to the working of financial institutions with policies based on profit making in international money markets, is by no means a new phenomenon in European social and political thought. What it reveals, however is not that there are too many people, but rather that there is a grave imbalance between the means available for the production of a material and social existence for all members of society, particularly in view of the technological advances of recent years, and existing political, cultural and economic arrangements.

These problems are not to be solved easily, for the removal from so many of the opportunity to earn their own living cannot be equated with increased leisure. Even if state benefit for the unemployed were adequate, the loss of the independence gained in our culture through earning and the loss of meaningful activity derived from working do not create the conditions necessary for leisure. The evidence presented in this book demonstrates this very clearly. The breaking of the political consensus on the necessity of full employment has in a very important way removed from many the expectation, even the hope, of a meaningful future. Beveridge, a Liberal in British politics claimed that 'the only sovereign remedy, yet discovered by democracies for unemployment is total war' (Beveridge, 1944, p. 112). Since such a remedy is conceivably no longer available, social scientists have a particular responsibility to use their skills not only to investigate the effects of unemployment but to discover the means by which new technologies can be harnessed to modes of social organization which allow the production and distribution of resources in such a way that all participate, and all can benefit.

This book is mainly concerned with the effects of unemployment on individuals, families and households. It says little of resistance, organized or spontaneous, to unemployment or the threat of unemployment, though there are brief references in the paper on Asian Youth (Brah) and on Women's unemployment (Hurstfield). There is a clear need to record and analyse the resistance which has taken place and continues to be undertaken by workers against forced redundancies. There is also a need to focus on the communal and collective efforts of the unemployed and the never employed to organize and lobby against their treatment by state and government.

Dennis Marsden formulated the question as follows 'But as unemployment grows we must at last begin to face up to the question: how much freedom will remain in a society where the workless are numbered in millions?' (Marsden, 1982, p. 270). The chapters in this book do not give a full answer to this question. Indeed, they answer it only indirectly, but the evidence they present speaks directly to the kind of answer we require. They also indicate some of the directions in which social scientists must go if their work is to be relevant to the crucial issues of society in the late twentieth century.

THE CONTEXT OF UNEMPLOYMENT

Seaton, in a comparative analysis of the 1930s and the 1980s, examines the ways in which the ideological context of unemployment has changed. She charts the way in which unemployment was displaced during the 1970s and 1980s as a central issue. Inflation became the prime economic bogey threatening the national well being. Unemployment, previously a major economic and social problem in its own right, now came to be represented as a solution to the problem of inflation. This downgrading of the issue of unemployment was part of a social process in which academics, politicians and in particular, the media presented revised explanations of the events of the 1930s and reformulated central political problems, and thus proceeded to marginalize not only unemployment but the unemployed. Such marginalization entails stigmatization in which unemployment is seen as the fault of an individual and not as a social pathology. Of course, it is possible to over-estimate this process. There was then, as there currently is, some sympathy for the unemployed, but the ill-informed scare of stories of 'welfare scroungers' reported by Seaton testify to the reality of the process of denigration and marginalization.

Her claims are reinforced by evidence of the extent of the unemployment since the phenomenon does not simply present itself as a 'fact'. Evidence has to be collected, data analyzed and statistics compiled. Most of this is done by government agencies.

Officially recorded unemployment rates present problems of interpretation both in terms of the techniques used for compiling the data and in the assumptions underlying the concept of employment. If we seek to understand the causes, consequences and extent of unemployment, whether in times of rapidly increasing and high unemployment as in the 1920s or 1980s or in periods of near full employment such as the two decades following the 1939–45 war, then due regard must be paid to the different uses of the everyday words, 'work', 'employment' and 'unemployment' in various situations and relationships. Official statistics are based only on certain forms of paid work and must always be treated with caution.

Many commentators have indicated that official data are far from being an accurate and objective record (see Purcell, 1985). The shortcomings do not, of course, only affect data on unemployment but apply across a whole range of official statistics relating to the size of the labour force, its distribution and its characteristics (Hyman and Price, 1979). The sociologist seeking to understand unemployment is thus faced with a plethora of omissions and systematic distortions. These relate to the extent and duration of unemployment and especially to its rate where the actual size of the labour force is unknown, as with the black population. Much the same can be said of all sections of the population of working age systematically marginalized by the methods of official data collection and their underlying assumptions.

Several papers raise these issues. For example, *Hurstfield* discusses the assumptions made in relation to women. She details the ways in which analyses and explanations of unemployment in the 1930s, whether governmental or compiled by social scientists and independent bodies, systematically ignored or denigrated the experience of unemployed women, thus reinforcing further the view that women's proper place was in the home. Hurstfield compares this situation to that in the 1980s and notes that, although official statistics and social science show some improvement, they are still far from adequate. Rules governing who counts as unemployed have been subjected to several changes by government ministers in the 1980s, in ways which seem to deliberately seek to minimize the total. Other papers in the volume underscore this point. Both Coles and Brah remind us of undercounting of the young unemployed, and the need to take account of those who remain in school or college because no jobs are available. If all the categories of those not presently in full-time employment who are looking for full-time jobs were included then it is estimated that the figures would be two or three times as high so far as young people are concerned.

Hurstfield emphasizes this point with regard to women, noting how much more difficult it is for women to be recognized as unemployed compared to men because of the assumption of female dependancy, particularly in the case of married women. The effects of such policies reinforce ideologies of sex and gender differences at the same time as they systematically distort the reality they claim to represent.

The consequences of this distortion are wide ranging. Platt, for instance, in explaining why he has restricted his analyses of parasuicide to males makes the point that the reliability of the employment status classification of female parasuicides (particularly married women) is extremely doubtful. But his difficulties do not stop there. An investigation of the relationship between parasuicide and unemployment amongst women is also rendered problematic because women, and especially married women, may not register as unemployed because they are ineligible for benefit. Even if they register they may be deemed not to be looking for work or not genuinely unemployed (Smith, 1981), and since 1982, unless they can actually claim benefit, they are not counted as unemployed in any case. This is yet another example of how methods of determining who is employed and who unemployed render women invisible in studies which seek to explain the consequences of unemployment. Whether it is enough to say that women cannot be studied in such circumstances because the methods currently used make them difficult to classify, is a matter of considerable dispute, and the conclusion for sociologists must be that, where official statistics are so designed as to obscure investigation of central problems, other methods must be devised.

YOUTH UNEMPLOYMENT

A key component of recent discussions of unemployment has been the issue of youth unemployment, and there is no disagreement about its rapid rise since 1980, nor about the very high levels recorded since then, despite training and job-experience schemes which removed large numbers of young people from the unemployment statistics. What is less well understood, however, are its causes. Raffe considers one of the major explanations advanced to account for this phenomenon – the 'structural explanation' of youth unemployment, which holds that young people have been so hard hit because of changes in the nature and composition of labour-force requirements, to which they have failed to adapt. Through a detailed analysis and critique of this argument, Raffe concludes that the case remains unproven and that the weight of available evidence suggests that theories based on the changing level of employment (demand for labour) are more convincing. A fall in demand for labour affects adults as well, but for a number of reasons hits young people harder. When firms stop, or slow down, recruitment, entry to the labour market is more difficult and 'Last in, first out' practices affect younger people more when redundancies do occur. Raffe suggests that policy measures which try to improve the position of young people in the labour market by imparting new skills or modifying behaviour will prove to be ineffective, and that youth unemployment will decline as unemployment in general declines. It is to this latter end that employment policy must be directed.

Whatever the level of the demand for labour, however, the problems of which young people get jobs, where and under what conditions remain, as do questions regarding what happens to those who fail to find paid employment. These issues are discussed in three papers which deal with the experiences of, and responses to, youth unemployment. Each deals with a specific location – Brah with an inner-city area of Leicester, Coles with four rural or small town locations within a large Shire County, and Allatt and Yeandle with a ward of a city in North-East England. Each uses different methods. Brah concentrates on group discussions and in-depth interviews with unemployed Sikhs, Muslims and Hindus. Coles uses survey methods to collect information on two cohorts of young people. Allatt and Yeandle conducted interviews with young people entering the labour market and with their families. Each investigates the position of young people in slightly different age groups and at different times – Brah those aged 16–25 in 1983, Coles those reaching the age of 16 in 1978 and 1982, and Allatt and Yeandle those entering the labour-market since 1980.

These differences in location, method and populations researched afford different emphases in their analyses, and indicate a wide range of issues, often difficult to compare, which are significant for the field of youth unemployment. Nevertheless some common points emerge. One of the most significant is the financial constraints imposed by being unemployed. Though the extent of this varies with the family background of the individual, it was a major factor for all except a small minority in the rural study. They felt that the freedom gained by leaving school counterbalanced every disadvantage, including the shortage of money, and this negative experience of education is a factor reported not only in Coles study but by some Asians in the inner city. However, for these Asians unemployment is not experienced as freedom but as further alienation, in which they are explicitly excluded from the labour market much as they were implicitly excluded from the mainstream in their educational experience.

All three studies raise questions concerning the structuring of dependence and independence for young people without jobs. The transition from dependant statuses – associated with residence in the parental household, reliance on parents for material support and thus subject to their normative controls – to an independent and adult status has in general been closely correlated, at least among working class youth, with getting a job, earning a wage and paying for one's keep. Without a job and a wage, this process of transition is disrupted, and this affects all members of the household. It leads, according to Allatt and Yeandle, to a reinforcement of parental control, and to feelings of shame and embarrassment by and on behalf of the young unemployed. Brah's study indicates that such feelings weigh heavily upon Asian men unable to provide for widowed mothers, younger siblings and, in some cases, wives. Asian women are keenly aware of the loss of independence entailed in being unemployed – those who are married are unable to contribute financially to the household, and so do not experience the independence from husband and family which a job provides, whilst the unmarried are further penalized by being unable to contribute towards their own marriage provision. Relations of dependance promoted by high unemployment negate the personal and social development of young people and distort relations within families, between young people and their parents and between men and women. This forced dependance is confirmed by the legal rules and administrative practices entailed in unemployment and social security provisions. The enforced dependancy of young unemployed people in relation to their parents, siblings and spouses should not be construed as a return to traditional close-knit family relationships, but as a denial of the processes by which independent adult statuses are achieved.

There is little evidence in these studies that lack of motivation is even a partial explanation for unemployment. Indeed the contrary seems to be the case, and the search for jobs continues in the most unpromising circumstances. Both Allatt and Yeandle and Brah found that families encouraged job search through a variety of means. Brah points to the obstacles for Asians in getting jobs through informal means (such as 'word of mouth' recruitment) where the employed are virtually all white. In the North-East the deep commitment parents had to finding a job for their child indicates a belief in such particularistic recruitment practices which, though they may work for some, by definition exclude many others. In the search for jobs being the right colour and choosing your parents and where you live very carefully may help. It also helps if you do not suffer from physical or mental disability, do not have a police record or are the appropriate gender. These factors, while providing some explanation of why young person 'x' gets a job while 'y' does not, operate within a given level of demand for labour. Where jobs are scarce any or all of these factors may be crucial. A high level of demand for labour may reduce (though it does not remove) their significance. At no time do these factors explain rates of unemployment and employment.

Search strategies are a somewhat different matter and, while 'getting on your bike' is of little use in areas or regions of very high unemployment, there is plenty of evidence that young people undertake the modern equivalent. 'Getting out' of areas of high unemployment through education, by moving elsewhere, or by joining the armed forces are part of the strategy of some teachers, parents and young people themselves. In the North East the forces could be said to be something of a traditional male escape from unemployment. For Asians geographical mobility is not unknown, nor is the path into higher or further education, but for them, as for others, these routes are increasingly restricted by higher rates of unemployment and cutbacks in education. While a minority of young people may still be able to follow such strategies they cannot serve the need for employment of the majority. The restrictions placed on mobility by the level of social security provision, the lack of accommodation evidenced by homelessness among young and single people and the attacks on some who do move are difficulties of which some commentators appear unaware or choose to ignore.

Rather than move up or out, however, there is some evidence of pressure on young people to take a job, any job, however poorly paid and however long the hours, or to accept a place on Manpower Service Commission training schemes for a nominal wage. Allatt and Yeandle organize their argument around the idea of 'fairness' – a concept constantly invoked by their respondents, especially as young people and their parents expressed their sense of *unfairness* about the lack of job prospects, or the poor pay or poor conditions on offer. Nonetheless, all those involved developed mechanisms to cope with this situation, as did the young people documented by Coles and by Brah. All of them did so in the context of a tradition, which, throughout the twentieth century, has been evident in various legislative measures to secure fair wages and working conditions. Since the Second World War a broad measure of agreement has existed in Britain across political parties, trade unions and employers' associations that the provision of jobs with fair wages was necessary, through collective agreements or statutory machinery, not only to ensure an adequate living wage, but to protect employers themselves from the unfair competition of others undercutting wages (Low Pay Unit, 1983; Winyard, 1982). The case for a living, fair or minimum wage has been put forward throughout this century on economic grounds, quite apart from consideration of a social or moral nature (Churchill, 1909; Craig *et al.*, 1982). Successive governments of all parties until 1979 introduced or strengthened legislation to promote wage protection and prevent unfair competition.[1] Though the implementation of these issues has always fallen short of their ends, the general expectation on the part of both employers and workers has been that a fair wage was reasonable.

Since 1979, the conservative administration, having already abolished the Fair Wages Resolution, is actively seeking to abolish the Wages Councils indicating a disregard for both fair and minimum levels of pay. Indeed the exclusion of young people from Wages Councils' regulations seriously considered by Ministers in 1981 (Low Pay Unit, 1983, p. 35) was announced in 1985. The argument that lower pay would produce more jobs, particularly for young people, is a controversial one. As Raffe argues, the evidence is far from conclusive, and whilst one can point to very low rates of pay – in 1982, for instance, the average minimum wage was £38 a week for 16 year olds and £44 for 17 years old (DoE, 1982) – there is little suggestion that these low rates increase the level of employment for young people. They do, however, worsen an already vulnerable bargaining position and increase the feelings of unfairness and resentment in both young people and their parents, particularly when they are accused of 'pricing themselves out of jobs'.

These feelings are further reinforced by the suggestion that individuals should move to where it is believed employment is to be obtained or may exist, a suggestion which not only raises issues of individual competence and initiative but also of the relation between people and their communities. This was a major issue in the 1984–85 coal dispute. Forty years ago Beveridge was in no doubt about what to recommend.

> It is easier for men and women to change their occupation and it is much easier for boys and girls to choose their first occupations, with reference to the demand in particular industries, than it is for work-people of any age to move their place of residence. For some people age and family ties make movement almost impracticable. Leaving home in pursuit of new occupations is often a tonic in individual cases, but is a poison if taken in large quantities involving destruction of communities. (Beveridge, 1944, p. 25)

The discussions of youth unemployment in this volume indicate that individuals and families have made conscious and rational decisions to allow them to cope with the economic effects and stigma of unemployment. How far in the longer term the various forms of family and social stress can be managed within the limits of the resources available to them is an issue of some doubt.

THE EFFECTS OF UNEMPLOYMENT

Links between unemployment and a wide range of social problems have been made by academics, politicians and journalists. Ill-health, premature death, attempted and actual suicide, marriage breakdown, child battering, racial conflicts and football hooliganism are a few of the examples that have been cited in the last five years. As frequently, suggestions have been made of alternatives to paid employment which, through the constructive use of the time available to them, are claimed to be able to enhance both the lives of the unemployed and their economic chances. Among these are increased leisure pursuits, educational or training courses, caring work in their neighbourhoods, and establishing small businesses to fill gaps in product or service markets. Finally there have been those who claim that many of the unemployed are not really out of work, but are already fully occupied in the 'informal' sector of the economy.

Several of these themes are explored in the papers in this volume. Three papers in particular deal in depth with aspects of these popularly promoted links and suggestions on which hard evidence is only now emerging. Not surprisingly, each points to a complex of interacting factors which belie any simple cause – effect relationship promulgated in popular debate. Two of these contributions take very cautious positions on what is currently known about how the unemployed order their relationships to cope with economic and social constraints, including not least the State's interest in their activities.

McKee and Bell report a study of 45 Kidderminster families in which the man is unemployed, there is at least one dependant child and the partners are mostly in the early stages of family building. Illustrating the narrowing of options forced on these families, they point out that the combined effects of poverty, of stage of the life cycle and of unemployment are not easily disentangled, but note that several changes could be directly related to the unemployment of the man. In a number of cases women gave up their employment when their partner became unemployed since their earnings were deducted from the benefit received by him. As they received no benefit in their own right, they saw no point in registering as unemployed. Only women in highly paid occupations could afford to remain in employment in such circumstances and there were few of them. Simultaneously, this loss of employment by women reinforced the conventional patterns of the division of labour between the sexes, in large measure due to the need (perceived by women as well as men) to support the man's identity as the provider for the family. In McKee and Bell's study, it was clear that the women were expected to meet household needs on less money. Managing unemployment is very much women's work, even where there is the sometimes unwelcome presence of a male in the house all day. The interest taken by the State in the activities of the male unemployed reduce the possibilities of men carrying out tasks for others and receiving any form of remuneration, and the fear of State investigation is compounded by the fear of being informed on by neighbours.

Wallace and Pahl's 1981 study of a random sample of 730 households on the Isle of Sheppey included both the employed and unemployed. They were thus able to investigate the differences between these groups particularly in terms of the work activities engaged in, and to discover whether unemployment in the formal economy led to the acquisition of skills and the exploitation of opportunities within the informal economy. Their conclusions, contradicting earlier optimism (Gershuny and Pahl, 1980), indicate a polarization between households with multiple earners and a relatively high income in which both formal and informal work is carried out, and those with no earners and a very low income, which are systematically denied places in both the 'formal' and 'informal' economy. Wallace and Pahl's conclusions reinforce those of McKee and Bell and suggest that the unemployed are 'poor, isolated and unable to engage in any more than marginal informal activities thus casting doubt on the notion that alternative activities are open to the unemployed'.

Though these two studies are comparable neither in scale nor scope the exploration of gender relations is a key factor in both. Their evidence demonstrates that if we are to understand the consequences of unemployment, then gender together with age and class must be taken into account. Unemployment among men has clear consequences for them, but it also has consequences for women which can only be understood in the context of the differential relations of men and women to the labour market and to domestic labour. Hurstfield raises this point in relation to the difficulty some women have in identifying themselves as unemployed. The consequences of unemployment among women are little understood because of a general lack of recognition that women can be unemployed, allied to the belief that for most women marriage is their main career and the dearth of research into the experience of those who do see themselves as being unemployed (Coyle, 1984). There is even less knowledge of the effects which having an unemployed wife, mother or sister has on male kin, though Allatt and Yeandle discuss attitudes towards the unemployment of daughters. The papers in this volume make a contribution to the recognition that unemployment is not simply a male problem and provide some evidence which can form the basis of research into a long neglected aspected of unemployment.

Platt presents an analysis of evidence from a study of the relationship between unemployment and parasuicide (non-fatal deliberate self-harm) among the male unemployed in Edinburgh over the period 1968–83 and situates this within the context of other work on the relation of health and unemployment. The statistical relationship of morbidity and mortality to unemployment has been demonstrated by a number of studies but, given the range of variables involved, establishing causation is a matter of some complexity.

None the less Platt's findings are entirely consistent with the hypothesis that unemployment is a cause of parasuicide. Despite some contrary trends, an overall positive and highly significant aggregate association was found between unemployment and male parasuicide rates in Edinburgh. Throughout the period investigated the rate amongst the unemployed was considerably higher than that for the employed. Importantly, whilst those recently losing their jobs were characterized by a marked increase in their rate of parasuicide, the highest relative risk was found amongst the long-term unemployed. Platt's conclusion, that parasuicide is almost certainly the effect of a complex interation of many factors, supports a conclusion of the Black Report (Townsend and Davidson, 1982) that unemployment is one of a range of social and economic inequalities with significant effects for morbidity and mortality, and signals the need for further long term enquiries into the role of predisposing and precipitating conditions among the at-risk population. His observation that many male parasuicides live chronically marginal existences, and that unemployment (especially when it is long-term) reinforces this marginality suggests that not only research but practical action is called for.

Over the past few years policies aimed at providing temporary work, and in some cases training opportunities, for the long-term unemployed have been introduced by the Manpower Services Commission and the Department of Employment. They can be seen as a response to the rapid increase in long-term unemployment as a proportion of the high levels of registered unemployed. As Brah suggests, the unemployed do not always experience such provisions as uniformly beneficial and there is evidence that they are sometimes regarded by employers as sources of cheap labour and by the young people themselves as comestic, resource-wasting exercises whose main function is to reduce the unemployment statistics.

None the less the notion of a hard-core of long-term unemployed, who constitute a particular problem, has a long official history. During most of the post-war years, registered unemployment was less than half a million and only a small proportion of these were long-term unemployed (that is, unemployed for more than a year). The existence of an alleged hard-core of 'unemployables' was never established by official surveys (Ministry of Labour, 1962, 1965; DoE, 1974) and independent studies (Hill *et al.*, 1973) mainly concentrated on the supposed personal deficiencies of the long-term unemployed. Both popular and official notions that such unemployment was caused by the inadequacies and failures of the unemployed themselves has to be set against the facts of the variations in the annual rates of unemployment and, in any one year, against differences between regions. In brief, while age or skill or mental and physical disability played some part in determining who was unemployed, and for how long, this was very minor relative to variations in labour market conditions. Nevertheless the strength of the belief that causation lay with personal characteristics rather than with the demand for labour in the market persisted and persists. It is one more facet of the process whereby those marginalized by unemployment are further marginalized by the processes to which this condition subjects them.

Buckland and Macgregor discuss this argument and investigate the role of Re-establishment Centres, founded to deal with the long-term unemployed in the 1950s. In particular, their paper presents findings derived from research on one such Re-establishment Centre, which had been upgraded to provide training. Their conclusions are based on interviews with men attending the centre, with those referred but not attending, on group discussions with unemployment officers, who had the task of referring individuals, and with staff at the centre, and on an analysis of case records. Despite positive aspects of the Centre, including the conscientious and relatively sympathetic approach by staff and the chance it gave to 'get out of the house', talk over problems and share experiences among those attending a course, there is little to suggest that, either as a mechanism of control or as means of improving job prospects, such Centres actually work. 60 per cent of those referred did not attend, but for some who did the Centre often functioned mainly to show that they could play the game and observe the rules, helping to safeguard payment of their social security. Very few left the Centre to go into a job, and few had a job three months later, though their plight was marginally better than that of the non-attenders.

Significantly, women are not referred to such Centres. Buckland and MacGregor comment on the consequences of this for the sexual division of labour, and, as with McKee and Bell, note how conventional gender divisions are reinforced by official policies. But it is interesting to ask why women are not referred. Is it because they are not normally able to claim social security in their own right and are therefore not seen as part of the problem of control? Or is it due to women not being recognized as unemployed and therefore not requiring the services of the centres to improve their skills or job search activities? Or is it that women's unemployment is seen as having a lower priority? Once again, questions concerning the conceptualization of unemployment are raised.

With the rise of unemployment in the 1980s an increasing number of people are experiencing long-term unemployment. Attempts are still being made to categorize them along the lines of earlier official and popular notions of who was without jobs and why, but such stereotyping flies in the face of much of the evidence recently gathered and analysed. This book presents some of that evidence, and indicates directions for future research and analysis. The work here represents a mere fraction of work-in progress and that being planned. Despite the massive cut-backs in social science funding, we confidently expect this work will be developed to enrich our understanding of the relations of work, employment and unemployment. Beveridge wrote that 'the greatest evil of unemployment is not physical but moral, not the want which it may bring but the hatred and fear which it breeds' (Beveridge, 1944, p. 15). None of us can afford to ignore his advice.

NOTE

1. Article 4 of the European Social Charter which includes the right to 'fair remuneration' and the International Labour Office Convention No. 26 which requires governments to create and maintain machinery for fixing minimum wages where no effective regulation such as by collective agreements exists and where wages are exceptionally low are already part of the British Government obligations as a Member State in the one case and as a signatory in the other.

2 The Media and the Politics of Interpreting Unemployment

JEAN SEATON

INTRODUCTION

Are the unemployed protesting less during the 1980s slump because they are more fragmented, isolated and apathetic than they were in the 1930s? Are they doing less because they know so little about their shared plight? Similarly, can the lack of political concern for the unemployed be explained by ignorance, and a failure of empathy based on inadequate information? Are citizens becoming less altruistic, and politicians less anxious about unemployment, at least in part, because they are uninformed about the real condition of the unemployed – whose experience is becoming increasingly remote from everyone else's?

Or, on the contrary, has the resistance of the unemployed been eroded by their surfeit of 'knowledge' so that, understanding only too well from their repeated exposure to the media that governments can do nothing to ameliorate their condition they have sunk into rational, *over informed*, fatalism? According to this kind of explanation, the unemployed, as well as policy makers, politicians and the public all share in a consensus about the possibilities of political and economic action to deal with unemployment. Such an explanation depends on views about the media's capacity to dominate ways of thinking about social and economic issues, and its capacity to exclude alternatives. Or finally have the protests of the unemployed been stifled because they have accepted and internalized the perjorative image of themselves as 'welfare scroungers', unemployables, and union militants who have 'priced themselves out of a job'?

17

Such questions are prompted by the need to explain the 'failure' of the working class as a whole to protest more radically about their conditions. The political journalist Robert Taylor explains it in terms of the increasing 'sectionalism and selfishness of the trade union movement' (Taylor, 1982, p. 5). More romantically Jeremy Seabrook has argued, yet again, that the culprit is working class consumerism, and a decline in community values (Seabrook, 1981). Bill Jordan, expressing the revolutionary position, maintains that the working class has yet to mobilise, but that when the situation becomes worse, it will (Jordan, 1982). More soberly Peter Golding and Sue Middleton explain the lack of working class protest against unemployment in terms of media social control (Golding and Middleton, 1979), while Alan Deacon has pointed to the mechanisms which depoliticise unemployment (Deacon, 1981). Many commentators have thus implicitly compared the 1980s unfavourably with the 1930s, which becomes in retrospect a glorious 'red united fighting front' of a decade (see Pimlott, 1977).

In particular it is the revolution of attitudes that has made current levels of unemployment tolerable which needs closer examination. As recently as 1978 John Goldthorpe was arguing, as part of his account of inflation, that governments continued to find high levels of unemployment politically unacceptable (Goldthorpe, 1978, p. 202). It would be, he added, political suicide for any party to accept levels over 1½ million. Keith Middlemass commented that, although the supposed benefits of consensus had come to be seen, not, as in 1940, as high aspiration, but as the lowest common denominator of policies designed to avoid trouble, the key area of 'trouble avoidance' for all post-war governments was the maintenance of high levels of employment (Middlemass, 1979, p. 429). Alan Deacon has argued that over employment policy the politicians and 'opinion formers' moved swiftly from the caution and hesitation of the 1940s, to the swaggering confidence of the full employment era, and then, just as rapidly to the fatalism of the 1970s (Deacon, 1981, p. 85). Thus, by December 1984, although 72 per cent of a Gallup Poll sample thought that 'unemployment was the most serious problem facing the country', 43 per cent also thought that 'unemployment' was sometimes justified (Gallup, 1984) indicating, for the present at least, an acceptance of the problem.

It is in this context that the present essay considers the relationship of the media to the politics of unemployment. Through a discussion

of the ways in which the media can shape and disseminate information, influencing politicians, public opinion and the unemployed
themselves, and being influenced itself in turn, it is argued that the
role of the media is more complex, and more important, than usually
recognised. This can be seen to be particularly the case when current
arguments about and discussions of unemployment are set in a
longer-term perspective.

POLITICIANS, POLICY MAKERS AND UNEMPLOYMENT

A paradoxical aspect of unemployment is that, as it increases, its
news value tends to fall. Within the context of narrow conventions,
newspapers look for the unusual or the unexpected. Steadily rising
unemployment figures, reaching new records every month, lose their
power to shock, and editors react accordingly. Thus headlines on
joblessness are least often to be seen when unemployment is high.
An examination of *The Times* shows an inverse relationship between
the percentage out of work and the front page attention given to the
subject: between 1958 and 1978 main leads about unemployment
were comparatively frequent; by contrast in the 1980s, as in the
1930s, they have been virtually non-existent. During an era of full
employment, fairly small increases in the number out of work caused
governments to tremble and Fleet Street to react. In a series of
articles in *The Times* in 1970, writers like Michael Young and Asa
Briggs examined the social problems caused by youth unemployment, discussed the plight of the long term unemployed, and
considered the long term effects of the decline of opportunities in
the country (*The Times*, 1970). Fifteen years later, with the situation
incomparably worse, these issues are discussed in surprisingly similar
terms. What has changed is the political context. No longer is unemployment seen as *the* major political or economic problem. In the
1980s, as Eatwell and Green (1984) have pointed out, even radical
critiques of government policies tend to be presented in monetarist
terms.

The reasons for this rapid shift in opinion about unemployment,
as with the switch in economic orthodoxy, remain to be fully
explained. Part of the answer, however, lies in the way interpretations of the decade of the 1930s have changed.

The old adage that generals base their strategy in any given war

on the assumptions of the previous one seems particularly apt in the
case of unemployment. In the 1950s and 1960s expectations and
responses were conditioned by the events of the 1930s, changing
only gradually. In the early 1950s, an imminent return to high unemployment was still widely feared. Politicians entered the decade
hoping to keep unemployment below its pre-war levels, but not to
eradicate it. They did not expect to produce anything near recent
definitions of full employment. Indeed, Keynes' own definition of
full employment, which allowed for a 9 per cent unemployment rate,
was in general what was thought realistic (Skidelsky, 1965).

When unemployment failed to rise, one response was to reinter-
pret the slump of the 1930s. Unemployment, it was claimed, had
been an avoidable disaster. Two strands of historical work emphasised the decade as the 'mistaken years'. The first blamed the incom-
petence of the 'guilty men' in government (Cato, 1939; Calder,
1968), the second suggested that an economic remedy was available,
if only politicians had had the imagination to see it. The second
strand is developed most clearly in Robert Skidelsky's *Politicians
and the Slump* (1965) which emphasised the availability of political
solutions to the economic problems of the decade and discusses why
they were not seized earlier. Thus the 1930s became characterised
historically and for politicians as an 'absent' decade when solutions
were available, but politicians failed to act.

This view of the 1930s as a decade of failure was enthusiastically
embraced by the intellectual establishment and the media in the
1960s and early 1970s, bolstering a fragile uneasy optimism. A
number of re-examinations of the 'error' of the pre-war period
appeared, in diplomacy, economic and social policy, and it is no
accident that there developed a new interest in the early writings of
George Orwell, with their savage indictment of the indifference of
public opinion and of the authorities to poverty (Orwell, 1933, 1937).
Politicians were seen to have greater responsibilities, a view accepted
by them, reinforced by academic analysis and given wider currency
by the media.

But this interpretation has in its turn been challenged. The claim
that governments had *no* policy for unemployment during the 1930s
has been disputed (Stevenson, 1983). The view that there was a
solution, a miracle cure available but not used, has been met by the
counter-argument that, in reality, there were a variety of opportunities, with partial successes and partial failures (Miller, 1976). The

responsibility of the 'guilty men' for the mistakes of the decade has been questioned, and the 'rejected prophet' assumption in economic policy countered by the argument that Keynesian methods could only have been applied under certain conditions that were, in the main, not present. Finally, it has been argued that the simple model of the 'hungry decade' is inappropriate: depending on where you lived, the 1930s was, for many people, a period of prosperity and rapid material progress (Stevenson and Cook, 1979).

Whether these revisions are a product of a more sophisticated use of evidence or of a changed climate of opinion, that extends beyond the world of academic debate, they reflect a change in the terms and the tone of discussion of the political responsibility for unemployment. As a consequence we have, in practice, both a different view of the scope of government intervention in the 1930s, and reduced expectations of the possible alternatives.

This continual revision of history, of interpretations of the events and possibilities of the past, operates as an important influence within the media, since it helps shape the interpretation of current events provided by the 'quality' press and 'serious' current affairs and documentary broadcasts. These, in turn, help monitor the limits of public expectation of government, since what politicians are likely to be blamed in public for *not* doing acts as a parameter of what they are likely to do. In a very real sense, revisionist views of the 1930s have helped set the scene for more unemployment, and less being done about it, *in the present*.

That the change appears to have happened so swiftly, and so totally, however, needs some explanation. Neither Mrs Thatcher, nor the leading members of her government, began as monetarists. Indeed, all were products of the earlier consensual politics. And the press and broadcasting were an important part of this consensus. Yet, as one critic has pointed out, 'the rapid transformation of the monetarist doctrine from fringe medicine to new orthodoxy has been one of the wonders of our age' (Pimlott, 1984, p. 6).

It is worth comparing the 'monetarist revolution' with its earlier, Keynesian, equivalent, for the change of outlook that accompanied the acceptance of Keynesian techniques was similar in significant respects. In both cases, a comparatively small number of individuals led opinion, and courted publicity (for the case of Keynes, see Skidelsky, 1983). In both cases, the seminal ideas had been advanced decades before their widespread acceptance. Crucially, however, for both Keynesianism and monetarism, it was the action of government that was of critical importance in establishing the new orthodoxy.

Here, however, the similarity ends. The Keynesian revolution was legitimated in practice before it was legitimated in ideology. With the outbreak of the Second World War, Keynes and his disciples took over the economic and fiscal management of the war effort. Indirectly, requirements of war induced the government to take responsibility for the allocation of goods, and people became accustomed to state 'planning'. By 1945, there was widespread media support for increased intervention. This support, a product of various influences, sought a theoretical justification. In the 1940s, as now, journalists were interested in the authority which economic experts gave their own, popularly derived, statements, and were on the whole prepared to use expert opinion precisely in as far as it confirmed views they already held.

The monetarist revolution was in contrast led by journalists who happened to be economists. It was successful partly because, like the Keynesian revolution, there was a somewhat frayed orthodoxy to replace, but also because there was desire for a new fashion, as it gave journalists a whole new battery of things to write.

Indeed, the Thatcherite experiment was not the result of a surprise putsch by a few fanatical monetarists. Rather, as Colin Clark the (ex Fabian) market economist, revealed in a collection of essays marking the twenty-fifth anniversary (in 1981) of the Institute of Economic Affairs, there was a long term plan to take over the establishment by gentle persuasion (see Clark, 1981, p. 204). The monetarists learnt from their enemy. It was the Fabian Society which provided the model for the Institute, and organisations like the innocuously named Centre for Policy Studies. These worked by commissioning papers, holding seminars, and publishing articles. The new right found inspiration from social as much as economic thought. As Sir Alfred Sherman wrote in the preface of CPS pamphlets 'Out object is to re-shape the climate of opinion' (Keegan, 1984, p. 153).

It was the inflation of the 1970s which provided the catalyst. Keynesian orthodoxy had no solution and 'into the vacuum of economic policy' as Robin Murray put it 'monetarism marched with the confidence of a zealot' (Murray, 1984, p. 208). Ideas which had seemed marginal and absurd became respectable and orthodox, and it was ideas which led to the monetarist revolution, not just an advertising agent's campaign plan.

One of the key areas which monetarism won first was the media.

In the popular press this took the form of an attack on the welfare state, while the quality papers elaborated the new theories. Between 1976 and 1979 *The Times* may have had a few headlines about unemployment, but it had nearly 170 major articles and leaders developing 'monetarist' theories. In policing the boundaries of the permissible the media helped to change the levels of unemployment which were seen to be a threat to governments.

In addition, the media provide the cultural background for political changes. They establish, or amplify, political moods. As one newspaper put it 'in all the places where opinion is formed and influenced, packaged and marketed, to be on the Right now is not merely respectable: it is fashionable' (*Sunday Times*, 1984).

INFORMATION, COMPARISON AND POLICY

Journalists, writers and broadcasters have always been aware of the influence they may exert. In the 1930s and 1940s reformers believed that more would be done to alleviate the condition of the unemployed if their situation was made known to the politically active classes. In this way Orwell's *The Road to Wigan Pier* (Orwell, 1937) and Humphrey Jennings' films on housing and health were seen as revelationary reports. They were to expose the previously unknown truth to the protected middle classes, which incidentally mobilised sympathy and support for progressive policies.

As Paddy Scannel shows in his study of the 1930s BBC programmes on unemployment, the voice and tone of the work depended on broadcasters' images of the audience. The intent of the programmes was always the same: 'they were an appeal to the conscience of the nation and call for voluntary efforts to mitigate the worst consequences of unemployment' (Scannel, 1980, p. 17). BBC reporters imagined that their audience was composed of middle-class suburban families. Their treatment of unemployment (which caused far more vigorous opposition, and was regarded more seriously than now) involved talks by experts, with important advances in documentary broadcasting. Almost for the first time working class unemployed people were allowed to speak (scripted, but self-scripted), directly to the public. The programmes were not intended for the unemployed, but to mobilise knowledge of and sympathy for them. One significant effect was to mobilise programme makers into political action as well.

The innovative style of these 'progressive' programmes was inevitably the subject of parody: 'Have I told you chaps what I heard last night at the unemployment club?' 'Yes, it was about lace-making to keep the chaps cheerful' joked one contemporary play produced for a BBC Northern regional audience that knew a little more directly about unemployment (see Scannell, 1980, p. 15). More importantly, the rigid distinctions between political and social issues, fact and comment, had not developed, so the programmes were wider in their impact than is now possible, and were timed with less political discretion. On the evening before a parliamentary debate on benefit rates in 1933, the BBC broadcast a programme about the conditions in which the unemployed in different parts of the country actually lived.

The idea that 'exposure' and 'revelation' are the key role of the media in presenting political issues has remained dominant. The tone of the 1930s programmes may seem patronising to the modern ear but their implicit argument and style is recognisable and familiar. Unemployment and its social consequences have been explored in numerous documentary and current affairs programmes and have provided the theme in five major fictional series in recent years. The aims of current affairs coverage in the 1980s have been similar to those programmes on the same subject in the 1930s – to inform in order to mobilise someone other than the subjects of the programmes. What might have been expected to have changed rather more than it has is the approach to the unemployed. In the 1930s what they had to say was scripted. In the 1980s they talk direct to camera – but what they say is edited and organised – to demonstrate the argument of the programme, to expose, to reveal.

In some respects the fictional series have broken traditional convention in presenting the unemployed, and have examined the impact of unemployment within the communities and groups which experience it. Yet they have been limited by their failure to escape from the cliches of experience, emotion, personal crises and private life which form the convention of television drama. Even such innovative series as *The Boys from the Blackstuff* ultimately personalised the issues, resulting in unemployment being characterised as an affliction which affects individuals, thus under-representing the systematic nature of unemployment in the 1980s.

In the 1930s the aim of the 'literature of conscience' (and the journalism associated with it) was to demonstrate the injustice of the condition of the unemployed to 'the public', who would then be moved to alleviate their condition. In the 1980s at least some part of this tradition seems concerned to demonstrate that the unemployed are recognisably normal. Yet the capacity of information to mobilise sympathy or action is by no means direct. Indeed writing and broadcasting which was both an influence on and an expression of the reformist tone of progressive thought in the 1930s and 1940s may now have a different function. The tradition of 'revelation' in the media handling of welfare issues and the implicit assumption about the kinds of political action needed to solve problems now operates in a climate where the welfare state is being increasingly rejected.

SCROUNGERPHOBIA AND BLAME

There is considerable evidence that attitudes towards welfare and the unemployed are more hostile and more divisive in Britain than elsewhere. Research has suggested that the British are more likely than other Europeans to perceive poverty and unemployment as the 'fault' of its victims, rather than the result of any structural injustice (Eurobarometer, 1982). Paradoxically, as unemployment worsens, individuals here are blamed more, not less for their situation (Economist Intelligence Unit, 1982b), while unemployment in Britain is more fiercely concentrated amongst the poorest than anywhere else in Europe or America (Sinfield, 1981).

The role of the media in elaborating hostile stereotypes of the unemployed has been well documented. Attacks on the welfare state in the popular press started before alterations in public and political opinion. Golding and Middleton suggested that the current period of economic recession was at first particularly unacceptable because 'it followed a period of widespread belief in universal prosperity and progress. The deepening gloom thus required explanation and management, a task for which the news media are strategically placed' (Golding and Middleton, 1979, p. 5). They demonstrate how a series of popular newspaper stories about fraudulent social security claims led to a general questioning of the purposes of the welfare system, in which the interests of tax payers were increasingly posed against those of 'claimants'. The media presented criminal images of the unemployed and produced a set of derogatory images of welfare. Whatever the existing popular anxieties about the welfare system, the researchers argued that such 'focusing of moral outrage does as much to create concern as to reflect it' (Golding and Middleton, 1980, p. 79). The campaign created an apparent unity between taxpayers and workers as it implied they were being exploited by feckless claimants. Bea Campbell has pointed out that there were special targets for the media's scroungerphobia – single mothers and homeless men. These two categories, she argued, were at risk because they disturbed conventional notions of male and female roles. Both these groups, she suggests, 'are subject to the most intense state scrutiny because they are both in greatest need of state support and represent the greatest challenge to 'normal' masculinity and femininity within the family' (Campbell, 1984, p. 22). Unemployment, it is implied, is a problem for the marginal and unstable. It is not part of normal experience. A media campaign launched in the popular press was then taken up, initially quite uncritically, by broadcasting, and in turn reflected on by the 'quality' press.

An effect of these stereotypes is to reduce the numbers that are seen as genuinely unemployed. This is done by suggesting that many without paid employment are 'unemployable', not willing to work, better off on benefits, or scroungers. Similar images can be found in the press of the 1930s (Deacon, 1980; 1981) and then, as now, helped politicians to de-politicise the issue by making it personal. But in the 1930s, unemployment was characterised as an unfortunate state which politicians could do little to control. 'It is a sad fact', claimed Stanley Baldwin, the Conservative Prime Minister, 'but unemployment is not something the government can claim to be able to affect' (quoted in Middlemass and Barnes, 1971). In the 1980s unemployment has become a tool which governments claim they have to wield in order to combat the greater ills of inflation and recession. Unemployment is used, and is justified as for the good of the country as a whole.

In the 1980s images of the unemployed as lazy, work-shy or criminal operate in a different press climate from the 1930s. Newspaper stories imply that the state is beleagured by false and fraudulent claimants, and that those who claim welfare benefits are not full citizens. Yet this 'witch hunt' is occurring against a background, at least in the popular press, of an obsession with the irrational. As Phillip Elliot pointed out, the popular press contains very little news at all by the 1980s, and is concerned rather with the manufacture of scares, scandals, and stories of magic, the unpredictable and inexplicable events (Elliot, 1982). In this context, the popular press seem to be operating as a mobiliser of fears rather than of hopes or action.

Unemployment is thus often portrayed, not as a political problem, but as a social threat.

These perjorative images of the unemployed have a complex impact. For policy makers the media apparently reduce the urgency of the problem by removing large numbers of people from the category of 'deserving unemployed'. For those with little or no direct experience of unemployment it distances unemployment and isolates the unemployed even further, while for the unemployed it may confine them in apathy.

CONCLUSION

When images of welfare and the unemployed are put in historical context, other aspects of their political effect become clear. The images of the unemployed developed in the 1980s are clearly related to images of the role of the public in the inflation that preceded depression. Both issues have proved particularly susceptible to moral interpretation. Both are conditions which have been seen as corrupting or as the product of corruption. These interpretations have sustained and been used by a Conservative government which has tended to transform most policy issues into more general problems of values. Rather than concentrating on solutions to particular problems, it has answered criticisms by escalation up the moral scale to issues of compassion and authority. This has done its media image less harm than might have been expected. Broadcasting in particular has numerous devices for demonstrating normative style and reporting images, but it is less good at investigative reporting (Seaton, 1985). The media prompted by the new political consensus that higher rates of unemployment are both necessary and irreversible, have been particularly concerned with allocating blame. They have, in comparison with the previous period, lodged more of it with the public. The media have also provided an imagery to accompany and reinforce the argument.

In particular, the link between the media's interpretation of the politics of inflation and the politics on unemployment is important, because the imagery of the first established the conditions for the latter. Initially both phenomena are explained, for different reasons as being beyond the power of governments. They have both also been interpreted as leading to political apathy. Yet unemployment is now seen as the 'cure' for inflation. Perceptions of both problems have changed. What is clear, however, is that there is apparently a remarkable breakdown in the link between what the public perceive as urgent political problems and the willingness of the public to hold the government responsible for their solution.

The media have not merely reflected social and political change, nor have they simply been manipulated by governments. At the same time they have not been an overriding independent influence on attitudes towards unemployment. All of these models propose far too crude a relationship between politics and the media. That a new orthodoxy has been established with startling rapidity is incontestable, yet its emergence remains puzzling. Views about the role of the state, the effects of the market, the responsibilities of politicians, and the scope of political action to remedy unemployment have changed with considerable speed. The changes were as dramatic amongst the political elite as they were in the public. This paper only begins to identify the problems of analysing the media's role in such a complex revolution. But it has established that there was a shift in the consensus about the proper political response to unemployment, and that the media played an important part in these changes. In doing so the political role of the press and broadcasting itself was altered. The media elaborated the shift in the consensus about unemployment, and crucially acted as the catalyst of the new popular orthodoxy.

3 Women's Unemployment in the 1930s: Some Comparison with the 1980s

JENNIFER HURSTFIELD

INTRODUCTION

In the inter-war period in Britain, registered unemployment never dropped below 10 per cent of the insured labour force. At its peak in January 1933, official estimates were of nearly 3 million people unemployed – about 22 per cent of insured workers. If the unregistered and uninsured had been included, the totals would have been much higher. Today, when government estimates for the numbers of unemployed have topped 3 million, parallels between the 1930s and the 1980s are frequently evoked. Mass unemployment and the absence of any imminent sense of economic recovery are strongly reminiscent of the early 1930s.

In this situation, a number of studies have raised theoretical issues about the impact of unemployment on sexual divisions at work and in the family. There has been a debate about the differential impact of the recession on male and female workers (see e.g. Bruegel, 1979; Rubery and Tarling, 1982). Have women been the first to lose their jobs, reflecting their more tenuous hold in the labour market as the reserve army of labour thesis would suggest? Or has the restructuring of the economy in the last fifteen years meant that women's concentration in the service sector has cushioned them against the worst of the decline in jobs in the manufacturing sector? The answer seems to depend both on the region and the industry being examined. But certainly as several studies have pointed out, the rigidity of sex segregation in the labour market means that in times of unemployment, women can not easily be replaced by men (Rubery and Tarling, 1982).

The same questions can be raised about the 1930s, and this paper will examine the levels of unemployment among men and women, and how these are related to the restructuring of the economy in that period. But the central focus is concerned with the differential representation of male and female unemployment in social surveys in the 1930s. It will be argued that most of them ignored the seriousness of women's unemployment and reproduced rather than contradicted the popular view that, while unemployment was a terrible thing for everyone, it struck at men's identity as workers, while women were affected not primarily as workers, but as wives and mothers. The paper will explore some of the reasons for this treatment including the role of the state in marginalising the significance of women's unemployment. The last part of the paper will highlight certain parallels and contrasts between the 1930s and the present day.

RESTRUCTURING IN THE 1930s

To set the social surveys from the 1930s in context, it is necessary to provide some background on the character of the economic crisis. There is a substantial body of research by economic historians which throws light on the restructuring of capital which occurred during the inter-war period.[1] The main features were a long-term downturn in demand for the products of what had traditionally been Britain's staple industries. Ship-building, iron and steel, coal, and cotton textiles all suffered a severe decline. With the exception of textiles, this collapse particularly affected men's jobs.

The depression also had a regional character. South Wales, Central Scotland and Northern England were hardest hit. In contrast the Southeast and the Midlands were less affected, in part because they became the sites for what contemporaries referred to as the 'new industries'. By this they meant industries such as electrical engineering, motor manufacturing, food processing and rayon. Some of the industries incorporated new mass production technologies, such as assembly lines, and in many instances they were located on the suburban edge of cities – for example, GEC and Austin in Birmingham. Although the growth of these new industries did not offset the much more dramatic decline in the traditional staple industries, this restructuring did play an important part in determining the distribution of unemployment between men and women. Employers in the new industries often drew on young single women for their labour force, and much of the semi-skilled assembly work was sex-typed as 'women's work' from the outset (for a discussion of this see Glucksmann, 1984). There was also some expansion in the service industries such as catering, and retail distribution, which were also predominately women's jobs. The uneven impact of unemployment mirrored this sexual segregation in the labour market.

The form of this restructuring might therefore lead one to expect that men would be more vulnerable to redundancy and long-term unemployment than women. Certainly the official estimates of unemployment rates lend support to this impression. Although the two main sources collected the data on different bases, they both show a higher proportion of men unemployed. The 1931 Census reported an average unemployment rate for men of 12.7 per cent and 8.6 per cent for women, based on the numbers of unemployed as a percentage of the occupied population aged 14 and over (UK Census, 1931). The Ministry of Labour statistics were based instead on the numbers of insured workers who registered at Labour Exchanges as a proportion of the total number of insured workers. For most of the inter-war period they show a rate for women of between a half and two thirds that of the male rate. A series of articles by William Beveridge in 1936 and 1937 drew upon the Ministry figures to argue that women had a lower unemployment rate than men and also suffered less from long-term unemployment (Beveridge, 1936, 1937a, 1937b).

It will be argued in a later section that these official figures incorporated a particular construction of unemployment which distorted both the extent and the nature of women's unemployment. The point here is simply that those statistics that were widely available tended to confirm the view that men had a much higher unemployment rate than women.

SOCIAL SURVEYS IN THE 1930s

In the 1920s and the 1930s there were a large number of industrial surveys documenting the economic conditions in areas of high unemployment. These studies, often commissioned by the government, provide a wealth of data on patterns of employment in different regions. This article is not concerned with analysing these studies which contain considerable valuable information on the industrial distribution of male and female unemployment. Instead I am concerned with the social surveys which had widened their focus to encompass the social and psychological repercussions of unemployment. Such studies were attempting to depict something of the subjective dimensions of unemployment, and the way in which the unemployed themselves were experiencing and responding to unemployment. These surveys were often conducted by teams of researchers based at the local university. In some cases they were done by individuals. I have selected a few examples to illustrate the argument that they contributed to the denial of women's unemployment as a problem meriting research.

E. W. Bakke's study of unemployment in Greenwich, London, is regarded as a pioneering study, because it took as its central theme the issue of how the unemployed themselves viewed their situation, and the system of unemployment benefits (Bakke, 1933). At the time Bakke was an American graduate student, and later he became Director of Unemployment Studies at Yale. He based his study on observation, interviews and diaries kept by the unemployed. However, as his title, *The Unemployed Man*, makes clear, he sought and reported only the experiences of men. He does not seem to have interviewed women and even the discussion of family and home life is based exclusively on what the men say about family life. When he comes to look at work opportunities for young people, he deals only with boys and the effect of having an unemployed father. Bakke does make mention of the fact that very few women had paid employment after marriage even if their husbands were unemployed. But he does not enquire into the situation of women to uncover how they might feel about the lack of opportunities for paid employment. His interest was in the effects on men as the breadwinners in becoming unemployed, and their loss of energy and direction as the period of time without work lengthened. He uses his research to challenge notions of the unemployed as 'work-shy' and to argue for adequate systems of national insurance provision. With respect to male unemployment his analysis was progressive and empathetic. But within his analysis women and girls were largely invisible.

A second example is the *Social Survey of Merseyside*, published in 1934. Edited by D. Caradog Jones, it was a major three volume study based in part on the results of a 1:30 household survey. Statistical data on both male and female unemployment is presented showing that the numbers and proportion of men unemployed are considerably larger than those of women. But the undeniably higher male rate is then used to legitimate an analysis which continually stresses the demoralising consequences for male workers only. The human cost of unemployment, 'expressed in terms of the deterioration which a man is liable to suffer when his labour is not used for some time – cannot be measured' (Jones, 1934, p. 3). There is a discussion of clerical work, which notes that employers preferred a succession of young girls as employees to either men or older women. The official statistics show a higher rate of unemployment for men and the report comments: 'A pathetic demoralisation begins to reveal itself when a clerk is long out of work. He becomes shabby, down-at-heel and unemployable' (Jones, 1934, p. 328). The survey found that in 1931 of a sample of 471 claimants of unemployment benefit, 391 were male and 80 female. This leads to a detailed discussion of the men, but the author comments that the number of women is too small for more than 'passing reference'. The numbers argument is consistently used to provide the rationale for the focus on men.

A study of a South Wales mining village provides the third example. *Brynmawr: a Study of a Distressed Area*, by Hilda Jennings was published in 1934 and based on a survey conducted in 1929–32 by the local Community Study Council with some academic consultants. The introduction states that 'All sections of the community have taken part in the Survey, which has been planned as a community self-study in which the experiences of the employed and unemployed and the point of view of men of every shade of opinion should have its due weight' (Jennings, 1934, p. v). The emphasis on men is understandable given that Brymawr was a small village dependent on mining. But even so it is remarkable that in the chapter on the extent and effect of unemployment, women should receive no mention at all. There is a discussion of the psychological consequences for men, and their experience of financial dependency and sense of being wasted. There is also a discussion of the perpetuation of this cycle of deprivation in the school; but, as in Bakke's study, only boys are discussed and girls are not referred to.

Even in Sheffield, a city where registered unemployment reached 40 per cent among men, and 20 per cent among women in 1932, the debilitating impact on women is not examined. In 1932 A. D. K. Owen wrote a report entitled *Unemployment in Sheffield* based partly on a survey of 1:10 on the unemployment register. In many ways it is an excellent report which succinctly documents the collapse in demand for iron and steel and its impact on male employment. But the section on the psychological effects reiterates the same theme: 'The effect of unemployment on most men is to create a feeling of insecurity which amounts – among some older men – to a haunting dread of the possibility of never getting a job again (Owen, 1932, p. 64). What about the effect on older women? The question is neither asked nor answered. Owen categorises his male respondents into three groups according to their responses to unemployment, but does not discuss the women's responses.

These are a few examples to which others could be added (e.g. Lush, 1941) to illustrate the argument that social science surveys of the period consistently neglected researching the issue of women's experience of unemployment. There is also extensive American literature from the 1930s specifically on the psychological effects of unemployment. In a thirty page review of this literature, Eisenberg and Lazarsfield (1938) devote only one paragraph to women and are able to cite only half-a-dozen references specifically on women. There is only one major exception to this uniformity in Britain, and that is the study commissioned by the Pilgrim Trust and ironically published under the title *Men without Work* in 1938 (Pilgrim Trust, 1938).

The focus of *Men without Work* was on the long-term unemployed – i.e. those who had been unemployed for more than one year. While other studies had defined this as a predominantly male issue, the authors of the study set out to ensure that the sample included enough women to be able to say something about the problems facing the long-term unemployed woman. Therefore, while official figures indicated that women comprised about 6 per cent of the long-term unemployed, in this survey women made up 14 per cent of the sample.

One chapter is devoted to a discussion of women. The survey was conducted in six areas where women's expectations of having paid employment varied considerably: the Rhondda and south-west Durham where women did not usually work outside the home; Blackburn and Leicester where women expected to be in paid employment all their lives; and Liverpool where women were believed to regard work as a stop-gap between school and marriage. In the sixth area, Deptford, there was very little long-term female unemployment. The report argues that the effect on women of losing their jobs depended in part on their expectation of working after marriage. Thus in cities like Blackburn and Leicester where women had expected to work all their lives, unemployment came as much as a shock as it did for men. The discussion of Blackburn where unemployment was concentrated in the cotton mills, provides a vivid sense of the ways in which women were undermined. The investigators describe young women with small children missing the factory company and wanting to get back to work. For them as for men, work is about social life as well as money:

> Though she does not say much, it is easy to see that being out of a job is a great blow to her, and that not entirely on financial grounds. She says she misses the company, and evidently she feels very keenly being told that she is too old for work. [Age 47. Interviewer's notes.] (Pilgrim Trust, 1938, p. 239)

The interviews also exposed the ways in which women, like men, began to lose their confidence as the months went by. Many women said they did not feel up to returning to work after a period of unemployment. The report comments perceptively: 'The strain of being out of work for a long time has told upon them mentally and physically. They have lost confidence in themselves as workers. . . . They are convinced that their eyesight or their nerves would not be equal to it' (Pilgrim Trust, 1938, p. 241).

There is thus much valuable material in the report. The analysis is shot through with value judgements in which evidence that women are giving their families priority and staying at home is seen as an 'indication of social progress'. But despite such assumptions, the interviewers clearly listened to enough women and took seriously what they said, to allow them to acknowledge the debilitating effect of unemployment on women who wanted to work. It indicates what might have been picked up in the other social surveys had the investigators asked different questions. In the discussion that follows, *Men Without Work* must be considered the exception.

GOVERNMENT STATISTICS ON UNEMPLOYMENT IN THE 1930s

In this section I want to consider in what respects the majority of social surveys can be argued to have presented a partial and misleading impression of women's experience. One of the major limitations of the social surveys is that they relied heavily on official statistics both to measure and to understand the relative importance of women's unemployment. Whereas today the validity of government statistics on unemployment is openly challenged, in the 1930s there was little critical discussion of their limitations. The figures usually quoted by the surveys are for registered unemployment in insured occupations. At that time several categories of workers, including domestic servants, public employees and white collar workers earning more than £5 per week were not covered by National Insurance, and therefore did not feature in the Ministry of Labour calculations. Although the figures for men and women were affected by this practice, by far the largest category of workers excluded were domestic servants.

More important, however, are the specific state measures which sought to restrict women's eligibility for Unemployment Benefit. Since these measures had an important effect in discouraging married women from registering, I shall briefly outline them. In the 1920s eligibility for extended benefit (the term given to payments to those who did not qualify for the standard benefit) was dependent on a number of conditions. One of these was the household means test which provided that a claimant could be refused benefit on the basis of the total household income. According to calculations by Alan Deacon, approximately 3 per cent of men and 15 per cent of women were refused on income grounds (Deacon, 1977, p. 16). A second condition was that the applicant be 'genuinely seeking whole-time employment', a test which put the onus of proof on the applicant. Deacon notes that by 1927 one in ten of all claims were being disallowed, and of these the proportion for men was 14.9 per cent and 34.3 per cent for women (Deacon, 1977, p. 32).

As a result of widespread opposition from the labour movement, the 'genuinely seeking work' clause was repealed in 1930. But a year later the 1931 Anomalies Act was passed and it is significant that this measure, more than others, struck primarily at married women's right to benefit. The Act stipulated that a married woman had to have paid a certain number of contributions *after* marriage to qualify for benefit. The only exceptions were if she could prove that she was normally employed, would seek work *and* could reasonably expect to obtain work in the district.

The impact of these regulations was devastating. By April 1933 of 299 908 claims refused under the anomalies regulations, 84 per cent were claims by married women (Deacon, 1977, p. 27). But the consequences can best be seen from Table 3.1 which shows that when the 'genuinely seeking work' clause was dropped, the female rate of registered unemployment shot up from 63 per cent of the male rate in 1929 to 90 per cent in 1930. After the anomalies regulations came into force the female rate dropped back in December 1931 to 66 per cent of the male rate.

TABLE 3.1   *Rates of unemployment of males and females, 1927–36 in GB and NI*

	All insured industries		
	Mean unemployment percentage		Rate for females as
Year	Males	Females	per cent of males
1927	11.0	6.2	56
1928	12.3	7.0	57
1929	11.6	7.3	63
1930	16.5	14.8	90
1931 Jan.–Oct.	22.4	18.4	82
1931 Nov.–Dec.	23.1	15.3	66
1932	25.2	13.7	54
1933	23.2	11.4	49
1934	19.3	10.0	52
1935	17.7	9.8	55
1936 Jan.–Aug.	15.6	9.1	58

SOURCE   Beveridge, 1936, p. 358. The table was derived by Beveridge from Ministry of Labour statistics.

The statistics indicate the numbers of women whose claims were disallowed. The introduction of the qualification that a claimant could expect to obtain work established a double standard of eligibility for men and women. In areas of high unemployment there was little hope of fulfilling such conditions. What cannot be assessed, of course, is the number of women who were deterred from even trying to claim benefit. But the very high rate of registered female unemployment in 1930 and early 1931 does at least point to the existence of a huge pool of female labour who, according to their own definition, were unemployed and eligible for benefit.

The significance of this does not appear in the social surveys of the 1930s, as the interviewers did not attempt to talk to women denied benefit, nor did they consider the impact of such treatment on women's identity as workers. The *Social Survey of Sheffield* gives a measure of the impact of the regulations in one town. In the space of two months, October to November, 1931, 2954 insured people were refused benefit, and of these 98.5 per cent were married women. But Owen confines his discussion of the anomalies regulations to an Appendix, and simply notes that after November 1931 very few cases were heard and most of these were married women 'who appeared to have returned to domestic life and to have had little or no intention of taking up employment outside the home again' (Owen, 1932, p. 72).

The extent of female unemployment thus remained concealed. The surveys tended implicitly to legitimise the state's sleight of hand in removing large numbers of women from the category of unemployed. This can be seen in the 1934 study of Merseyside. This household survey recorded a man as unemployed if he was normally engaged in regular work but had been unemployed in the previous week. Women had not only to fulfil that condition but in addition 'Any woman, of whom no evidence was recorded that she was seeking work, was also relegated to the non-earning class', i.e. she was not classified as 'unemployed' (Jones, 1934, p. 384).

The social surveys also tended to reinforce the impression given by the official statistics that women were much less affected by long-term unemployment than men. The figures for registered unemployment certainly show that trend. But it is also highly likely that women were discouraged from registering by the measures discussed above. Furthermore marriage bars in many occupations prevented some women from maintaining their jobs after marriage. These bars operated selectively as Ray Strachey pointed out: 'It is a significant fact that the barriers apply almost entirely to the stable and better-paid employments, and vanish at the level where cheap labour and casual work are the rule' (1934, p. 335). Certainly in clerical work, the professions, and in some skilled manual work married women found themselves excluded from their jobs. This is not the only factor but a significant one in accounting for the fact that between the wars only about 10 per cent of married women were in the labour force – compared with 70 per cent of single and 40 per cent of widowed and divorced women. These figures from the censuses are undoubtedly under-estimates of the numbers of women in paid employment, (excluding as they do women who worked part-time or in seasonal work) and it is also the case that some women retained their jobs after marriage by concealing their status. However, the proportion of married women in the recorded labour force was undoubtedly small, and it is arguable that the marriage bars constituted a form of coerced and long-term unemployment. It was not a form of unemployment which received attention from researchers in the 1930s.

I have argued above that the majority of social surveys reinforced rather than challenged the ideology which denied many women unemployed status. The question remains: why did they do this? Social research in the 1930s has to be situated in an ideological climate hostile to married women's claims to a place in the labour force. The women who were most severely affected by unemployment were married women. In 1931 married women made up 13.6 per cent of employed women, but 31.9 per cent of the total of unemployed women (Davidoff, 1956, p. 313). Yet outside the campaigns of some women trade unionists and women's rights groups, there was little sympathy for the unemployed married woman (Davidoff, 1956; Lewis, 1980; Strachey, 1935). As Deacon (1977) has shown, there was comparatively little opposition to the passing of the Anomalies Act in 1931 because the regulations were directed at married women. Married women workers were seen as a threat in that they might displace men and undercut their wages. There were several contemporary articles debating whether or not women were 'taking' men's jobs (e.g. Davies, 1931). As unemployment reached its peak in 1932–33 popular opposition grew to the idea that any home might have two wages going into it while others had none.

These ideas were frequently expressed by married women themselves. In a series of BBC talks in 1934, based on interviews with eleven unemployed people, one of the two women interviewed says: 'The women nowadays don't want the work if it gives the men a chance. I feel our job is to be at home.' (Green, 1935, p. 83). It is perhaps hardly surprising that married women's unemployment was not easily defined as a problem requiring investigation. By 1938, H. W. Robinson could casually note that 'married women are not not considered to be unemployed' as if no explanation was required (British Association for the Advancement of Science, 1938, p. 96).

But secondly, the underlying framework for the studies undoubtedly reflects the backgrounds and disciplines of those who conducted the research. In the 1930s Sociology had only one recognised base which was at the London School of Economics, and even there it met with considerable opposition. Elsewhere the discipline had no secure foothold. As Philip Abrams has shown, Sociology 'languished' until after the Second World War, and institutional resistance to the discipline drove many potential sociologists into the expanding opportunities in government administration or politics (Abrams, 1968, p. 149). Social research was characterised by an empirical, fact-gathering methodology, and largely carried out by those with backgrounds in economics, statistics and administration. For those with such backgrounds there were opportunities for mobility between government posts and academia, and many of the studies reflect an internalisation of the frameworks within which government policies were debated rather than a more independent, critical stance. Furthermore, the fact that the majority of the studies of unemployment were directed by men no doubt played its part in shaping the research assumptions about the appropriate roles for men and women. It is perhaps instructive as well as interesting to note that in the Introduction to the Pilgrim Trust report, the Chairman notes that it was the Secretary to the Committee, Eleanora Iredale who 'devoted special attention to that part of the enquiry which relates to women's unemployment' (Pilgrim Trust, 1938, p. ix).

PARALLELS BETWEEN THE 1930s AND THE 1980s

In the last part of this paper I consider what parallels may be drawn between the 1930s and the 1980s. My discussion is necessarily brief but the discussion of the situation in the 1930s will hopefully suggest many more points of comparison and difference than those which can be dealt with here (see also Walby, 1983).

A major issue is the extent of unemployment and the differential impact on men and women. There has been far more analysis of this dimension than there was in the 1930s. The research done in the 1970s on sex segregation in the occupational structure has provided the basis for understanding the uneven impact of unemployment (e.g. Hakim, 1978). The expansion of the service sector in the 1970s with its recruitment of part-time workers as a crucial part of the labour force, the majority of them married women, meant that when the recession struck first at manufacturing industries, women were in relatively protected sectors of the economy. The down-turn in the services sector came later resulting in a growth in the unemployment rate among women. Now, in 1984, the small increase in employment that is occurring is apparently concentrated once again in the service industries, and has been made up of part-time women workers.

These changes can be, as in the 1930s, set in the wider context of a restructuring of the economy. Doreen Massey has summarised the salient aspects of this transformation, and describes how 'de-industrialisation' and changes in the labour process in certain industries (some of them the 'new industries' of the 1930s), have been accompanied by a recomposition of the labour force. Her comment that 'The archetypal shift is from male manual workers classified as skilled to female assemblers classified as unskilled or semi-skilled' is reminiscent of changes occurring in the 1930s at a different stage of technological development (Massey, 1983, p. 23).

Once again the official statistics tell the same story of men being worse affected than women. Government figures for September 1983 showed an average unemployment rate of 8.6 per cent for women compared with 15 per cent for men. But in the 1980s government statistics have been subject to a barrage of criticism (see e.g. Irvine *et al.*, 1979). These criticisms have highlighted the means by which the government has artificially reduced the numbers of the unemployed by changing the methods of compiling the statistics. A number of groups have been rendered invisible in the last two years including school leavers and men over sixty. But, as in the 1930s, it appears that married women comprise the largest group among the 'hidden unemployed'. Many married women do not register as unemployed because they are not eligible for unemployment benefit. Until October, 1982 those who did register for work were counted among the unemployed even if they could not claim benefit. Unemployment is now measured on the basis of those actually claiming benefit. According to the 1983 Labour Force Survey, over half of those who were seeking work but not claiming benefit, were married women (DoE, 1984b). The level of women's unemployment is also extremely hard to quantify because the criteria used in recording the labour force results in an under-estimate of women's involvement in paid work. Large numbers of women who engage in homework, casual or seasonal work never appear in the official statistics (Allen, 1982b). It is therefore very difficult to estimate the proportion of the female labour force who are unemployed, since both the numbers in paid work and the numbers unemployed are underestimated.

There have also been measures which have further affected women's eligibility for unemployment benefit. Claimants can now be questioned on their availability for work and arrangements for child care. In addition if a claimant is specifically seeking part-time work he or she can be refused benefit on the grounds that they are placing 'unreasonable restrictions' on their availability for work. The application of this regulation seems to be discretionary as is the interpretation of 'unreasonable'. Since about 40 per cent of women work part-time compared with 5 per cent of men such regulations embody forms of indirect discrimination against married women reminiscent of the Anomalies Act of 1931.

The consequences of such measures today are similar to the past: they divide on a sex basis the ranks of the unemployed; they undermine women's claims to be unemployed, and implicitly loosen their foothold in the labour market. Ideologically such state strategies reinforce the identification of masculinity with the breadwinner and femininity with caring for the home and children. They shore up sexual divisions in the family as well as in the labour market. Unlike the 1930s, however, there is more resistance to such measures, and the state now operates in a context where the definition of who is unemployed has become a more overt arena of struggle. For example, women's groups have organised campaigns aimed at encouraging women to sign on, claim benefit and in general identify themselves as 'unemployed'.

There is a further aspect of the comparison between the 1930s and the 1980s, which throws some light on the contradictory nature of the struggle to assert women's equal right to be defined as unemployed. As in the 1930s there have been a number of sociological studies of the impact of unemployment on the identity of those without work. As Gordon Marshall (1984) has pointed out, most of these studies in the 1970s focused on groups of male workers and attempted to explore the consequences for them of unemployment.

The attention to men yet again mirrors the 1930s. However, more recently, there has at last been a shift of attention and a number of studies are now surfacing which throw light on women's subjective experience. Of these the most substantial to date is the *Women's Employment Survey* (Martin and Roberts, 1984). The report on the survey has a chapter on unemployment which does full justice to the complexity of women's self-perceptions. Particularly interesting from the perspective of this article is the light it throws on the refusal by many women to define or even see themselves as 'unemployed'. In careful detail the report documents the way in which women's relationship to the family means that some married women reject the notion of themselves as unemployed because they see themselves as busy and occupied in the home. Whereas the single women can identify with the term, for married women it becomes yet another way in which the labour they do in the home can become devalued. Case studies were commissioned to supplement the main survey

(Cragg and Dawson, 1984; Martin and Wallace, 1984). The in-depth interviews by Cragg and Dawson further amplify the survey findings. They quote women as perceiving a radical divergence between their own situation and that of an unemployed male worker. Wanting, sometimes desperately, to get back to work themselves, they none the less perceive the man as suffering more hardship because he has no role, nothing to do, his identity is stripped. Thus they end up identifying with an ideology which prioritises male claims for preferential treatment:

I think women are silly to think of themselves as unemployed because running a home is a job. In fact it's a full-time job. It's a job that's unpaid but I still don't see that I'm unemployed.

At least when a woman's unemployed she can do housework. She can generally busy herself, whereas if a man's got no hobbies, he's worse off.

If I were a man and I had a family to keep, I'd get a bit emotive about a married woman taking a full-time job that a man could do. (Cragg and Dawson, 1984, pp. 18, 64 and 65)

This complex process of identification means that now, as in the 1930s, attempts to affirm women's claims whether to unemployment benefit or simply to be counted among the unemployed have to take account of the ambivalent identification with domesticity which mediates any simple relationship of women to unemployment. Such parallels should not, however, mask an important difference between the periods. The transformation of married women's relationship to employment has been one of the central changes since the Second World War. Nearly all women now expect to engage in paid labour for long periods after marriage. This expectation of paid employment means that women do not lightly accept redundancy. Angela Coyle's study of workers made redundant in two Yorkshire clothing factories found that the women as well as the men were acutely aware that it was hard to survive on one wage alone. Many of the women strongly affirmed both single and married women's right to a job, and the crucial role their earnings played in the maintenance of their families. What is also clear from Coyle's interviews is that work represented financial independence and a level of personal autonomy that unemployment removed:

For once in my life I feel as though I'm being kept and I've never had that feeling, I've always been very independent . . . I've felt it terribly, that loss of independence. (Coyle, 1984, p. 107)

This study throws light on the overlapping but different experience of unemployment for men and women. The difference now, as in the 1930s, reflects the continuing gap between the level of men and women's involvement in domestic labour. As Beatrix Campbell writes:

It is not that redundancy is worse for men than for women just because they are men or because their work matters more to them. But there is still a difference, and it explains much of what makes redundancy a crisis for men. It rests on their relationship to the home, because it is unemployment that puts men firmly in their homes, full-time, for the first time in their lives. (Campbell, 1984, p. 171)

She is writing of the 1980s, but her words could equally apply to Britain in the 1930s. In times of recession these divergent experiences are there to be drawn upon, to be interpreted and used in different ways, both by the state and by women and men themselves.

NOTE

1. There is a vast literature on the growth of the new industries in the inter-war period. See especially Aldcroft, 1970; Branson and Heinemann, 1971; Buxton and Aldcroft, 1979; Hannah, 1983; and Plummer, 1937. However, none of these studies gives attention to the question of how and why employers in the expanding industries turned to female labour for its semi-skilled workforce. A substantial contribution to analysing the sexual division of labour in the new industries is the paper by Miriam Glucksmann (1984).

4 Change and Continuity in the Youth Labour Market: a Critical Review of Structural Explanations of Youth Unemployment[1]

DAVID RAFFE

THE STRUCTURAL EXPLANATION OF YOUTH UNEMPLOYMENT

An orthodoxy of pessimism dominates the current debate about youth unemployment. The massive increase in youth unemployment since the early 1970s, according to many commentators, results from factors over and above the recessionary influences which caused adult unemployment to rise. Even if adult unemployment were to fall to the levels of the 1960s, it is argued, youth unemployment would remain high. This is the 'structural explanation' of youth unemployment.

In conventional economic analysis '[s]tructural unemployment may be said to exist when there is a mismatching between the unemployed and the available jobs in terms of regional location, required skills, or any other relevant dimension' (Lipsey, 1979, p. 736). It is usually defined in opposition to demand-deficient unemployment. The structural explanation of youth unemployment claims that jobs have increasingly demanded workers with skills or other attributes not usually possessed by young people, and that young people have failed to adapt to this situation. The structural explanation therefore attributes rising youth unemployment to factors over and above the declining aggregate demand for labour which recession entails, and is advanced in opposition to the view that the present level of youth unemployment is wholly or largely recession-induced. The structural explanation is therefore based on changes in the composition rather than the level of the demand for labour; it maintains that the demand for young workers would have fallen even if total employment levels had remained constant.

The term structural has a narrower meaning here than in many other social–scientific explanations. It does not refer to factors which depress the aggregate demand for labour, or to factors which make young people disproportionately vulnerable to the recessionary process (although both might appropriately be termed structural in other contexts).

Most structural arguments refer to alleged changes on the demand side of the labour market.[2] They correspond to the first two of Lee's (1981) three categories of industrial, occupational and cyclical shifts. Lee's third category, cyclical shifts, is analogous to the alternative, recession-induced explanation. In what follows a variety of structural explanations are examined and found to be deficient. It is argued that the evidence for such explanations is generally weak and inconclusive and that it frequently rests upon a misinterpretation of the effects of recession. The effects of structural changes on levels of youth unemployment are uncertain, but they are probably variable in direction and small in their net quantitative impact. Overwhelmingly the main explanation for the present high level of youth unemployment is the recession.

THE INDUSTRIAL-SHIFT ARGUMENT

The industrial-shift argument claims that young people's employment has been concentrated in industries whose total employment has declined faster than average. Specific versions point to 'a general decline in manufacturing employment' (BYC, 1979, p. 8; Rees and Gregory, 1981, pp. 9–10; Sawdon and Taylor, 1980, pp. 30–2) or to the recent reduction in apprenticeships (Ashton and Maguire, 1983, pp. 5–6).

The industrial-shift argument assumes that the industrial composition of youth employment is very different from that of adults. This is not in fact the case. Only in one industry (construction) did teenagers comprise more than 12 per cent of male employees in 1971; the average for all industries was 7 per cent. Teenagers comprised a larger proportion of the female workforce (11 per cent), but still accounted for less than one in five of workers within each industry (Jolly *et al.*, 1980, pp. 81–2). More importantly, there is little evidence that young people have been disproportionately employed in declining industries. In an analysis of all manufacturing industries for the period 1968–75, Jolly *et al.* (1980, p. 131) find no significant association between the rate of change of employment within each industry and the proportion of either male or female employees aged under twenty-five. Further analysis of their data reveals that, between 1961–71, only 0.2 per cent of jobs held by male teenagers, and 1.8 per cent of jobs held by female teenagers, were lost as a result of the disproportionate employment of teenagers in declining industries. Similar analysis of more recent Scottish data shows that, between 1979–83, only 1.3 per cent of school-leaver jobs were lost for the same reason, although forty-five per cent of school-leaver jobs were lost over the period (Raffe, 1984b). In other words, any disproportionate tendency for young people to work in declining industries was very slight, and very little of the reduction in youth employment can be accounted for in this way.

In a recession youth employment tends to fall faster than adult employment within each industry, as well as in the economy as a whole. Young people, therefore, tend to lose jobs most rapidly in those industries which decline fastest, and the industrial composition of youth employment therefore changes faster than that of adult employment, since young people tend to be excluded from industries which stop recruiting. Such industrial changes may be misinterpreted as evidence of structurally determined youth unemployment, but they are, in fact, simply effects of recession. Were there no recession – that is, were total employment to remain constant – young people would benefit disproportionately from new recruitment into expanding industries, just as they suffer disproportionately from the suspension of recruitment into declining industries. Only if expanding industries employ smaller proportions of young people than contracting industries are young people affected by structural change. The available evidence suggests this has not been the case to any significant extent.

The industrial-shift argument also assumes a substantial degree of rigidity in the age distribution of employment both within and across industries. However, youth employment appears to be flexible with respect to the local industrial structure (Makeham, 1980); just as it is flexible over space, so is it likely to be flexible over time. Implicit in many of the structural arguments is the view that the labour market is segmented in terms of age and that this entails the absence of competition between young and adult workers; if the youth labour market is insulated from the adult market, it is implied, the level of youth employment must be separately determined. But in practice segmentation simply means that competition exists at a group, rather than an individual, level (Ashton *et al.*, 1982). Competition occurs at the point where jobs are designed and recruitment policies formulated, rather than at the point of selection. To the extent that the labour market is segmented in terms of age, employers still have flexibility to switch the age groups from which they recruit.

OCCUPATIONAL SHIFTS: THE ARGUMENT FROM DETAILED ANALYSIS

A parallel argument alleges that young people are adversely affected by changes in the occupational structure. Different versions of this argument, discussed in the following sections, refer respectively to an upskilling process, to a deskilling process, and to the effects of competition from adult women. This section examines arguments which make no prior assumption about the nature or direction of occupational change. Such arguments must analyse occupational changes in detail since they lack a theoretical base for identifying broad occupational categories in terms of which relevant changes might be measured. The NYEC (1974) report refers to the only detailed study of this kind. This analysed the occupations of fifteen to seventeen year olds, as revealed by the 1961, 1966 and 1971 Censuses, and concluded:

> Where the largest numbers of young people's jobs were lost, this was because young people were concentrated in certain occupations where the job loss was high for adults and young people alike. (NYEC, 1974, p. 13)

This study appears to offer strong evidence for a structural effect, but there are three major problems in interpreting its findings. First, the period covered, 1961–71, was a time when the youth labour market was still in a state of excess supply (Merrilees and Wilson,

1979; Wells, 1983) and when levels of participation in full-time education were rising rapidly. Changes in youth employment over the period were largely supply-led, and of doubtful relevance to the structural explanation which seeks to explain more recent changes in term of changes in demand.

Second, the NYEC report neither presents detailed results nor describes the methodology employed in its study. My own analysis (of the data reported by Jolly *et al.*, 1980, pp. 94–5) comes to very different conclusions. Between 1961 and 1971 only 1.5 per cent of male teenage jobs and 1.6 per cent of female teenage jobs were lost as a result of the disproportionate employment of teenagers in contracting occupations. The discrepancy between my results and those of the NYEC may result from the narrower age band studied by the latter, from methodological differences or from the use of different occupational categories. Even if the NYEC conclusions are accepted, this would suggest that young people were only affected by occupational change at the most detailed level; as soon as occupations are aggregated to the twenty six occupational orders of the OPCS (1970) classification, most of the effect disappears. In other words young people were largely affected – if the NYEC's conclusions are valid – by small shifts in the occupational structure between functionally similar occupations. This is consistent with the view that many of the shifts were supply-led; occupations may have changed their titles as they came to be performed by adults rather than young people.

The third problem echoes a point made about the industrial-shift argument. When expressed in terms of detailed occupational categories, the occupational-shift argument presupposes a rigid age distribution of employment within and among occupations; but, again, group- or individual-level competition may make this distribution flexible.

OCCUPATIONAL SHIFTS: THE UPSKILLING ARGUMENT

Other arguments concerning occupational shifts detail the nature or direction of these shifts. The first of these, the upskilling argument, claims that skill demands have risen in the economy as a whole, and that young people are now more likely to be unemployed, as they are less experienced and less skilled than adults and have traditionally worked in the declining, less skilled jobs. Three main types of evidence are used to support this argument.

First, the increasing link between qualifications and employment, and the concentration of unemployment among the unqualified, are alleged to reflect occupational demands for higher levels of skill and ability (NYEC, 1974; Williamson, 1983). However the concentration of unemployment among the unqualified can be explained more convincingly in terms of a queue theory of occupational selection. Employers rank young job-applicants at least partly in terms of qualifications. In periods of low recruitment employers only take on young people from nearer the front of the queue; those at the back of the queue, with fewest qualifications, remain unemployed. At times of recession, therefore, youth unemployment (like adult unemployment) tends to be concentrated among the unqualified and unskilled, but, while this may enable us to say something about employers' relative preferences, it is no evidence of change in the absolute requirements of jobs.

Second, the upskilling argument points to aggregate occupational changes, and especially to the rising proportion of employment in non-manual and nominally skilled occupations. However, these changes are again partly the (reversible) results of recession, which tends to destroy less skilled jobs at a faster rate than skilled jobs. Moreover it is debatable whether skill levels in general have been rising; some non-manual or 'skilled' jobs have themselves been deskilled, and in any case, any upskilling of labour requirements is from a very low base. The levels of skill demanded in a variety of jobs have been very low (Blackburn and Mann, 1979) and many employers have declared themselves more interested in recruiting on the basis of the personalities, motivation and attitudes of workers than of their pre-existing cognitive or technical skills (MSC, 1978; Ashton *et al.*, 1982; Hunt and Small, 1981). There is no evidence that employers have increased their emphasis on ability or skill, relative to other characteristics of job-applicants, as the upskilling theory would predict. Young people are disadvantaged when occupations are restricted to graduates and thereby removed totally from the youth labour market (Ashton and Maguire, 1983, p. 7), but the effects of such changes have almost certainly been outweighed, in recent years, by the growing numbers of young people continuing in full-time education. Between 1972–82 full-time enrolments in non-advanced further education in England rose by 81 per cent (DES, 1983); over the same period the school-leaving age was raised to sixteen, and the proportion of 16 year olds staying on at school also rose towards the end of the decade.

The third source of evidence for the upskilling argument is provided by studies of employment trends within particular industries. These studies have access to more sophisticated concepts of skill than aggregate studies of qualification requirements or occupational titles, but their evidence suffers from two main limitations. First, it usually rests, not upon repeated observations of employers' recruitment behaviour over time, but on employers' own judgements of how recruitment patterns have changed and their expectations of further changes in the future (Ashton *et al.*, 1982; MSC, 1978). Such 'second-hand' evidence of trends can be unreliable. For example, if one accepted such evidence one would have to believe, against all other available evidence, that educational standards have been in a process of continuous decline at least since 1900 (Reeder, 1979). Second, much of the evidence actually identifies effects of recession rather than trends that are structural in the sense used in this paper. For example, a survey of employers in three local labour markets concludes:

> Within the banks, building societies and insurance companies there was an expectation that the introduction of micro-processors and visual display units, together with increased computerization, would improve the productivity of existing staff and so reduce the demand for additional staff. These organisations expect to be able to cope with an increased volume of work without substantially increasing staffing levels. As they have traditionally taken large numbers of school-leavers, such a change would reduce opportunities for those seeking entry, particularly for clerical occupations normally held by females. (Ashton *et al.*, 1982, p. 46).

Nothing in this account suggests that the specifically *occupational* changes – changes in the organisation of work – make young people any less suitable for the work tasks required. The problem is the changing level of employment, not its composition. Since the level of employment is falling, recruitment is cut back and young people are less likely to be taken on. This is an effect of recession, not of structural change. Were total employment levels (across the economy) to remain constant, young people would find jobs instead in the expanding areas.

Occupational changes do not necessarily disadvantage young

people. Many employers prefer to train new workers rather than re-train those who have developed habits associated with older work practices (Livock, 1983, p. 15). School-leaver employment has been high in several new occupations, such as those in manufacturing industries based on information technology. Moreover, to the extent that occupational change proceeds through redundancy and indus-trial re-structuring, adults lose the competitive advantage currently given them by employment protection legislation.

The upskilling argument is not completely unfounded. There is evidence that some firms, at least, may have switched recruitment from young people to more highly qualified or skilled personnel (Ashton *et al.*, 1982). However, most of this evidence is based on a limited number of firms within a very few industries; it does not substantiate the claim that there has been a general process of upskil-ling in the economy, with aggregate effects on youth employment. In any case the pace of any upskilling has been slow, and thus cannot account for the collapse of the youth labour market since 1979.

OCCUPATIONAL SHIFTS: THE DESKILLING ARGUMENT

The second specific argument concerning occupational shifts is that of deskilling, summarised thus:

> Changes in the labour process are putting a premium on experi-enced, self-disciplined workers, who are at once responsible and malleable. Labour process analysts usually treat these changes in terms of deskilling, but from the perspective of young workers the crucial process is 'semi-skilling': tasks are being simplified and routinised, apprenticeship training is becoming increasingly irrelevant for the jobs craftsmen are actually asked to do, but there is, nevertheless, an increased demand for 'responsible autonomy', for workers who will do these simplified, routinised tasks without needing constant supervision and control, who will willingly subject themselves to, and service, costly machines. (Finn and Frith, 1981, p. 75)

Unfortunately deskilling theorists often appear more concerned to explore the theory's political implications (interesting and important as these are) than to provide detailed empirical justification for their claims. We are usually expected to take on trust their interpretations of any research to which they refer (eg Frith, 1980; Finn and Frith, 1981). Seemingly, their accounts owe more to a theoretical extrapolation from a highly generalised theory of trends in the general labour market than to direct observation of trends in the youth labour market. Such evidence as they do refer to is obtained largely from employers' own accounts of their employment policies, and none of their evidence is based on direct study of trends through repeated observations over time. At best the alleged trends are either supported by 'second-hand' evidence, subject to the limitations mentioned above, or based on allusions to an unsubstantiated past, such as Finn's (1983) description of a 'casual' youth labour market which is supposed to have disappeared.

Recent discussions of the deskilling debate have emphasised the difficulties of generalisation, and have suggested that different processes may be found at work in different localities or in different sectors of the economy (Wood, 1981). The same point can be made of the deskilling hypothesis as applied to the youth labour market. It is particularly worrying that the argument rests so much upon a study of a single local labour market, Coventry (Frith, 1980; Finn and Frith, 1981). Not only are we asked to take on trust the authors' own conclusions from that study, since we are not provided with sufficient data to form our own conclusions (they cite the published report of the MSC, 1977, study of Coventry but this provides no evidence either for a semi-skilling process or for an increased demand for responsible autonomy); but the Coventry labour market is highly atypical, with an exceptionally small services sector, an employment situation for young people that was unparalleled even within the West Midlands, and an historically high rate of unemployment among women and girls (MSC, 1977, p. 16, pp. 22 4). This is an unsatisfactory basis for a generalised theory of labour-market trends.

Perhaps the weakest part of the deskilling theorists' argument is the claim that deskilling, where it occurs, disadvantages young people. Whatever the situation in Coventry, this is unlikely to be true of the economy in general. Some commentators have pointed to a trend, if not towards deskilling, at least towards a proportionate growth of 'secondary' forms of employment characterised by insecurity, low wages, poor conditions and low unionisation (Goldthorpe, 1983). It may be too soon to say whether such a trend is secular or recession-induced, but young people have conventionally been seen as participants in the secondary labour market (Bosanquet and Doeringer, 1973), so an expansion of this market might be expected to enhance youth employment. There is tentative evidence that such jobs may have recently increased as a proportion of young people's employment (Jones, 1984).

OCCUPATIONAL SHIFTS: COMPETITION FROM ADULT WOMEN

The third specific argument concerning occupational shifts is that adult women, who have increased their participation in the workforce over the post-war period, have displaced a number of young people from jobs (Casson, 1979; Sawdon and Taylor, 1980, pp. 33–4; Ashton and Maguire, 1983, pp. 6–7). There is evidence that some employers perceive adult women to possess qualities that suit them for jobs which might otherwise have gone to young workers (Ashton and Maguire, 1980). It is therefore probable that the increased participation of adult women in the workforce has had some effect on the youth labour market, but the size of the effect remains to be determined. An analysis of data for 1971 and 1979 concludes that women have only displaced male employees in the services sector, and then mainly in professional services, miscellaneous services and public administration (Bell *et al.*, 1981). However these findings are less than conclusive since they rest on assumptions about the rigidity of demarcations in the labour market of the kind questioned above. Ashton and Maguire (1983, pp. 6–7; Ashton *et al.*, 1982, pp. 45–6) are the main recent advocates of the view that young workers are affected by competition with adult women, especially part-time workers; yet they base their judgements largely upon a single industry (distributive trades) and they report at least one counter-example within the same industry where a firm changed its employment policy to increase recruitment of school leavers (Ashton *et al.*, 1982, pp. 20–1). Moreover, Wells (1983, pp. 61–3) finds stronger evidence that young males compete with full-time women workers than that they compete with part-time women workers; his results for young females are inconclusive.

In any case, increased competition from adult women cannot explain the largest and most recent increase in youth unemployment. Adult women's labour-force participation levelled off for a period in the early 1980s, a time in which youth unemployment rose sharply.

A NOTE ON YOUTH WAGES

One of the more controversial explanations for youth unemployment is that young workers have become less attractive to employers because their wages have risen relative to those of adults. The econometric evidence is inconclusive,[3] but it seems likely that relative wages have some effect on youth employment, in view of the extent of individual- and group-level competition between adults and young people in the labour market. However, any effect is likely to be modest, because this competition is based on many considerations other than the relative costs of employing young people, and because non-wage costs (such as supervision and training costs) may be more important (Markall and Finn, 1981). Moreover, the relative wages of young people cannot account for trends over the last few years (when most of the decline in youth employment has occurred) since they have remained steady, or even fallen slightly, since 1975 (Wells, 1983).

However, to the extent that the relative level of youth earnings influences the demand for youth labour, the case for a structurally determined rise in youth unemployment is made even weaker, since changes in relative wages would be one mechanism whereby the relative demand for adult and youth labour could be kept in balance with the supply. This may not be as unrealistic as is sometimes supposed; there is tentative evidence that recent policies have reduced the relative wages of young people and consequently increased levels of youth employment relative to the employment of adults (Jones, 1984).

THE STRUCTURAL CASE: AN OVERVIEW

The first general point about the structural case is that it often receives no justification at all; it is simply taken for granted by many commentators. Although the arguments of a number of writers have been criticised in this paper, it should be acknowledged that they have at least attempted to justify their views. That said, structural arguments share at least four main general weaknesses.

The first is that their accounts tend to be based on inadequate evidence of trends. Their arguments centre on the identification and interpretation of trends, yet very little of their evidence consists of genuine trend data, obtained through repeated observations at successive points in time. Much of it consists of second-hand reports of changes, a much less reliable source of data. In other cases, commentators extrapolate unjustifiably from one-off studies, in which the present is contrasted with an implicit (and sometimes fictitious) past.

Second, there is widespread confusion of recession-induced and structural effects. The term 'structural' as used here identifies factors which contribute to youth unemployment over and above the effects of a declining aggregate demand for labour. Structural effects in this sense are distinct from the effects of the recession, but in practice the two are often confused. For example, youth unemployment arising from a falling *level* of employment (associated perhaps with new technology) is mistakenly identified as structural change, even when there is no evidence that the *composition* of employment has changed to the disadvantage of young people. Occupational and industrial changes accompany any recession, but commentators discussing such changes rarely pause to consider which are permanent and which are likely to end with the recession. Similarly, rising unemployment among the less qualified is a predictable consequence of recession, given employers' preferences for the qualified, but it is often mistakenly interpreted as evidence of rising skill demands.

A third reason for treating the structural explanations with some scepticism is that they contradict each other. Some theories, or at least their supporting methodologies, assume a relatively fixed age structure of employment across industries and occupations; others assume group- or individual-level competition between adults and young workers. Some presuppose a general process of upskilling of labour requirements; others assume a deskilling process. That rising youth unemployment should be attributed to several different and often opposing processes is not in itself sufficient reason to dismiss all such accounts. However, the disparate nature of the structural argument suggests that different processes are at work in different parts of the economy. There are serious problems in generalising from much of the evidence, based as it is on particular local labour markets and particular industries. It is probable that any long-term trends which have affected youth employment have not been general to the youth labour market, but have varied in nature and direction across localities, industries and employers. These different trends may not have precisely cancelled each other out, but it is unlikely that they have all worked in the same direction. Many students of the (adult) labour process now agree that 'the quest for general trends, such as a progressive deskilling of the work force, or general conclusions about the impact of new technologies are likely to be both theoretically and practically in vain' (Wood, 1981, p. 18). The same is likely to be true also for the youth labour market.

The final weakness of structural arguments is their lack of historical specificity. The evidence is rarely related to concurrent trends in the labour market, and it is often imprecise in its historical reference. Most of the evidence refers to the 1970s, or even the 1960s, but by far the larger part of the current problem of youth unemployment is attributable to changes that have occurred in the 1980s. This is a crucial point – for all structural explanations assume a relatively steady process of change over a period of decades rather than years. None of them can explain why youth unemployment should have risen so suddenly after 1979 – except in terms that actually identify effects of recession rather than structural changes.

CONCLUSION

Most of the arguments which attribute the recent rise in youth unemployment to structural economic changes refer to shifts in either the industrial or the occupational structure of the demand for labour. It has been shown above that changes in industrial structure have had very little effect on recent levels of youth employment. The evidence for an effect of changes in occupational structure is more substantial, but nevertheless equivocal. The impact of both types of change is in any case likely to have been substantially cushioned by the flexibility of the labour market in switching recruitment between age groups. Moreover, the different industrial and occupational changes have had different and often opposing effects on the demand for youth labour. Had aggregate levels of unemployment remained constant since 1970, there is little reason to believe that youth unemployment would have been significantly affected by these changes. The *net* explanatory power of the structural explanation is therefore small.

Since the structural and recession-induced explanations are defined in opposition to each other, the latter must therefore account for most of the recent rise in youth unemployment. Analyses of recent trends in youth unemployment point to the same conclusion (Layard, 1979; Makeham, 1980; Hirsch, 1983; Raffe, 1984a; 1984c).

If the recession – the decline in aggregate demand for labour – is mainly responsible for youth unemployment, why then has this risen faster than adult unemployment? The answer is simply that it always has done in a recession. Young people, especially school leavers, are most affected when firms suspend new recruitment. Moreover, their lack of skills and experience makes them less attractive than adults to many employers, and although this does not matter at times of full employment it means that young people tend to lose out at times of unemployment when employers can be more selective. Young people are also affected disproportionately by cutbacks in training, by last-in-first-out redundancy policies and by the tendency for the least skilled jobs to be cut during a recession. These processes largely explain why youth unemployment rises more rapidly than adult unemployment during any recession, and thus why youth unemployment has risen so much since the early 1970s, over a period when adult unemployment itself has risen sharply.

The recession-induced explanation of youth unemployment is most directly concerned not with the level of youth unemployment but with the relationship between youth and adult unemployment rates. It claims, not that the differential between these rates has been constant (it has risen in this recession just as in previous recessions) but that the underlying relationship between this differential and the total level of unemployment has been relatively stable. Had the level of adult unemployment remained constant, the level of youth unemployment would also have remained more or less constant. Were adult unemployment now to return to the level of the 1950s or 1960s, youth unemployment would also return to those levels.

The implications of this conclusion depend upon whether and when adult unemployment is expected to fall. Both structural and recession-induced arguments speculate about the consequences of such a fall, so both implicitly accept that such a fall is conceivable if not necessarily imminent. If it is accepted that in the long run there is nothing inevitable about high adult unemployment, then youth unemployment need not be permanent. Several policy conclusions follow.

First, the practical case for policies specifically to reduce youth unemployment is weakened. If youth and adult labour markets are closely linked, the most realistic way to reduce youth unemployment substantially is through measures that reduce unemployment among all age groups. Defining the problem of unemployment in terms of separate age categories is neither economically justified nor politically desirable. Moreover, the priority currently given to youth unemployment might be properly shared with other groups such as the long-term unemployed.

Second, in the long run there need be no demand for schemes to keep large numbers of young people off the register and out of trouble. Whatever its public objectives the political case for the Youth Training Scheme derives largely from concern about youth unemployment. If this is not a permanent problem then the future YTS, or any other permanent education or training scheme, should be designed more exclusively on educational or training criteria.

More generally, actual and proposed policies for adjusting the supply of youth labour to the scarcity of jobs need to be examined critically. As well as education and training programmes these include work-sharing schemes and various work or leisure alternatives to full-time paid employment. In the short term such measures may be desirable palliatives. In the longer term, however, they must be evaluated on their own merits, according to whether the educational or social innovations they introduce are intrinsically desirable. Many of these measures risk institutionalising low-employment patterns of activity among young people, and thus the prophecies of low employment upon which they are based may become self-fulfilling. If the proposed alternatives are intrinsically less desirable than full-time paid employment – and many of their supporters see them only as second-best – then they may help to prepare a second-best future for coming generations of young people even when a preferable future, based on full employment, is available.

Finally, the policy-making and research communities should consider the quality as well as the quantity of youth employment. At times of high unemployment there is a tendency to treat employment as an undifferentiated good and to focus only on the distinction between it and unemployment. But if in the long term there need be no quantitative problem of youth employment, both researchers and policy-makers should be more willing to examine its qualitative aspects. In the long term the important issue may be, not the level of employment among young people, but whether or not that employment provides sufficient opportunities for their personal, social and vocational development.

NOTES

1. Work on this paper was carried out under the ESRC-funded programme of research on the Effectiveness of Schooling. The author is responsible for all opinions expressed in the paper.
2. Certain other influences on youth employment levels are not directly discussed in this paper. These include government policies, including YOP/YTS and employment protection legislation (see Markall and Finn, 1981, p. 33; Livock, 1983, p. 33), demographic trends (which in any case appear not to be influential: see Makeham, 1980, and Raffe, 1984c) and the alleged failure of schools to prepare young people for working life. Raffe (1983) discusses several of these factors. Moreover, the argument of the paper is restricted to Britain. There is at least superficial evidence that the youth labour market is less vulnerable to economic recession in other western countries (OECD, 1980).
3. A number of studies (Layard, 1979; Merrilees and Wilson, 1979; Lynch and Richardson, 1982; Wells, 1983) all report an effect of relative earnings on youth unemployment. Other studies (Makeham, 1980) have found no effect, or no effect among males (Hutchinson *et al.*, 1984).

5 Unemployment and Racism: Asian Youth on the Dole

AVTAR BRAH

INTRODUCTION

Black unemployment has risen dramatically over the last decade. Between 1973 and 1982 while total unemployment in Great Britain increased by 309 per cent registered unemployment among black people rose by 515 per cent. The proportion of the unemployed in 1973 who were black was 2.7 per cent. In 1982, the figure was 4.1 per cent (Runnymede Trust, 1983).[1] A survey carried out by the Policy Studies Institute found unemployment rates of 13 per cent for whites, 25 per cent for people of Afro-caribbean origin and 20 per cent for those of Asian origin. Asian women were found to have an unemployment rate twice as high as white women, and Afro-caribbean women a rate one-and-a-half times that of white women (Brown, 1984).

The high increase in youth unemployment since 1979 has attracted much publicity. Yet high levels of unemployment have been common among young blacks for a long period. There is evidence too that British-born young blacks may be especially vulnerable to unemployment (Runnymede Trust, 1981; Campbell and Jones, 1981). The view that young blacks born and brought up in Britain would face a more optimistic future than the immigrant parental generation has therefore remained unsubstantiated by fact.

In this paper I am concerned to describe and analyse the experience of one category of unemployed black youth, namely those young people whose family origins are in the Asian sub-continent.[2]

61

Before doing so I shall outline the broader context of their experience of unemployment.

ASIAN BUSINESS ACTIVITY AND THE YOUNG UNEMPLOYED

Until recently little attention has been focused on the plight of Asian youth in the labour market. This category of black youth was assumed to be faring well in the competition for jobs. Apparent complacency about the job prospects of young Asians is at least partially related to one popular image of Asians as 'successful entrepreneurs capable of looking after their own'. This image has some basis insofar as the last three decades have witnessed a rapid proliferation of Asian business enterprises (Allen *et al.*, 1977; Aldrich *et al.*, 1981). Nevertheless, as has been noted:

> Commercial growth is not necessarily to be equated with commercial success and high levels of rewards are confined to a small fraction of the community and won at an extremely high cost. (Aldrich *et al.*, 1981, p. 188)

Exaggerated claims about the success of Asian business, though frequent, are misleading. According to available evidence much of Asian entrepreneurial activity is limited to the level of circulation and distribution rather than production of commodities. The large firm operating at a high profit margin and employing a substantial workforce is not typical of the Asian enterprises which are generally small in size and are often dependant on household labour. Despite impressionistic newspaper reports that enterprises owned by Asians are poised to develop into big capital this is not very likely. The Asian entrepreneurial class constitutes a very small section of the Asian population in Britain and its ability to provide employment on any appreciable scale to the growing numbers of unemployed, whether Asian or others is extremely limited. Furthermore, to deduce the future of Asians as a whole from the experience of a very small minority is a gross distortion of reality. Not only are the great majority of employed Asians still to be found in semi-skilled or unskilled manual occupations, but there is growing evidence of substantial levels of poverty among them (Sills *et al.*, 1982).

ASIAN YOUTH UNEMPLOYMENT

Evidence from studies carried out during the 1970s shows that unemployment rates among young Asians were generally higher than young whites, and that young Asian women were disproportionately unemployed relative to young men (Brooks, 1983). The employment prospects for young Asians have deteriorated rapidly since 1979. For instance, Department of Employment statistics for 1980–81 reveal that among young black people aged 16–24 the rate of increase in unemployment was highest for Bangladeshi young women followed by Indian and Pakistani young men (Runnymede Trust, 1981).

A study of employment prospects of young Asians in Bradford found extremely high unemployment levels amongst this group (Campbell and Jones, 1981). Twelve months after leaving school in 1980, 41 per cent of the Asians were unemployed and a further 31 per cent were on YOP schemes. In comparison, of all 1980 school leavers (the cohort of which the Asians were a part), 19 per cent were unemployed and 14 per cent were on YOP schemes. Therefore, while only 28 per cent of the Asians had obtained a job, some 67 per cent of the total had done so. The study also shows that a place on a YOP scheme did not necessarily lead to a job for Asians. For every graduate of a YOP scheme who was able to find employment, three were unemployed. A survey carried out in Leicester found that in all age groups unemployment was higher among Asian and Afro-caribbean groups. In the 16–19 age group, for example, the unemployment figure for Asian and white young people was 38.5 per cent and 23.6 per cent respectively (Leicester City and County Council, 1984).

In general, any unemployment figures for young Asians must take account of a marked tendency on the part of this group to stay on in full-time education beyond the minimum statutory school leaving age (Brooks and Singh, 1978; Anwar, 1982). According to one study this tendency was greater amongst Asian young women than Asian young men, and amongst Asian young men born in East Africa relative to those born in Asia or in the UK (Lee and Wrench, 1983). There is some evidence to suggest that the greater propensity of young Asians to stay on at school longer or go to college is in part a reflection of their realistic assessment of the restricted job opportunities available to them. If this indeed is the case, and a substantial proportion of young Asians are opting to stay on in education because they anticipate problems in gaining employment, then the available unemployment figures for this group may under-estimate the size of the problem.

UNEMPLOYMENT, RACISM AND DISCRIMINATION

A number of factors account for the rapidly accelerating rates of unemployment among Asian groups. Firstly, a high proportion of Asian workers are employed in the generally contracting manufacturing sector, and within this sector are more likely to work in those industries and at those levels of skill which have been especially vulnerable to decline. Secondly, a greater proportion of Asians live and work in regions where unemployment levels have recently been among the highest. Thirdly, the current high unemployment is in part a consequence of the restructuring of the world economy involving an accelerating trend towards the internationalisation of capital and labour. This development is especially significant for black workers for they are concentrated in occupations that are vulnerable to technological change and relocation (Sivanandan, 1979; Frobel, 1980).

Important though these factors are, they do not provide an adequate explanation for disproportionately high black unemployment, except perhaps in the case of the textile industry (Smith, 1981). And even in relation to textiles, one must be cautious about giving primacy to arguments which attribute high levels of Asian unemployment to the effects of an industry in decline. Asian workers need not have been affected disproportionately by job losses, especially if they had had parity with whites in terms of access to retraining provision for new work. The issue of racism and discrimination is thus part of the explanation even in textiles.

A considerable body of evidence, dating from the late 60's onwards points to widespread direct and indirect discrimination against black workers in terms of access to employment, promotion, training, etc. (Daniel, 1968; Smith, 1974; Allen *et al.*, 1977; Commission for Racial Equality, 1978). The future facing young blacks looking for work is certainly no brighter than the one their parents had to contend with. There is extensive discrimination against them, such that even when they have equivalent or better qualifications than their white counterparts their search for jobs is less successful (Brooks and Singh, 1978; Hubbuck and Carter, 1980; Troyna and Smith, 1983; Lee and Wrench, 1983).

There is a striking similarity in the employers' perceptions reported by Allen *et al.* (1977) of mainly an adult immigrant generation of Asian workers and employers' attitudes towards young Asians in Birmingham studied by Lee and Wrench (1983). Both studies found that employers were likely to hold a variety of stereotypic perceptions of the aptitudes and abilities of Asian workers and job seekers which were in turn used to rationalise discriminatory behaviour towards them. Clearly, this is an important illustration of one of the ways in which the reproduction of labour is mediated through racism. At the same time, racism cannot be seen merely as an ideology affecting individuals (Hall *et al.*, 1978). Of greater significance is the way in which racism permeates all the major institutions of British society. It is a structured feature of the social system rather than a phenomenon of individual prejudice. It needs to be analysed as a set of material practices maintained by relations of power which constitute the conditions of black people's existence – where they live, which schools they attend, how they are 'skilled' or 'de-skilled' for the labour market, what positions in the labour market and the cultural system they occupy, what treatment they receive at the hands of the various state agencies, and so on. In other words how they are socially constructed at the economic, political and ideological levels (Hall *et al.*, 1978; Centre for Contemporary Cultural Studies, 1982). It is in this sense as we shall see in the following sections, that black unemployment is experienced through racism.

JOB SEARCH PATTERNS AND EXPERIENCES

The fastest growth in the number of unemployed in recent years has taken place among the under 25s; and leaving aside the over 60s, the highest rate of long-term unemployment is also to be found in the 18–24 year old group. Even so to find 70 per cent of the young men and women we interviewed had been unemployed for a period of between 1–2 years was a matter of serious concern. They reported that they had made a large number of applications – some as many as over a hundred. I was shown files full of copies of written applications and letters of rejection. Despite the disappointment and frustration resulting from this experience there was no indication that these young people had given up looking for work. Indeed the perseverance and tenacity shown was quite remarkable.

In the early stages of unemployment, the local newspaper, the Job Centre, and informal channels were cited as the most frequently used sources of information. Whenever appropriate direct applications were also made. With the passage of time, however, the attraction of the Job Centre tended to decline sharply so that local press advertising and direct application were the most favoured methods of job search among the long-term unemployed. These two methods of recruitment are reported to be the most popular with employers in Leicester (Ashton and Maguire, 1982). Where employers recruit through 'word of mouth' young Asians are at a disadvantage because this excludes them from firms with a predominantly white workforce. We found that the young men and women had explored all the available channels of information about jobs and their lack of success in the labour market could not be attributed to inadequate job search methods.

FINANCIAL AND SOCIAL DIFFICULTIES ASSOCIATED WITH UNEMPLOYMENT

The loss or serious reduction in income is, of course, one of the most difficult aspects of being unemployed. The Policy Studies Institute research demonstrates that Asian households are particularly badly hit by the loss of wage-earners through unemployment (Brown, 1984). This can be due to a number of factors including the higher rates of unemployment affecting Asian families, the comparatively high ratio of dependants to earners and the responsibility many of them have for supporting dependants outside the immediate household, sometimes overseas. On the one hand, Immigration law prevents these families from being able to live together and on the other, Social Security law penalises them financially for living apart, since persons with dependents in the country of origin can no longer claim benefit for them. The poverty associated with unemployment which many experience has particular features in the case of Asians through institutionalised discriminatory legislation as well as the other factors.

Most of the interviewees were long-term unemployed. Those who had been in work had consequently exhausted their eligibility to unemployment benefit and were now like those who never had a job, dependent on supplementary benefit. It is not surprising therefore that financial difficulty was at the core of the problems faced by the young people and their families. With the exception of a very small minority of young men, the interviewees lived with their families, which were often a variant of extended family. Loss of an income was experienced not merely as an individualised personal deprivation but as a reduction in the family's total budget. The level of material deprivation in a family varied according to the number of unemployed to employed members (and whether those were low-waged) and the number of dependants to earners and unemployed.

Of the 31 unmarried interviewees 8 were members of a family where parents and possibly siblings were in employment. For these young men and women unemployment was associated much more in the short term with frustration arising from boredom than with financial problems, though it did mean foregoing some forms of recreation and consumer goods. In such cases the family seemed temporarily to cushion young people against the full material and ideological impact of unemployment but it was clear that the working class Asian family was in a weak position to sustain this role over a period of time because even the pooled wages of employed members were rarely adequate to withstand the financial pressures of long-term maintenance of unemployed family members.

In contrast to the above minority most of the respondents were faced with acute financial problems. In some families there was not a single employed person and in others the mother was the sole bread-winner earning, like most female workers, a low wage. Unable financially to set up independent households, a large proportion of married young couples lived with their parents and siblings in over-crowded conditions. Those with a mortgage had great difficulty maintaining mortgage repayments. Some of those living in rented accommodation were in arrears with their rent.

The emotional upset caused by unemployment manifested itself through boredom, depression, anxiety and anger. The young people felt that their future was bleak.

> There is no future for me. I try *not* to think about my future. It is so depressing, you know. What future have I got? I become very depressed. You beat somebody just to let off pressure.

Arguments, conflict and tension at home were all too common, and this was especially the case when several members in a single family were unemployed. Whilst the hardships resulting from unemployment were borne by the family as a collective entity (Bradley, 1986) it was clear that the experience was mediated by gender.

Somewhat ironically, though, by no means surprisingly, the

ideology of male as the 'breadwinner' – constituting as it does a key element in the structuration and legitimation of male dominance – was central to many of the social and psychological pressures which the male respondents describe as underpinning their experience of unemployment. In analysing the experience of unemployed young white males Paul Willis has described this aspect as the 'male gender crisis' (Willis, 1984). In the case of the Asian male the obligation to 'provide' extends beyond spouse and children to include a range of designated kin in the extended family. Consequently, both married and unmarried men, particularly if they are eldest sons, feel under pressure to shoulder this responsibility. Hence, many male respondents spoke of feeling a sense of failure at not being able to contribute to the family income. One unmarried male, living with his widowed mother and a younger brother had been unemployed for two years. His younger brother worked as a packer and brought home a wage of £50. His own weekly supplementary benefit of £21.15 did not last beyond the Monday or Tuesday of the following week. As the eldest son without a father he experienced considerable guilt and unhappiness because he was a non-earning member of the family

> I can't live off my mother and younger brother. I am supposed to look after them and not the other way around. My mother thinks I am not trying hard enough to find a job. If I don't go to the Job Centre for just a couple of days she thinks I am not really interested in finding a job. Then we get arguments. I keep telling her there are so many people unemployed. It's not her fault. It's embarrassing for her that I don't have a job.

Another young man from a family of six younger brothers and sisters had also been unemployed for two years. No one in his family had a job. Whilst all members of the family who were of working age were under pressure to find a job he felt that the responsibility weighed more heavily on his shoulders because he was male. He expressed his anger and frustration thus:

> The worst is when your mother can't even buy shoes for the little ones. You feel so awful because you can't do anything about it. What future have I got. There are times you just want to kill yourself. Sometimes you get so angry you feel like going out and shooting everyone else.

Thus, unemployment brings into sharp focus the centrality of the wage as an affirmation of masculinity. Whilst the current high levels of unemployment should mean that the likelihood of this being readily attributed to personal deficiency should lessen, the stigma does not disappear. One young man had virtually stopped going to any family or community gatherings because people were bound to ask what kind of work he did.

For those unmarried young males contemplating marriage the lack of a job can mean reduced opportunities for, or a delay in, securing a suitable match. For the married male wishing to set up an independent household unemployment poses other kinds of problems. While a married Asian young man will not be under the same pressure to leave the parental home as his white counterpart for according to custom a married male and his family is normally expected to continue living with his parents, lack of suitable accommodation makes this difficult in Leicester where the need for separate accommodation has become very acute indeed. The majority of Asian households live in small terraced houses. Compared to the housing conditions of white families Asian are much more poorly housed (Leicester City and County Council, 1984).

Due to the sexual division of labour in the household which frees men from domestic work, it is largely the unemployed males rather than the females who can claim to have considerable 'free time' at their disposal. The young men spent this time engaged in a variety of activities such as watching television; going to a pub, youth club or a disco; walking the streets with friends or just hanging around the local park or at the City Centre; participating in community-based political activities; or attending activities sponsored by religious and cultural organisations. It was while on the streets that the young men came face-to-face with racial violence from their white counterparts and a number of the respondents had themselves been attacked. There was a general feeling that the police provided inadequate protection against racial harassment. Both male and female respondents expressed sympathy with Afro-caribbean youth whom they saw as facing the brunt of 'heavy policing'. The experience of youth from the two communities, they said, were becoming increasingly similar and there was growing solidarity between them.

The pressures on young women are different as well as more acute. The burden of keeping the family together under dire financial circumstances bore especially hard on women in the family, particularly those who were married. It was they who had to decide what economies to make in order to make ends meet. A 23 year old woman in a household which included not only her husband, herself and two young children but her husband's younger brother and his elderly parents explained:

> There is so much tension with my husband being out of work too. Money is a big problem. Lack of money creates a lot of tension, lot of bickering, lot of conflict. The wife suffers most. It's really depressing. You get pressurized from all directions – needs of children, family, other people in the house. Our house is not big enough for the whole family but we can't afford to have a home of our own. You can't go out for a meal or something. Children's needs cannot be fully met. You have to economise on everything – gas, electricity. House repairs – well you have no choice but to leave the house as it is or you end up borrowing money from relatives.

Divorced young women with children to support faced even greater hardships. One 21 year old divorced woman with a six month old baby had to meet all her expenses from the £32 that she received as her weekly benefit. She was on the council's waiting list for accommodation and in the meantime had no option but to live with her family in over-crowded conditions and at a time when three other members in the family were also unemployed. Women like her were extremely unhappy about the renewed dependence on the natal family which lack of a wage imposed upon them. Understandably, they did not wish to be a financial burden on their families who, as often as not, were themselves not very well off. Equally however, they were concerned about the stigma of divorce facing not only themselves but also their families. Economic reliance on the family meant that a woman would be under greater pressure to comply with the wishes and demands of the family. Indeed, the importance of waged work for women was a theme that was echoed throughout the interviews with the young women. Most of the single women said they would wish to work after marriage and the married women shared this view. There was in fact strong consensus about the desirability of paid employment because this was thought to give women a measure of independence.

> Having a job means independence. You don't have to rely on the husband for money.

I want a job. I hate staying at home. I want to be able to earn some money – buy clothes I want to, and not be a burden on my parents.

Of course, the women knew that paid employment did not by itself lead to equality with men. Either through their own previous experience of paid work or the experience of their mothers and of other female relatives, the young women were fully aware of the 'double-burden' of combing work outside the home with domestic duties. They knew too that they would earn less than the men, and that there were domains of the labour market from which they, as women, were excluded. Thus, these young women were not unfamiliar with the inequality embedded in the sexual division of labour at work and in the home. But they recognised that a wage did allow women to have a degree of autonomy and control; that it did prevent women from being totally dependent on a male wage. The women saw these as very real gains which they felt were being seriously threatened by their own unemployment.

The young women argued that in most Asian families a woman's wage was a very necessary part of the family's income; that it was not possible to keep up with the cost of living on male income alone so that women's paid work was a pressing economic necessity. Of course, for low income families generally the female wage has become a vital part of the household income. The number of households with income below supplementary benefits level would treble if it were not for this second source of income. But the concentration of Asian workers in low-paid work renders Asian women's wage that much more central to the household budget.

Unemployment also meant one less contribution to the family savings intended for the dowry of some of the unmarried women. In the absence of a job, marriage seemed to hold out the prospect of relief from the sheer boredom of life on the dole. Others felt robbed of the opportunity to embark on a career which they said they might or might not have wished to combine with marriage. For them unemployment meant a closing of options.

Work outside the home was regarded by the female respondents as important also because it provides social contact beyond family networks. A number of studies of women's employment have analysed female cultures in the workplace (cf. Pollert, 1981; Cavendish, 1982; Westwood, 1984). These cultures are shown to be deeply contradictory – shot through with divisions of gender, race and ethnicity. Encapsulating the potential for resistance at the same time as they confirm racist patriarchal relations in contemporary Britain. Whatever their limitations these cultures nevertheless enable women to force an identity outside the confines of the home. The workplace offers women the opportunity to socialise with a wider range of people, to break out of their isolation and to be able to share their concerns with other women. As one young married woman put it:

At work you are a different person. You are mixing with all kinds of people. You find out about their ways, they find out about yours. It's more fun than just being in one room, sitting around with children and just the husband.

Compared with men, the young women spent more of their time at home. As is the case amongst white families, there are important differences in the way daily lives of young women, including their 'leisure' pursuits, are structured (cf. Deem, 1983). While young men wishing to 'let off steam' could take part in a variety of outdoor activities there were greater constraints on the women. This is not to suggest that young women were confined to their homes by authoritarian families. In general, visiting friends and relatives and entertaining them in their own homes was common. When they went shopping with friends they refrained from 'hanging around' on the streets without purpose. This was due as much to the inhibiting influence of ideologies of femininity and the concrete demands of domestic responsibilities as the lack of suitable provision for young Asian women. Fear of racial attack was also cited as a factor affecting women's participation in activities outside the home, particularly in the evenings.

Contrary to the common ideological social construction of Asian cultures and family life as the *cause* of problems faced by young Asians in Britain, most young people said that their families were their major source of financial and emotional support, and that their Asian cultural life provided a strength that was not available to them outside their communities (Brah, 1982; Brah and Minhas, 1985).

It is evident that for both male and female respondents the social and economic pressures of unemployment were accentuated by the surrounding culture of racism. In addition to racial attacks, immigration and nationality laws were identified as particularly significant features of contemporary racism:

Many Asian people died for the British in the World Wars. My father used to be in the army. But now British people are trying to throw us out. They don't say direct but through laws like the immigration laws and the new one the Nationality one.

What I want to know is – and I get angry indeed – when people talk about immigrants they talk about Africans, Asians and West Indians. What about all those Australians, Canadians, Americans, German – are they not immigrants? No, because they are white when they talk about immigrants they talk about us. Disgraceful! Not a lot of people know that more people leave this country than come in. They never tell you that in the papers.

Unemployment seemed to have heightened their sense of group identity as blacks. Since leaving school their contacts with white people in other than official capacities had been minimal. With the closing of the school gates behind them, and without work most came to recognise the tenuous nature of relationships they had developed with white peers.

I tried to mix with white people for a few years. But no matter how much you tried to mix with them, at the back of their minds they always have this thing that you're black and they are white – that you're not the same. So taken in that sense you have to stick to your own. You could be born here but our colour doesn't change.

I see myself very much as an Asian. Of course you can go round flashing your British passport but you still get kicked over the head by the fascists 'cos you're black. It doesn't matter where you are born – it doesn't matter how many 'O' levels you have got. It doesn't matter, because your skin is black. I am very proud to say I am black.

Thus lack of social 'contact' between them and white people was not due to 'cultural encapsulation' on the part of the respondents as the popular view has it, but rather it was a consequence of racial divisions in society exacerbated by unemployment. These young people were not 'between two cultures'. Their cultural identity was secure and firmly based in the lived experience of Asians in Britain. Though emanating from the cultures of the sub-continent, these cultures are organically rooted in the local and national British context in which high levels of unemployment increasingly form a major part.

EDUCATION AND TRAINING

The great majority of the young men and women had left school with few or no qualifications. They argued, however, that their lack of qualifications was a reflection of the inadequacies of the education system, rather than of their own abilities and attitudes. They felt that the education system had failed them claiming that while few teachers were overtly racist the overall ethos of the schools conveyed the message that they were regarded by teachers as somewhat inferior.

> No one ever actually said this but you were made to feel that you were not meant to be more intelligent than your average British person. If you were bright the teachers saw it as some kind of genetic fault in you.
> They couldn't understand our problems, feelings and our ambitions. They kept pushing us towards factory jobs, almost as if we were not good enough for anything else.

Some felt that problems they had faced at school were also shared in part by white working class pupils.

> I think schools in Highfields suffer from the fact that it is a working class area. Teachers tend to think that pupils from this area are not clever enough, so they don't bother to train them. If you work very hard yourself, you may do well.
> Working class kids – black and white – face these problems more, because middle-class teachers like middle-class kids – they have more in common. I know no working class teachers around here.

Clearly, the part played by low teacher expectations and 'labelling' in the reproduction of black labour was not obscured from these young men and women, and for some the class nature of education was also evident.

The school curriculum came under severe criticism for perpetuating a Euro-centric world view that was seen to neglect the history and cultures of black groups and the issue of racism. Discontent was also expressed at the under-representation of Asian and other black teachers in the schools and the relative absence of black people from positions of authority and power. These experiences of schooling tended to elicit two broad responses from the interviewees both of which represent instances of resistance directed at educational structures and processes that they felt were stigmatising them as fit only for low-level manual work.

The first of these was to reject the school values as embodied in the perceived characteristics of a good pupil.

> We felt, why should we go through this humiliation just for a few qualifications. (We reacted) by not doing any work.

The second response entailed quite the opposite in that the interviewees became determined to try and achieve against all odds. As one young man stated:

> When I first came to this country my English was not very good. They put me in the bottom class. We were non-exam pupils. They didn't bother teaching us. There were other Asian kids in the class. They also had a problem with English. We felt we didn't belong in that class. We were not stupid. We used to get angry or mess about. In the third year I started fighting for my education. At the end of the year, we Indians got together and told the teacher we wanted to take Mock Exams. I didn't pass my English but I passed Maths, Physics, Biology, Chemistry and Metalwork. My careers teacher said I was stupid not looking for work. But I went to college to do 'O' and 'A' levels, and later got a degree.

He was one of three men and two women graduates in the sample. Only one of these was a recent graduate, the remaining four having been unemployed for a period of between one and two and a half years.

The young people in our study were aware that the possession of educational qualifications did not guarantee jobs. The collective experience of their communities in the labour market together with the difficulties they themselves had encountered during the course of their search for work had compelled them to recognise discrimination as a key constraining factor in the opportunities available to them.

> You have to be ten times, even a hundred times better than a white applicant.

> An Asian goes for a job and they say there's no vacancy, and a white person goes and they say you can start from Monday.

> What kind of person do you think employers tend to look for? I think somebody white.

Despite this, those with paper qualifications were determined to resist deskilling, and to repudiate the wider society's relatively low expectations of themselves. They held on to a residual optimism that educational credentials would be an asset in the long-term if not in the short-term.

The respondents also felt serious concern about the amount and quality of careers advice received by them both in school and from the Careers Service. They had found such advice offered infrequently, and not very helpful – a view that finds support in a study of local careers provision (Sherridan, 1981). One of their major complaints was that the careers teachers and careers officers were prone to underestimate the abilities of Asians and to discourage them from pursuing careers in higher education and the professions. As one put it:

> The careers teacher made you feel that you were at the bottom of the ladder, and no matter how hard you tried you couldn't get to the top.

A similar tendency was identified amongst some of the staff at the Job Centre. They said that a number of jobs for which they would express a preference were deemed by the staff as unsuitable for them. The problem of 'suitability' is a crucial one and may well be involved with subjective judgements in which both racial and gender stereotypes play a part.

The interviewees attitudes towards the MSC schemes for the unemployed were both critical and pragmatic. Since the interviewees were conducted before the new Youth Training Initiative became operative their comments referred to schemes which preceded the YTS. On the whole these schemes were seen as a poor substitute, indeed no substitute, for 'proper' training and 'proper' jobs. The following observations were typical:

They are not proper training schemes. Not like apprenticeships and that. They are just there to keep people off the street; keep the unemployment figures down. I have never met someone who came off a scheme and was successful in getting a job. I don't know what good they are doing.

You get £22.50 on the dole and 25 quid on a scheme. For a 40 hour week you get a paltry £25. It's cheap labour they are getting.

An average worker gets £75 a week. They stick an unemployed person on to a scheme for £25 and save £50. They don't train you, and when you leave 5–6 months later they stick in another one. They are using you.

There was an overall consensus that the employers did not value skills gained on these schemes.

Employers think these schemes are for dunces.

These schemes are seen to be for people who can't get jobs when they come out of school. They dump them on the schemes what they don't want on the dole. Employers think these people are second best.

Despite this overall disaffection with the schemes, there was recognition that schemes varied greatly in the quality of training and work experience provided. One of the local schemes was remembered with considerable pleasure by some of its former trainees. These young women said they had appreciated the friendly atmosphere of this scheme and had enjoyed being on it, even though they had not managed to get a job since leaving it. For some respondents the schemes provided an escape from boredom of staying at home:

It's better than being on the dole. At least you have somewhere to go every day and you might even learn something useful.

The views of the young people find resonance in a number of recent critiques of MSC schemes for the unemployed which stress that the schemes are not about training for jobs. These initiatives have been variously described as establishing the conditions to depress wages and wage expectations, an attempt to shift labour market control and resources away from working people and as seeking to redefine the cultural outlook of new generations (Green, 1983; Finn, 1984; Goldstein, 1984).

It is evident that the young Asians interviewed possess quite a sophisticated analysis of the 'hidden curriculum' of schools and other agencies that affect the unemployed. Their comments expose the hollowness of the ideology of equal opportunity and reveal some of the ways in which these institutions and agencies are implicated in reproducing Asian labour at the lower rungs of the socioeconomic formation.

The experience of unemployment for young Asians is mediated through racial, class and gender divisions in contemporary Britain, but they are not passive victims of structural determinations. They question, resist, challenge and repudiate structures and processes which serve to produce and maintain their subordination. Their political consciousness about the destiny of their labour power derives predominantly from their first hand experience of white dominated institutions but their political ideologies and responses are developed and elaborated within Asian communities and Asian peer groups and, increasingly, in discourse with young blacks and anti-racist young whites.

NOTES

1. Figures on unemployed black people were collected from employment offices and job centres from 1963–83 and were published quarterly in the *Employment Gazette*. The table was discontinued at the end of 1982.
2. This paper is based on research undertaken during 1983. In-depth personal interviews were carried out with 50 young men and women (27 male, 23 female) in the age range 16–25 living in an inner-city area of Leicester. Of these, 24 were Hindus, 16 Muslims and 10 Sikhs. Whilst 24 were born in the Indian Subcontinent, 19 in Africa and 7 in Britain, nevertheless half the sample came to Britain under the age of eleven. The majority (31) were unmarried. These interview data were augmented by four full-length group discussions with groups of between 10–15 young men. Thus, altogether 100 young people participated. A fuller report with Peter Golding (Brah and Golding, 1983) is available from the Centre for Mass Communications Research, University of Leicester.

6 School Leaver, Job Seeker, Dole Reaper: Young and Unemployed in Rural England

BOB COLES

INTRODUCTION

In describing the plight of the young unemployed much research has concentrated upon the inner cities where most are to be found (Watts, 1983; Roberts, 1984). The rapid rise in unemployment at the beginning of the 1980s now means that youth unemployment is widespread. Nationwide, youth unemployment increased more in a single year, 1980, than in the whole of the previous decade (see Raffe, Chapter 4 in this book). This increase occurred not only in the inner cities but in small towns, villages and rural areas. Early research conducted by Youthaid suggested that the young unemployed in rural areas faced special problems. Local rural economies offer only a restricted range of jobs, some of which are part time or seasonal, and further education colleges only a limited number of courses. Transport difficulties mean that the opportunities young people can reasonable explore are few and far between, and unemployment results in isolation and loneliness as school-leavers give up the only structured occasion in which they can meet people of their own age (Sawdon *et al.*, 1979). More recent research sponsored by the Department of Employment has also highlighted the fact that youth unemployment is often concentrated in regional blackspots, with some areas reporting as many as one in three young people unemployed, and others as few as one in thirty-three (Ashton and Maguire, 1985).

The basis of this paper is the first stage of a research project being carried out in four areas of one large Shire county in England.[1] The research has a number of specific features. First, we have deliberately concentrated upon rural communities and included only small to medium-sized towns, thus focusing attention away from the inner cities. Second we have studied four distinctive local labour markets, including both areas with high and low youth unemployment rates, and one area which is contradicting national trends by combining high rates of youth unemployment with relatively low adult rates (Makeham, 1980). Third the survey included all young people in particular age groups, rather than those who might be defined as 'unemployed' at the time the study was undertaken. We have done this not only because 'youth unemployment' is particularly difficult to define, but because, when market conditions prevent them from securing a full time job, many young people settle for temporary, short term alternatives in education or training schemes. The two cohorts discussed reached the age of sixteen in the school years ending in July 1978 and 1982, and were chosen because they straddle the big rise in youth unemployment which took place in 1980. Fourth, our research attempts to move beyond mere descriptions of the changing career paths embarked upon by sixteen year olds after the minimum school leaving age. Young people are here regarded as active agents, making informed decisions about their own lives. We argue that it is important to see the motivations and aspirations of the young unemployed within the overall context of local youth cultures. For it is only by understanding the aims, ambitions and motives of their contemporaries that the frustrations of those without work can be gauged.

Initially the different career paths followed by the two cohorts are described in order to illustrate that, in the short term, rising unemployment figures are not the only result of a collapse in work opportunities for young people. This is followed by an exploration of the major dimensions of 'life style' which are used by young people in explaining the decisions they took at the age of sixteen. In doing this we have relied upon what survey respondents wrote in their own words.

THE SHIRE COUNTY SCHOOL LEAVERS SURVEY

The data was collected by a questionnaire, mailed to both age cohorts in July 1983. Table 6.1 indicates the response rates of both populations[2].

TABLE 6.1   *The Shire County School leavers' survey*

	Total	1978 cohort	1982 cohort
Total number of people from whom sample was drawn	7 430	3 554	3 876
Number of questionnaires sent	2 442	1 159	1 283
Untraceable by Post Office	160	132	28
Effective sample size	2 282	1 027	1 255
Total completed questionnaire	1 582	652	930
Overall response rate (percentage)	69.3	62.5	74.1

In part the survey was intended to provide as accurate an account as possible of the social changes which had occurred in the areas over a period of four years. Official statistics give an unrealiable and incomplete picture, and careers service staff pointed out that their aggregate statistical records disguised the fact that many young people switched between the various categories of work, education and training throughout the year. A simple factual picture of what members of a particular age cohort are doing during the year after the age of sixteen is therefore not readily available.

The survey results show that those who register as looking for work with the Careers Service or the Job Centre are by no means the only young people seeking full-time work. At the time of our study, some twelve months after the 1982 cohort had reached the minimum school leaving age, substantial numbers had not registered as unemployed, even though they were eligible to do so. Much of this 'non-registered' unemployment, as is indicated by other studies, was short term (Roberts *et al.*, 1981). It mainly comprised those who defined themselves as 'between things' – either one job or another, college and work, or school and the next stage of their career. More often than not however, this 'next stage' seemed vague and unsettled. To these 'unregistered unemployed' we must add those who were on government schemes but who were still without a permanent full-

time job. It should be borne in mind that, according to some estimates, in some areas only about a third of those young people on
government schemes obtain full time employment when they finish
(Raffe, 1984b). Yet others had secured only part-time or seasonal
work and were, therefore, also looking for something full time and
permanent. Adding these categories to those who were registered as
unemployed with the Job Centre or Careers Service, the number of
young people seeking a full-time job is two or three times as many
as is indicated by official government figures.

TABLE 6.2   *1982 Cohort still 'seeking full-time work' in July 1983
(percentages given are of male and female subsets of area cohorts)*

	Blackstone Bay	Ackthorpe	Batwith	Kitchester
Male				
Registered unemployed with careers or job centre	10.0	7.0	15.1	8.7
Unregistered unemployed	10.0	3.5	6.1	4.8
On government scheme (YOP etc.)	8.6	5.3	7.1	8.3
In part-time or seasonal work only	4.3	1.8	3.0	3.5
TOTAL seeking work	32.9	17.7	31.3	25.3
Female				
Registered unemployed with careers or job centre	8.4	1.9	16.1	10.6
Unregistered unemployed	5.6	9.3	8.0	6.4
On government scheme (YOP etc.)	8.3	5.6	5.4	5.5
In part-time or seasonal work only	11.1	5.6	7.1	6.8
TOTAL seeking work	32.4	22.4	36.6	29.3

CAREER PATHS OF THE 1978 and 1982 COHORTS

Even the figures in Table 6.2 underestimate the problem. If we
compare the career paths followed by the 1978 and 1982 cohorts, it
is apparent that obtaining a full-time job on leaving school is an
increasingly uncommon occurrence. As the availability of full-time

work has decreased, the tendency to stay within education beyond the minimum school leaving age has increased. Figure 6.1 illustrates this trend. Fewer young people from the 1982 than the 1978 cohort report that they found a full-time job immediately after leaving school, and many more report that they stayed on in education after the summer holidays. Thus, at least in the short term, the lack of full-time work does not fully reveal itself in the unemployment figures, but in the increasing numbers of young people doing another year at school, or taking a course in further education.

These broad trends are further complicated by two important factors. The first concerns gender. In recent years more girls than boys have stayed in education beyond the minimum school leaving age, with fewer of them leaving to find full-time work at the age of sixteen (Burnhill, 1984). Whilst the decline in job vacancies now means that both girls *and* boys are increasingly finding it difficult to move straight from school to work, it is still girls who find this the hardest path to follow. Indeed in 1982 the proportion of young women able to take this route was very small indeed, as low as 5 per cent in Batwith, and 8 per cent in Blackstone Bay.

The second factor is the history of local labour markets and the sort of opportunities young people *think* may be available. For instance, in Blackstone Bay, where high rates of unemployment have been experienced for a decade, there is a very noticeable increase in the proportion of boys staying within education between 1978 and 1982, from 29 to 51 per cent. In Ackthorpe on the other hand, where unemployment rates have only just begun to rise appreciably, a much lower proportion of boys stay on – the increase here being from 18 to 28 per cent.

When both gender and area factors are combined we find, in Ackthorpe, that the 1982 bulge in post-sixteen education is predominantly accounted for by trends amongst young women in the area. In Batwith, however, more idiosyncratic trends are apparent. There is a small *decrease* in the proportion of girls taking the educational option in 1982, and a small *increase* in the number of boys who do so. It has been suggested to us that this 'anomaly' was caused by the aftermath of educational reorganisation in the area.

The career paths followed by young people during the twelve months after the end of compulsory schooling are, therefore, difficult to analyse. This is particularly so for the 1982 cohort, where the picture is complicated by movements in and out of education and training.

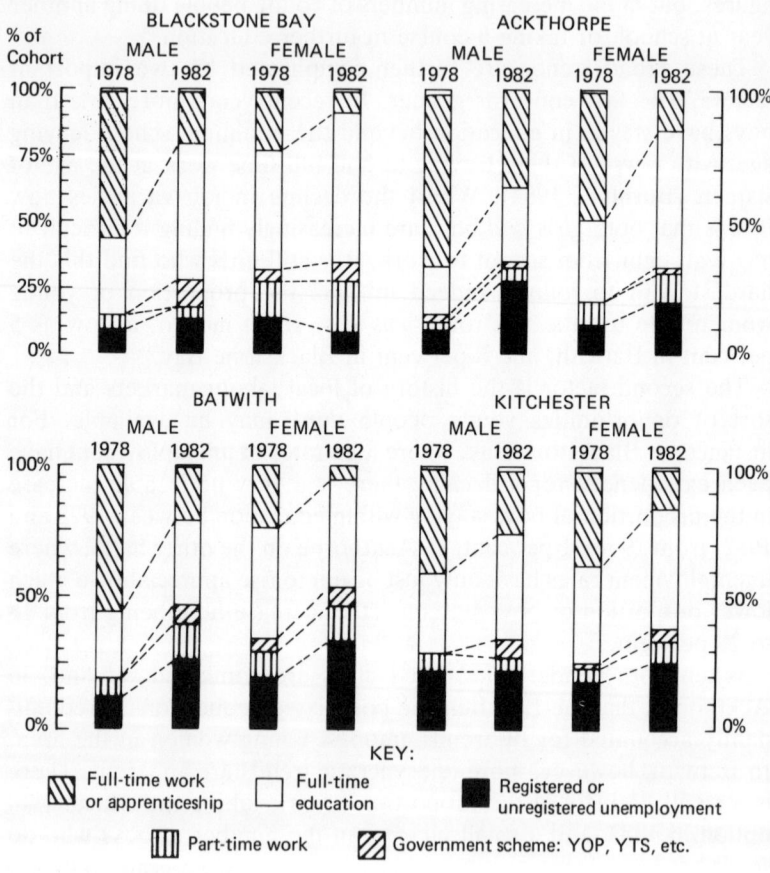

FIGURE 6.1 *Comparison of first moves made by 1978 and 1982 cohorts*

TABLE 6.3 *1982 Cohort movements through education (percentages given are of male and female subset of area cohorts)*

	Blackstone Bay	Ackthorpe	Batwith	Kitchester
Male				
In education October 1982	54.3	31.6	40.4	43.9
In education July 1983	40.0	21.0	27.2	32.2
Female				
In education October 1982	69.4	66.7	55.3	53.4
In education July 1983	30.5	46.1	35.7	33.9

In diagnosing trends in career paths, it is too simple to suggest that when jobs are available young people take them, and when work opportunities contract the education system expands to cope with increased unemployment. A grapevine of friends and relatives tells young people about the local labour market and they often make their career moves *in anticipation* of this. In Ackthorpe, for example, the boys who left school in 1982 did so in expectation that jobs would turn up. No extra time at school for them, even though 28 per cent of the cohort started their first year after school unemployed. They guessed that throughout the coming year, jobs would become available, (in all the areas we studied, except Blackstone Bay, unemployment amongst school leavers did decline throughout the year). Only 31 per cent of boys in Ackthorpe went straight from school into full-time work, but the majority still left school and searched for jobs. By the following July 61 per cent of them had full-time jobs or apprenticeships. The boys in Blackstone Bay, on the other hand, had heard differently. Although only twenty-five miles from Ackthorpe, they had learnt that very little work was likely to turn up during the year, and for a number of years had been told repeatedly at school that the only way for a boy to 'get on' was to 'get out' – that is get out of the area. To do this with any success, they were told, they needed qualifications. So, for the boys of Blackstone Bay, staying on at school or transferring into further education is both widespread and long term. This is in marked contrast to their female contemporaries. Many young women in this same area leave school to take up part time or seasonal work in the local tourist industry rather than persevere with education (See Table 6.3).

The significance of this use of education beyond the minimum school leaving age should not be underestimated. With the growth of the Youth Opportunities Programme, in its last year in 1982–83, and its successor, the Youth Training Scheme, some form of education or training has now very much become the norm for most post-sixteen year olds. If we simply add together those reporting these various forms of education or training, it is not too much to begin talking about the new 'unannounced raising of the school leaving age of the 1980's' as the most significant response to rising youth unemployment. What is also apparent is that this new post-16 education and training involves a new form of stratification within the education system in which the impact of gender-segmented labour markets is critical (Ashton and Maguire, 1980). It also implies that it is the fortunes of seventeen or eighteen year olds which should be the focus of attention in studies of youth unemployment, despite the fact that the statutory school leaving age is still sixteen.

TABLE 6.4   *1982 Cohort distribution within 'Rosla-1980s Style'*
*(percentages of male and female subsets of areas on each raising of the
school-leaving age track 1982–83)*

	Blackstone Bay	Ackthorpe	Batwith	Kitchester
Male				
In education	54.3	31.6	40.4	43.9
On government schemes	21.4	21.1	17.2	20.4
TOTAL in education and training	76.7	52.7	57.6	64.3
Apprenticeships	8.6	15.8	28.3	21.7
Female				
In education	69.4	66.7	55.3	53.4
On government schemes	23.6	13.0	22.3	20.3
TOTAL in education and training	93.0	79.7	77.6	73.7
Apprenticeships	6.9	5.7	1.8	3.4

CAREER CHOICES AND THE IMPORTANCE OF YOUTH CULTURES

This research involves treating the career paths of the young as the result of deliberate, though complex decisions. The perspective being employed thus avoids the assumption implicitly built into much research (especially where it has relied upon survey methods), which regards young people as 'cultural dopes'; the passive recipients of measurable attributes, whether these be educational qualifications, training or work experience. Such research ignores the fact that in making decisions about their future, young people employ a complex vocabulary of image and motive which defines for them the significance of taking one course of action rather than another. In deciding to leave school, or to take a course at a college of further education, young people take account of the impact of this decision upon the 'life style' it will invoke. The analysis of the career paths of young people must, therefore, take full cognisance of the context of 'youth cultures' in which such paths are given meaning. Their plans are premised upon 'images' of school, education, and work, and the costs and benefits which might accrue from participation in them.

There are several reasons why the perspective being adopted here should be distanced from the 'youth subculture' approach, and why the ethnographic methods associated with this have not been employed within the first stage of the project (Hall and Jefferson, 1976; Hebdige, 1979). Two criticisms of many studies of youth subcultures are that they systematically ignore young women and the *majority* of young men (McRobbie, 1981; Allen, 1982a). While we have detailed accounts of a range of 'folk devils' – the Teddy Boys, Mods, Rockers, Hippies, Skinheads and Punks, these studies have been criticised, not because they are necessarily inaccurate, but because they concentrate attention only upon the glamorous or glamorisable sections of youth, to the exclusion of the majority. Until recently, we had little insight into the 'life style' and culture of 'ordinary kids' (Jenkins, 1983; Brown, 1984). School-based studies, such as those undertaken by Willis (1977), and by Corrigan (1979), come nearer to recognising a full range of youth cultures, although the analyses have concentrated upon the culture of the 'lads' and not the 'ear oles'.[3] But we must regard the 'ear oles' as 'cultured' too. Other most recent attempts to study the range of 'life styles' followed by 'ordinary kids' have, however, been based only upon young people contacted through youth centres or community projects (Jenkins, 1983; Stafford, 1981). For all the young people who can be contacted in this way there are thousands who are systematically excluded. If accounts of youth culture are to be based only on those with whom ethnographers find it easy to make contact, then we are in grave danger of providing a distorted picture of contemporary youth.

The Scottish School Leavers Surveys have illustrated that equally rich qualitative data can be obtained from mail questionnaires (Gow and McPherson, 1980; Hughes, 1984). Encouraged by this, we also invited our respondents to write freely about their experiences of education, training and the labour market. It is to this evidence that we now turn in describing the parameters of motive which lie behind the early career decisions of young people.[4]

HATING SCHOOL AND GETTING OUT

By the age of sixteen about half the young people in the survey expressed a wish to leave school and get a job, although, significantly, more boys wanted to do so than girls. As we have seen, for many, the chances of leaving school and moving immediately into full time work are remote, but such is the antipathy for school and everything it stands for, that many male and female respondents say they want to finish their education no matter what the consequences.

This 'hatred' of school also figures prominently in the ways in which respondents write in their own words. 'Hate', a ubiquitous word in the vocabulary of sixteen year olds becomes translated into a variety of negative images of school life. The repertoire of words used includes 'boring', 'irrelevant', 'infantile', 'a waste of time', 'vindictive' and 'useless'. A selection of such statements, made by the 1982 cohort, helps to fill out the picture. A young woman in Batwith with a full-time job wrote:

School to me was full of violent and mean people, and they were always trying to be better than everyone else. Now you can relax and get on with what you want in your own way, without people criticising you all the time.

Many of the comments contrast school with the preferred 'life style' they have experienced since they left. A young man from Batwith doing an apprenticeship wrote:

School was a waste of time, everything was do this, and do that without any apparent reason. Teachers were just there to bug you. Life now is alright, I can see why I am doing things and what for – (money).

A young man from Kitchester, having left college after one year wrote:

School became boring towards the end. Most teachers treated you as infantile. (At College) tutors treat you like grown ups, and not like little bits of dirt.

An unemployed young man from Batwith adds to the complaints:

I hated school because some of the teachers thought more of the richer [meaning money] ones in our school. They also ignored us, even when we wanted to work. That made us not bother with school.

MORE COMPLICATED BALANCE SHEETS

Not all respondents remember school in a totally negative way. The comparisons they draw are not just between 'school' and 'work' but from a range of statuses which being at school or leaving it can bring. Some respondents suggest that the act of leaving school has involved careful and calculating decisions. One such account, written by a young woman from Batwith, reads like a balance sheet.

Life at school; too many restrictions:– a) school regulations b) parents – what time I had to be in c) how many nights out per week d) homework very tying and tedious e) friends and boyfriends not liked v much by parents.
Life Now; no restrictions:– a) money b) freedom to go as I like within reason c) not treated like a kid d) much better circle of friends – more mature e) much more confidence.

Other respondents indicate that, to them, the balance sheet is not so unambiguously stacked. Different vocabularies of image speak of school as security, the clear structuring of time, friendship networks which are valued and school as a place in which responsibilities and worries can be comfortably avoided. These are again best illustrated by using the respondents' own words.

A female apprentice from Blackstone Bay wrote:

> On leaving school you suddenly realise that you are on your own
> . . . at first I found it frightening.

A young man in full-time work, having spent one year at college, wrote:

> It's a big change leaving school and moving on – a lonely experi-
> ence – I now see no-one I went to school with. You're on your
> own. You're always marking time and waiting for something – I
> don't know what.

A young woman from the same town wrote:

> Life at school was much easier than life at work . . . no pressure
> on you. Work is a much more different atmosphere . . . not as
> many friends, different ages, and no choice of friends. You must
> try and get on with everyone you work with.

Importantly, the value of full-time work is not written about, by those who have attained it, in terms which express any intrinsic values it might have, but in terms of its fringe benefits: being treated like an adult, and as the source of money which can be used to purchase independence and participation in an enhanced leisure life. Again the contrast of 'life style' associated with school and work is apparent. A young man with a full time job in Ackthorpe wrote:

> I hated school. Life now is great. I've got money to sup ale and
> smoke . . . the change I have felt is I've started living . . . I eat
> what I want, and sleep where I want, and I can practise sly
> manoeuvres on my motorbike to irritate the neighbours.

A young woman in Batwith wrote:

> Life at school was horrible especially if you had a bad record.
> Comparing it to now, it's much better. You get everything you
> want except time. I can now go out and come in when I please.
> I earn my own money, and can have as many clothes as I want . . .

PRESSURES FOR THOSE STAYING ON AT SCHOOL

It is too easy to make a simple division between those who leave school at sixteen and those who stay on. Some of the respondents to the survey write that they drifted into the sixth form at school and never thought of any other alternative as a possibility. Others, who also stayed on at school, are more than a little ambivalent about doing so. They see friends who have left attaining things to which they too aspire. Sometimes this pressure is sufficient to lure them away. A male sixth former from Kitchester wrote:

> Staying on at school puts great pressure on your life, While most of your friends are employed or drawing the dole, they're receiving money. You are frustrated because of lack of money and lack of freedom. Whereas those on the dole are free to go out when they please you are not. This makes you feel left out.

A young woman from Blackstone Bay who had just left school after spending one year in the sixth form wrote:

> I didn't think it was worth my while staying on into the 7th year when I didn't do too well in the 6th form exams. I thought I was working hard . . . but I wasn't getting the perks that some of my friends were getting. The prospect of earning my own money lured me away – I was tired of being broke.

Even when young people feel set to stay in education for some time, it is often not for the enhanced occupational chances this might bring, but again for the fringe benefits. A young woman from Batwith who was continuing at school wrote:

> I think, being a grammer school pupil, I was more likely to be aimed at university or polytechnic, but that is what I want anyway . . . I do not want to take up full time work until I have experienced university life.

Those from the 1978 cohort who have taken the gamble, and stayed on within education, through polytechnic and university explain themselves in similar terms. A young woman from Blackstone Bay who had managed to find some sort of job in her home town after graduating from university wrote:

I feel I have been lucky in two respects since leaving school. . . . I have left with an education and an interest in learning for its own sake, that would see me through times of unemployment or a job I didn't particularly like – that is my free time would compensate me. Secondly I was lucky enough to find a good boyfriend and acquire a lovely home so my bad times could never be as bad as for some young leavers.

A young man from the same area wrote:

The time spent in obtaining my seemingly useless university qualifications was probably the happiest period of my life so far.

What is important to note is that many of the reported motivations (albeit reconstructed after the event), suggest that 'life style', as much as career aspirations, is a feature of the decision-making process.

VOCABULARIES OF IMAGE AND MOTIVE

In previous sections of the paper the replies of respondents have been used to explore some of the dimensions of decision making which lie behind educational and occupational path profiles. There is not, of course, a singular vocabulary, but despite variations, certain dominant themes seem apparent. It is clear that some of the choices made by young people are 'avoidance strategies'; decisions taken either to escape from school or to avoid the insecurities of the labour market for as long as possible. The decisions can be grouped around five main concerns; money, the attainment of adult status, security, the structuring and use of time, and access to friendship networks.[5]

1. MONEY	(a) independence from parental support
	(b) access to leisure opportunities
2. ADULT STATUS	(a) freedom to make one's own decisions
	(b) responsibility – being treated like an adult
3. SECURITY	(a) having a job – having gained a foothold in the labour market
	(b) sheltered by school or further education
4. TIME	(a) invested time: time filled usefully by work, training or education

<table>
<tr><td></td><td>(b) alienated time: time structured by someone else, and regarded as sold at a cost – but for some tangible reward</td></tr>
<tr><td></td><td>(c) anomic time: time-on-one's-hands, boredom</td></tr>
<tr><td>5. FRIENDSHIP
NETWORKS</td><td>(a) school and education as the source of friendship networks</td></tr>
<tr><td></td><td>(b) having the resources to go out and meet old and new friends</td></tr>
</table>

Many of those who stay within education, or who secure full time jobs, seem to attain an acceptable mix of the five 'life style' ingredients listed above. They may not win on all of them, but are able to make rational choices about the balance. Those in full-time work, for instance, may lose the friends they had at school – and some miss them very much – but they receive, as compensation, the economic resources to be relatively independent, and to find new friends. They also obtain, in return for the loss of security felt on leaving the shelter of school, an 'adult status' which contrasts significantly to being 'treated as a kid' at school. And their time is structured and filled. Those who stay within education may, in the short term, have few financial rewards for doing so, but their time is filled and many regard that time as an investment, not necessarily in qualifications, but in a 'life style' they would not wish to miss.

Not all those in education, nor all those in full-time work, attain such an easy balance. Some switch tracks in order to pick up a path that is more acceptable as some of the earlier quotations illustrate.

The five dimensions of 'life style' also help us to understand the experience of the young unemployed. In taking the avoidance strategy and leaving school, they end up with very little except time, and to most of them in non metropolitan areas this is very much time-on-their-hands – anomic time. They lose security, without being accorded adult status; they gain independence, without the resources to use it; they lose friendship networks, without the financial means of forging new ones.

FROM SCHOOL TO UNEMPLOYMENT

Not all the comments made by the unemployed fall neatly into this pattern. There is some evidence from the survey that being able finally to leave school counterbalances all other costs. An unemployed young man from Kitchester wrote:

> School life was a waste of time personally. My life now is good, but short of money. I do not mind working, but the change I have felt is excellent. Do what I want, and when I want, I really enjoy myself now. We got treated like kids in the fifth year. It's excellent now – worth living.

But for most of the unemployed such relief is not permanent, and they comment on the security they now miss, the structuring of time which is now absent, and the friendships which have disappeared. The 'unemployed' in our survey came from a range of different social and economic circumstances, lived in different types of non metropolitan communities, and had been unemployed for varying lengths of time. It is remarkable that, despite these apparent differences in background, the comments given to us about unemployment are made in such similar ways. An unemployed young woman from Batwith wrote:

> When I first left school it was just like a holiday for the first few weeks, then I started to get bored. Living in a village makes it worse. Nowhere to go. I go all over looking for jobs but its the same every time. I miss my friends most of all, I'd love to go out but you just can't afford it.

Another young woman, from the same area adds a similar story:

> When I was at school I had no worries, but now I have worries everyday. I hated it at school, but I hate being unemployed. I just spend my time in bed. My temper has changed and I seem to snap at everybody – Then I go out and get drunk which doesn't make me feel any better.

An unemployed young woman from Kitchester wrote:

> Although school was boring, there was a routine which I certainly miss. I miss all my close friends because there is no way we can meet, moneywise.

An unemployed young man from the same town wrote:

Life at school was boring . . . being unemployed is very boring, but if I had a useful job I would be happy.

Some of those who were unemployed in July 1983 had had some work experience during their first year, but had left or been made redundant. They round out the picture – for it should not be anticipated that all those in full time work are terribly happy with their lot, as youth unemployment has dramatically reduced the wages being offered to them. A young man from Batwith who was no longer in work wrote:

My job was the sort of job I wanted, but I left because I was not getting much money for a hard days work. (£20 for a 40 hour week). The dole is very boring and the DHSS office suspended my dole because I packed my job in.

Isolation in small towns and rural areas takes its toll too. A young woman from Batwith writes of this in the following way:

When I was made redundant I was glad because the work I was doing was very very boring and the boss was still living in the middle ages. Now with being at home all the time I eat thus putting weight on, thus I no longer go out because I am self conscious of being fat. The only times in the last couple of months I've been out is up to the market shopping, or round to my friends. . . . However I have decided to pull myself together, I am dieting, also I have been seriously thinking about going to night school to do my A levels.

It is not only those without work who are concerned about unemployment. The fear of it reaches back into schools and colleges, as the following quotations illustrate. A sixth former from Batwith wrote:

I did go and look for a job, just out of curiosity to see how many there were actually available for school leavers. I was amazed to discover that most of the few jobs available were only open to those either over a certain age or with previous experience. Surely, how are people leaving school meant to get a job with that sort of barrier?

A female college student from Kitchester wrote:

At the moment the employment situation is bleak so therefore because of the high competition for jobs I feel pressurised and compelled to do well with our exams. I feel because of the considerable weight of pressure, and the constant reminder of the situation from the media, school children are trying more than their best, but to little avail. Jobs are scarce even if you have the necessary qualifications.

CONCLUSION

This paper is based on the first phase of a research project conducted in four predominantly rural areas within a single Shire County. But many of the central points made about such non-metropolitan districts have a wider relevance. First, it has been shown that one of the most marked changes resulting from the collapse in work opportunities, has been the effective raising of the school leaving age, as more and more young people enter some form of education and training beyond the age of sixteen. Second, it has been argued that figures on 'youth unemployment' are particularly enigmatic. Thus any estimate of the number of young people wanting and seeking permanent full time jobs must involve a doubling or even trebling of the number registered as unemployed with Careers Services and Job Centres. Third, it has been argued that any attempt to understand the experiences of the young unemployed must start with an examination of the ambitions and aspirations of a wide range of all young people. In attempting to do this, use has been made of the comments respondents wrote in their own words, to sketch some major dimensions of 'life style' which are of particular importance to them.

The analysis presented is based only upon survey data so far, but survey material, when covering full year cohorts, can provide important quantitative *and* qualitative material as the starting point for further investigation. Conversely, to concentrate the spotlight *only* upon those who fall within the official, narrow, definition of unemployment is to turn the young unemployed into a homogeneous and easily identifiable 'pariah' group, when in fact youth unemployment is amorphous and widespread. Youth unemployment, and the fear of it, is not the prerogative of a specific section of young people. It is the experience of a whole generation.

NOTES

1. Acknowledgement must be made to several people who helped to facilitate the survey reported here. Thanks should be made to the Shire County chief education officer and all his staff who helped in the preparation of the sample, to Angela Vagnarelli for her help in the early stages of the survey, and Chris Smallwood for his help in coding the data. Mary Maynard and Robert MacDonald also helped with detailed comments on earlier drafts of this paper.
2. The four areas have been given ficticious names at the request of the County County. Blackstone Bay is a small coastal town which acts as a focus for the surrounding rural area. It has had high rates of both adult and youth unemployment for some time as its traditional industries of fishing and tourism have declined. Ackthorpe is a small market town at the centre of a rural area. It has been largely immune from the recession. Batwith has suffered mixed economic fortunes. It too is a small market town in a dominantly rural area, but it has recently become the focus of the growth of a large, but capital intensive, industrial development. Kitchester is the largest town in the area, and has been traditionally immune from recession. Whilst it has some large employers of labour, it also acts as a regional and commercial centre for the region.
3. Willis in particular makes a distinction between those who reject school culture ('the lads'), and those who are prepared to conform to it (the 'ear oles') (Willis, 1977). More recent studies have suggested that this dichotomy is too simple, and that a third group ('ordinary kids') have a much more instrumental attitude to school and qualifications (Jenkins, 1983; Brown, 1984)
4. We have not followed Gow and McPherson (1980) in leaving the grammar and spelling of respondents uncorrected. It was felt that to use their written words, in this context, without such correction was potentially patronising to the attitudes expressed.
5. There are some interesting similarities between the descriptions given below, and those made separately by Marie Jahoda and Paul Willis, even though the areas studied, and the methods used different (Willis, 1984; Jahoda, 1981)

7 It's not Fair, Is It?: Youth Unemployment, Family Relations and the Social Contract[1]

PATRICIA ALLATT AND SUSAN YEANDLE

INTRODUCTION

Extensive unemployment in a society which has become accustomed to economic growth produces discontinuities in social and cultural relations. People are suddenly jolted out of their social niches (Kornhauser, 1960). Not only are erstwhile patterns of daily life upset but also, as in war time (Allatt, 1981; 1983), latent beliefs about how social life should be conducted are exposed.

Of course, even in circumstances which lend them support, highly regarded values are not invariably acted out in the daily routines they are supposed to inform. Nevertheless, when, for example, normative expectations about economic life are not met, it becomes difficult, even impossible, for individuals and groups to maintain belief in idealised standards. A variety of consequences may follow: individuals may feel bitter, frustrated and let down; latent priorities may become exposed as resources become more limited; people may become aware of competing ideologies within their culture; and, in mobilising their collective and individual resources to sustain threatened values, institutions may demonstrate both strength and flexibility. In this paper we shall be considering the institution of the family and its members, and their invocation of the concept of fairness in the face of severely limited employment opportunities for young people.[2]

This notion of fairness arose frequently in our research data. Descriptions, anecdotes and stories commonly included it in response to questions on the search for jobs, labour market histories, kinship networks and family life. The concept of fairness is not peculiar to our respondents but is part of our culture at many levels. A 'fair day's pay for a fair day's work' has long been a claim put forward by authoritative figures as well as workers. Children are exhorted to be fair and complain of treatment which 'isn't fair'. The media abounds with examples. In a single issue of one newspaper the terms 'unfair', 'moral outrage' and 'a question of justice' appeared (*Guardian*, 25 September, 1984). It has been argued that moral outrage is a universal response to injustice; individuals know when they have had a 'raw deal' (Moore, 1978, p. 508).

For Moore, 'the fundamental idea behind popular conceptions of justice and injustice, fairness and unfairness is the conception of "reciprocity" or "mutual obligation"' (1978, pp. 508–9 and 506), the essential component of which is voluntary compliance with social rules, an obedience which is not based upon force, fear or fraud. The notion of reciprocity is one 'where services and favours, trust and affection, in the course of mutual exchanges are ideally expected to find some rough balancing out' (Moore, 1978, p. 509), but such balance does not exclude the existence of inequality, of hierarchy and of authority.

Inherent in the legitimacy of those in authority is the obligation to supply commodities and services such as protection, security, order and a tolerable distribution of resources in return for compliance (although not necessarily acceptance). Since superiors can rarely control all aspects of behaviour and performance, compliance to authority builds up over time as subordinates develop their own practices to protect their own interests *vis-à-vis* their superiors. Precedent confers legitimacy. A sense of moral outrage may occur when the authority of precedent is challenged from within or from outside the subordinate group (Moore, 1978, p. 30).

A sense of unfairness at the breaking of social rules, and anger and moral outrage can appear in two broad types of situation.[3] In one, individuals or groups perceiving each other as equals will experience a sense of unfairness if advantage accrues to one and not to all, for example, members of the same economic group, work grade or siblings. In the second, subordinate groups perceive unfairness from superiors, for example, between subjects and rulers, between employees and employers, between children and parents. Both were evident in our data.

Two further characteristics of reciprocity, that of its latent and dynamic qualities, are important. The implicit social contract of reciprocity (Durkheim, 1964) rests upon unwritten, unspoken and unspecified mutualities of obligation and understanding. In a stratified society, for both dominant and subordinate groups there are limits to what either party can legitimately do. All parties recognise the existence of limits but the precise location of boundaries remains unknown. Individuals and groups, in seeking to further their interests, test and discover the limits of obedience and disobedience. The terms of the social contract are constantly renegotiated.

In periods of rapid social change this process of renegotiation becomes more evident. Moore observes that 'the less stable the society, the wider and more diffuse the limits' (1978, p. 18) and the wider the range within which their testing and discovery takes place. Severe problems of unemployment for young people and the social and cultural dislocation referred to earlier, reveal the limits which some groups will accept and, simultaneously, the advantages in the bargaining process for those who control employment opportunities.

In such a situation, the essentially contested nature of a concept such as fairness can be seen more clearly. It is seen to be evaluative and as such its 'application is inherently a matter of dispute. It can, nonetheless, be "operational", that is, empirically useful in that it allows hypotheses to be framed in terms of it that are in principle verifiable and falsifiable' (Lukes, 1974, p. 9). We use the concept of 'fairness' as an heuristic device to explore several sets of changing social relationships: first, between society and the individual as a citizen and worker, second, between society and the individual as a family member, and third, between family members. We also use it to explore some of the far-reaching social and cultural changes produced by high levels of youth unemployment.

THE NORTH-EAST STUDY

We conducted a study of 40 families living in one ward situated in a city in the North-East of England. Employed and unemployed young people, aged 18–20 years, were interviewed during 1983 and 1984 and their parents were also interviewed separately. The levels of unemployment in the region have been among the highest in

Great Britain throughout the post-war years. In 1981 'Eldon' ward had 30 per cent of its economically active men unemployed and 12.5 per cent of its women. In January 1984 the unemployment rate for the region stood at 17.7 per cent, that is a quarter of a million individuals (OPCS, 1983; DoE, 1984a).

Our study could not be representative in a statistical sense. However, it provided a range and variety of experiences from a group of young people and their parents. All the young people had entered the labour market during the current recession and consequently they and their families had been faced with the problems associated with a contracting labour market. The study throws some considerable light on the perception of fairness of those living in an area of high unemployment. Further research, using a representative sample could be undertaken to test how far the concept of fairness is invoked by those living through economic recession.

ECONOMIC CHANGE AND THE SOCIAL CONTRACT

In qualitative research, the response of one informant may indicate a theme which runs through the data and thus prompt a shift from empirical observation to theoretical analysis. For instance, in one parent's description of his relationships with employers, fellow workers, family members and others, a pattern emerged of the reciprocities which are widely expected to imbue such relationships.

Mr Hughes, in his dealings with employers, had one overriding tenet, that of 'a fair day's work for a fair day's pay'. He saw himself as a good worker, aware of his value to an employer, and prepared to work hard for a proper reward. 'They need me as much as I need them. . . . They want their pound of flesh but they pay you a decent wage.'

This view of a fair contract and of reciprocity was central to his thinking which he spelled out in detail in a whole range of his relationships. For example, in his tasks in the store he made the effort to facilitate those of his co-worker, a consideration reciprocated and valued by her. His teenage children had ready access to his wallet, but left IOUs which were always honoured.

In his discussion of work, Mr Hughes made frequent reference to 'the carrot', the reward for effort or for going beyond the bounds of duty in his view of the normal social contract. For others, however, such 'carrots' were gradually becoming meaningless, mere symbols of promises unfulfilled, or in harsher instances being replaced by 'the stick'. These indicate that the social contract based on previous understandings was being renegotiated. Karen, an office junior, had been encouraged by her employers to qualify as a typist with promise of promotion. After successfully completing her evening course promotion was given only after she asked for a reference for another job. Not all, however, have a foot-hold in the labour market or the possibility of another job on which to draw when promises or obligations are not fulfilled.

While Mr Hughes' lucid view of the contractual nature of social relationships within employment was particularly systematic, others indicated an awareness of norms being ignored or eroded in situations of high unemployment. Parents vividly expressed a sense of injustice at the alleged exploitation of their young both on some government training schemes[4] and in 'proper' jobs. In many instances parents felt the need to intervene in the implicit social contract between their offspring and employers. One mother said she would refuse to permit her child to take a place on a government training scheme which, she had heard, involved shift-work, for £25 a week when fares cost £3 a day, '. . . and doing *shift* work. I thought it was *diabolical*. I wouldn't have let mine *go*. I would have told them straight, no'. Marie explained that her father complained when her employer regularly kept her working until ten o'clock at night, and did not pay her overtime rates. 'From eight in the morning . . . you had no choice, . . . he just expected me to stay. Oh, they [her parents] were mad. They were livid. Sometimes they used to phone up an' tell him what they thought of him, 'cos he went a bit beyond a joke.'

These complaints were not about the traditional wage differentials associated with age, which some young people resented, or about the fact that work was hard. Indeed, parents tried to make their children realise that work was not easy. As one commented, 'I think he's been made to realise – you know, because he's working eight hours a day, an' he *does* work hard, cos there's some nights he comes in shattered – that . . . working's not all a bed of roses'. Thus, among the critics of the treatment of their children were parents who had been able to offer effective advice in the search for jobs, who had found jobs for their children (although often at a lower level than they would have wished), who would have been ashamed had their children not found work, together with those who, when their children were unemployed, tried to keep alive their work ethic by joking, 'nagging', and finding and paying them for household tasks.

In some circumstances a strong work ethic and a sense of justice combined to expose irreconcilable contradictions. Mrs Price felt helpless in the face of those contradictions posed by low wages and even lower unemployment benefit, and her sense of justice.

I don't know how they justify it, I don't. Some job Richard [married son of 21] went after was *£40 a week* . . . 'Mam', he says, 'they expect you to *work* for it.' I says, 'Well, even there again, it's better than £23.' He says, 'I'm not doin' all those hours and this and that and the other, for *that*.'

Unfair treatment in jobs and schemes was also referred to by young people themselves. Bryan, for example, disclosed both that, as a YOP trainee, he had had to complain to the Careers Office about working a 47 hour week, subsequently reduced to 40 hours after intervention by a senior Careers Officer, and that he had not received the promised training, 'I was in the stores for the full six months, so I didn't do what I was supposed to do.' He had been kept on by his employer following the scheme, but, although when interviewed he had been with the firm for almost two years, he was still only taking home approximately £38 for a 47 hour week. 'It works out that I'm actually getting paid under a pound an hour to come out with, . . . which is a bit bad.' Another young person, who had lived abroad most of her childhood and spoke good German, had obtained a job as a clerk-typist with a German-owned firm. Although she now enjoyed her work there, she had been asked to translate reports and felt less than fairly treated with regard to her linguistic ability. She knew a translator's wage was more than double her own and commented that 'they never even say thank you'.

A sense of injustice was additionally offered by one mother as a possible explanation of property crime by unemployed young people, a sentiment echoed widely in popular debate.

I think, probably they've got a grudge against society because they think like, well . . . what's the matter with us? Why can't *we* work? Because, I mean, they're bound to know that their parents at one time have worked . . . and probably older brothers and sisters have worked. And they'll be looking at themselves . . . and saying . . . why am I so different?

To take matters into their own hands in this way could accord with the notion of vengeance, that is, in this instance, a retaliation against a society which has not fulfilled its obligations.

Some young people were unable to conceal their disappointment, but we found very little evidence of jealousy or resentment *per se* at other people's success in obtaining work. Indeed, one girl said her unemployed friends 'thought it was great' when she got a job. Nevertheless, as jobs became scarce, latent priorities emerged in respect, for example, of gender. Of the general job market this same girl felt it was unfair that girls did not have the same opportunities as boys. 'I think there's more things for *lads* than what there is for lasses . . . I think they could give a girl a chance as well. An' when lads get the opportunity of getting a job first . . . I think that's *wrong*. They should treat wer the same . . .'. For some parents, however, unemployment was not as critical for a girl. Mrs Hughes felt unemployment was a 'crushing' experience for all young people but qualified her statement.

> I mean, it breaks my heart to see them, *especially boys*, . . . *especially* boys.
> *Why do you think more with them?*
> Well, I mean . . . it's always been – that's been the role of a boy . . . that's what they function for. . . . They leave school, they get a job, they get married, they look after a family. I mean, that's their whole purpose in life, is work. . . . And . . . to me, it's soul-destroying. . . . It really is cruel . . .

Nonetheless, it should be noted that not all mothers shared this view; some believed that unemployment was equally damaging for a young woman.

The cultural dislocation of economic recession not only makes visible deeply held values, as noted above with respect to gender, but also tends to undermine pre-existing challenges to the social order and to erstwhile dominant values.[5] Douglas (1975) has observed that societies can tolerate cultural ambiguity to varying degrees. The evidence from this study, however, suggests that within a society such toleration may vary over time; in economic recession, as some power bases are eroded and others strengthened, less tolerance may be shown to ambiguities which disturb deeply held classifications. For example, the economic and domestic categories of gender, deeply held although not necessarily immutable or undisputed, are 'contaminated' by the visible presence of married women in paid work or of men carrying out certain domestic tasks. 'Cultural intolerance of ambiguity is expressed in avoidance, by discrimination, and by pressure to conform' (Douglas, 1975, p. 53). The manner in which political voice has been given to the proposition that women should 'return to the home' and the fact of discrimination against girls in many government training schemes for young people, both in terms of work content and the fewer opportunities offered, would seem to support this view (Rees, 1983; Brelsford *et al.*, 1982, pp. vii, 1).

FROM RATIONAL TO TRADITIONAL

The rising expectations which characterised the post-war period of economic growth include those of occupational opportunity and personal development. These infuse, if not always in practice, at least the theory and rhetoric of the education system. While some parents felt that schools could offer very little anyway, others had come to believe in the benefits to be derived from education, especially formal qualifications, in a modern society. Parents referred to 'pushing' their children, 'being on his back all the time'. Consequently, a sense of being let down was apparent in comments about education, especially with regard to qualifications.

Some parents found that, despite qualifications, their children were unemployed or in unskilled jobs. Any extra years at school were deemed wasted; moreover, certain parents clung to the outmoded view that their sons missed the chance of an apprenticeship by staying into the sixth form. Some still held to their belief in the value of education, but others who had earlier regretted their children leaving school at sixteen were, in retrospect, thankful that they had done so. They felt continuing at school would have been either irrelevant or counter-productive. Mrs Robson commented, 'I mean, they stayed on for their . . . CSEs, are they? But nobody even *asks* for a *look* at *them* do they?' She had persuaded her boys to stay on at school but now reflected, 'Well, you feel like you wasted their time.'

Hopes of upward occupational mobility for their children, however modest, were also shattered. Mrs Robson, whose husband had worked his way up from labouring to a supervisory position, spoke of her sons' occupational descent. 'It's labouring, it's not what you wanted for them . . . I don't think you hope any more that they'll get a decent job, you're content with them getting a job.' Thus confidence inspired by apparent educational change in recent decades had been destroyed. It is depressing to note that over twenty years ago similar observations were being made about working class children remaining at school to obtain minimal qualifications (Miller quoted in Allen, 1968, p. 326).

Furthermore, people felt they could not afford to make a mistake; one false move and a foot-hold on any worthwhile job was lost. Phil Matthews, from a family in professional and skilled work, had become dissatisfied in the lower sixth and left school mid-term. He was now doing a heavy unskilled job with no prospect of advancement. Mrs Matthews felt bitter about his experience, '. . . I mean, you're encouraging them to stay on at school, an' then they miss their chance for an apprenticeship'. She found other training opportunities were also denied her son. 'We rang up from here the other day . . . but it was just for either unemployed people or sixteen year olds. You see, he's missed out there.' Such instances firmly underline the salience of the concern in current educational debate about the need for opportunities for education and training throughout adult life.

This orientation to education constitutes a strand in what seems to be a shift to enforced reliance on more traditional modes of behaviour in which access to work draws upon ties of kinship and affectivity, now more strongly supplementing bureaucratic procedures. This emerged in young people's and parents' feeling that, 'rational' means of access to jobs, that is, selection on the grounds of qualifications and ability – the 'fair' means of obtaining work in our respondents' eyes – are fast disappearing. It was repeatedly summed up in the phrase, 'It's not what you know, it's who you know.'

Even in a buoyant economy access to jobs through personal contact (through family, relatives or friends) has been a feature of some occupations, especially as a means of gaining a first job (Freedman, 1969, p. 29). As jobs have become scarcer applicants and potential applicants for each job have multiplied, forcing firms to place more reliance upon informal modes of recruitment which reduce the burden of selection for personnel departments and carry their own advantages for employers (Jenkins *et al.*, 1983, p. 266; Morris, 1984, p. 343). Mrs Pearce pointed out, 'You know, they say, "Well, the father's a good worker, therefore the son *may* be." I mean, it doesn't always work out, but it could be, you know.'

In addition some measure of responsibility for good performance implicitly falls upon the employee introducing the new recruit, especially a young one – the reason for reluctance on the part of some to speak for anyone at all. This tacit contract with an employer has significance for the power relationships within the family. As Mrs Hamilton explained,

> Well, we've had *no* trouble with him . . . from when he started the job because I mean . . . apart from anything else he doesn't want to let his dad *down* . . . after all his dad . . . got him the *job* and . . . he was *told* that before he started. . . . Me and my husband said, 'Now, whatever you do, don't let *me* down. You've been *lucky* enough – *very* lucky to get a job . . . stick at it.' You know how you do – you *talk* to them, 'Oh yes dad, I know.'

Thus, at a stage when a young person could anticipate a certain slackening of familial control, an increased sense of obligation to the parent is imported into the labour market. It would be seen by all parties as 'unfair' should the young person fail to keep his or her side of the bargain. When fewer job vacancies are notified through the formal institutional channels those seeking employment must rely increasingly upon personal contact. Despite the limits which such constraints impose on the personal autonomy of young people, they are considered fortunate to have links with the labour market. One parent was 'sorry' for those with no links at all.

The overriding imperative of familism is summarised in the view that 'You've got to look after your own.' Our informants were aware that, even in a contracting labour market, such actions are at odds with a sense of fairness. 'Aren't we a selfish world now?' Mrs McGuinness said, when asked if help in the search for jobs for her two children had come from personal sources beyond the kin network. 'I think if they'd heard about jobs they would have sort of grabbed them themselves because they've all got families.'

In the families we studied, familial commitment echoed the 'amoral familism' described by Banfield,[6] but was modified in two important ways. There was a saddened awareness that when the option lies between doing something for your own child or for another in greater need familial obligation contravenes the principles of both equality and compassion. Mrs Robson pointed to this,

> Well, I think everybody's got to look after theirself, you know . . . Mike's friend, he's nearly 19, he's still not working. I mean

we feel sorry for him [from a family with no-one in work] . . .
and his [Mike's] dad says to him, 'I'll try and get you a start next',
he says, 'but I had to look after Mike first', which you've got to,
look after your own.

At the same time there was an acceptance of the limits to which
family obligation can go. Mrs Pearce spoke of her uncle, whom she
had not seen for six years, who was a manager at an engineering
works,

I phoned him a few times but as he said, 'Well I *can't*. In fact
today you phoned me up, tomorrow I've got to go into work and
decide about 40 who we've got to finish.' So he says, 'I can't very
well finish 40 people and then take on a nephew.'

Some of the families said they had not drawn upon kin for help
but were quite confident that they would be able to do so if in dire
straits. The re-kindling of dormant kinship ties gave another hint of
enhanced traditionalism. For example, Mrs Pearce's uncle, after she
had contacted him for help, was invited to her son's engagement
party and, to her surprise, 'because they don't mix with the family
much', accepted the invitation. As he had been unable to help with
a job he probably felt obliged to demonstrate some kind of family
commitment.

FAMILY LIFE AND FAIRNESS

Within the family itself the idea of fairness emerged as a major
underlying assumption of family life, as Backett (1982, p. 34) has
noted. This fairness does not necessarily imply equality. Indeed the
idea of fairness was both vague and flexible, an important characteristic of such generalised values or norms (Parsons and Bales, 1956;
Backett, 1982, p. 21). This allows the generalised notion of fairness
to embrace a wide range of interpretations and behaviours. Economic recession, with its apparently arbitrary and differential impact
upon family members, is an ever present threat to this value. Our
study revealed how deeply the notion of fairness was held as families
attempted to ward off threats to the self-esteem of the vulnerable
individuals and to family relationships.

Families constantly attempted to prevent feelings of resentment and inadequacy without generating a sense of unfairness. This is illustrated by the negotiations and expectations surrounding the amount of money young people contributed toward household expenses. In some families fairness was sustained by a flat rate system, and all the children of working age who had left school paid the same amount of board money irrespective of the source or size of their income. One mother spelled out her reasoning by claiming that both children received the same household goods and services. In other cases, fairness was incorporated in a system of relativities; graduated rates were paid according to the size of a young person's income or what parents perceived as young people's needs. Caroline's mother, recounting arrangements in her family, explained, 'Bobby was on the lowest wage. He gave the lowest . . . and Stuart got the most . . . and then Richard got the most when he was working at Mallinson's and so his . . . went up.' Young people who were saving up to marry were allowed to contribute less board money than their earnings would seem to merit.

There were further hints of the practice of the philosophy 'from each according to his ability, to each according to his needs'. Working brothers and sisters would sometimes attempt to mitigate material differences between their own circumstances and those of an unemployed brother or sister. Borrowing clothes may occur amongst siblings in normal circumstances, but it was also seen explicitly as a way of helping those on low incomes. Unemployed young people were given money by brothers and sisters, a service which was reciprocated if the situation was reversed.

Parents who said they could afford it gave their unemployed children money and gifts. But some of their attempts to mitigate a young person's situation created tensions in the family. The 'prodigal son' effect of the different personalities of her two sons was clear in Mrs Robson's account. When her employed elder son David, a quiet reserved boy, was unemployed he had neither asked for nor received any extra money from his parents – 'He wasn't a one for going out when he was on the dole.' Yet Mrs Robson saw her younger, more lively, unemployed son Mike as 'needing' more money. Of his '£15 a week or so' social security money he gave her £10 board money, but received £5 a week pocket money from her, and 'then his dead would give him a fiver'. In addition to legitimate pocket money, she gave him a further £5. '. . . I feel a bit guilty giving Mike, so I sort of sly it to him (laughs). David knows Mike gets it. . . . But I sort of give it him on the sly.' She justified her actions by adding, 'But as I say, I used to buy David's cigarettes.' The father in this family also expected David to subsidise Mike. According to their mother, during the first few weeks of his job, David 'was slipping Mike a couple of pounds. But that stopped, you know. That causes a bit of aggro here, 'cos his dad thinks he should sort of give him a bit of pocket money. David doesn't think he should. He thinks Mike gets enough off us'. The boundaries of reciprocity were being tested.

In their relations with their parents, children also had a sense of fairness. They, like their parents, were often aware that what they contributed to the household budget did not cover their costs (see Leonard, 1980, p. 62; Cusack and Roll, 1985) and one girl had even lowered her job aspirations from hairdresser to shop assistant because she knew her parents could not afford to pay for the equipment she would need. 'I mean, me dad was working on a little wage, and there was a canny few of us in – living here at the time, I suppose I didn't want to upset, like, and let them fork it out and . . . suffer, really.' Thus economic recession creates situations in which deeply held values are brought to the surface and have to be managed in the routines of family life.

CULTURAL CHANGE

The discussion of the concept of fairness in family and work relations has revealed some of the implications economic recession holds for contemporary British society. The shift in the balance of power in the labour market evident in times of high unemployment may also denote a shift to a more traditional form of social organisation. Change in the labour market enhances the familial power of some parents fortunate enough to have access to the job market (Wallace and Pahl, *Chapter 8* in this book). Paradoxically, and even within the same family, the basis of parents' power in their role as advisers and counsellors to their children may be eroded when they feel they have unwittingly given them bad advice.

Reduced opportunities in the labour market also facilitate a clearer ordering of apparent priorities as they relate to family and gender. Mary Douglas' work on the way societies deal with threats to their structure is particularly pertinent as a way of understanding this (1975, p. 241). In a society where the work ethic is an important value but where recession has followed a period of rising material and cultural expectations, unemployment may be characterised as such a threat. In this situation it is hardly surprising that families with a strong work ethic exhibit anger and frustration at the treatment of their young. Very low pay, 'slave labour', and unemployment itself undermine a major orientating principle of their lives.

The encouragement parents give their children, the nagging, the threats, the irritability when their off-spring seem to be constantly watching television or spending long hours in bed, the 'job creation' within the household, joking about 'dole wallahs' are not only means of keeping a work ethic buoyant but, from a parent's point of view, an attempt to keep at bay the danger which threatens the principles by which they claim to have ordered their lives and brought up their children. 'Martin'll work because . . . that's just – he's been brought up in a house where you have to work.' This is perhaps not a comment on any generational differences in values (which may indeed exist), but rather is evidence of a feeling that widespread youth unemployment may erode existing values and provide the preconditions for unwelcome cultural shifts. For in this view the threat posed by unemployment is not so much that the unemployed can survive without working, but that they may be content to do so. That some of them 'are quite happy to get on with it', 'quite content', is more an accusation than an expression of relief that one's conscience need not be disturbed.

Parents in this situation tread a tightrope between compulsion and protectiveness and in some cases the uneasy tensions between these two aspects of parenting have been brought into sharp focus. When Phil Matthews left school abruptly at seventeen, 'Naturally we were disappointed, and Dad said, "Right, no work, no home, *out*" ' (Mrs Matthews). 'He got his marching orders' (Mr Matthews). Here Mr Matthews' paternal authority was used to effect (Phil obtained unskilled work next day), but Mrs Matthews' role in averting further conflict over the issue was also evident. She felt 'very sympathetic' towards her son, and stressed that, 'I didn't want him and his Dad to break over it.'

The pressures applied by parents which we have discussed may not be as strong as 'rules of avoidance' which make visible a public recognition of a structure of ideas (Douglas, 1966, p. 159). Nonetheless, they are part of the same phenonomon. Mrs Pearce's comments about the shame she would have felt had her son been unemployed, and her embarrassment (revealed both in what she said and her mode of expression) in the face of unemployment amongst others is a case in point:

I didn't tell *anyone* that Martin had been given the, er, you know [four months notice]. Now at one time it wouldn't have bothered me, but nowadays with jobs being difficult, I think it *is*, you do feel a little bit – ooh there's something *wrong*, if you can't *work*, sort of thing, or they can't *get* a job. . . . I thought 'Ooh, Mark [neighbour's son] mustn't be working' . . . he's a mechanic and I know he's a good mechaniç, and I – I don't know, I just find it very embarrassing, the whole, you know, I just never mention . . . when Martin's friends come in the house, I never say, 'Have you got a – any work now?' I just, you know, skim over the subject, don't mention it at all.

Despite this awareness of job scarcity, people's thinking about their own children is structured by the displacement effect which characterises powerful ideologies. Thus, in the last example, Mrs Pearce is tacitly suggesting that she would hold her own son, if unemployed, in some way responsible for his predicament; structural problems and contradictions inherent in the society or system are defined as the personal failings of the victim (Mills, 1959, p. 14; Douglas, 1975, p. 240; Allatt, 1981, p. 194). Similarly, in current political debate, the structural basis of unemployment is not always acknowledged by powerful groups and the lack of unemployment is attributed in some significant degree to the inadequate or inappropriate skills of the young themselves.[7] Not only in political rhetoric and government policy but, from our evidence, in the everyday interpretations and mundane routines of day to day existence, dominant ideologies about work and non-work are sustained and reinforced.

CONCLUSION

The idea of fairness, around which this paper has been organised, arose from its constant invocation by our respondents. Indeed, their insights into the nature of reciprocity and its structural role preceded reference to more academic investigations of the issue (Moore, 1978). Fairness was a concept which ordinary people drew upon in describing and interpreting their experiences of social change and, in so doing, revealed a sense of social dislocation which illuminated critical characteristics of, and potential trends in, our society.

Underlying the notion of fairness was a recognition of the reciprocities or mutual obligations which formed for them an implicit social contract between equals and were integral to a hierarchy of relationships. In the responses of young people and their parents to reduced employment opportunities, the continuously negotiated nature of obligations became apparent and the limits of what was considered fair were tested and revealed. In this process individuals became aware that the world was changing, bases of power were shifting, norms were being eroded, authority was losing its legitimacy and the principles and categories by which they had ordered their lives were threatened.

In their response to this situation individuals assessed their priorities and searched for alternative resources upon which to draw. Fundamental to this reaction was a deep commitment to familism. As opportunities diminished latent priorities reappeared, denoting a shift towards more traditional forms of social organisation, but still drawing upon a concept of fairness which went well beyond the kinship network. For some, the preferment of young males over females in the competition for scarce jobs seemed only fair in view of what were seen as young people's ultimate familial roles. Similarly, the rational bureaucratised means of access to jobs, only ever partially established, was modified by a renewed emphasis upon and recourse to informal networks, and ties based upon kinship and affectivity became dominant. For parents this was part of an attempt to do what was right by one's own children. Within a family such practices reveal and sustain structures of power and authority of parents over young people, of those in work over those without work.

As the respondents themselves realised, familism often contravenes other important values; in an economic recession such contradictions are highlighted. The contradictions between familism, equality, individualism and patriarchy generated unease and tension in these families. Beliefs about how parents should help their children, infused as they were with the imperative of maintaining the work ethic, paradoxically were in danger of shifting the blame for unemployment from problems of social structure to the victims themselves. While providing fertile soil for an inward looking and, therefore, a more fragmented society as 'each looks after their own', and reinforcing power relationships within the family, recession simultaneously revealed the resilience and resourcefulness of some families as they struggled to retain their principles of family life.

These contradictions and difficulties which families experienced are placed in context by a further paradox central to the role of the family itself – as both upholder of tradition and mediator of social change. Land (1979, p. 141) has noted the importance attached to the family as 'the key institution for creating and structuring continuities from one generation to the next', a notion which implies that the family is not only a 'powerful force for the transmission of the status quo', but also 'an institution which manages, or is expected to manage, the tension between order and change, thus facilitating rather than inhibiting change. Hence, paradoxically the family both transmits culture and provides a counter culture'. The current responses to the difficulties their younger members are experiencing in work and unemployment brings this duality into sharp and distressing focus.

NOTES

1. The study on which the paper is based, 'Family Structure and Youth Unemployment in an Area of Persistent Decline', is funded by a grant from the Leverhulme Trust. Interviews were conducted by the authors, assisted by George English and Peter McMylor. Alison Bloomer provided valuable administrative support. All the names used in the text are fictitious. All emphasis is that of respondents.
2. It is widely acknowledged that the use of the term 'family' presents problems of definition. Here we refer to those households containing young people and their parents which we selected for our study and the network of kin to which our respondents referred as family.
3. This is not to deny that in some cases the objective circumstances of the relationship between dominant and subordinate groups can generate awareness of injustice (even when existing social rules are kept) or that the legitimacy of the social system itself may be queried.
4. The Manpower Services Commission, established and funded by central government, operates a range of training schemes for school leavers and young people. Many of our respondents had participated in the Youth Opportunities Programme (YOP), in which placements were normally of six months' duration. This has been superceded by the Youth Training Scheme (YTS) offering twelve-month placements.
5. It has been observed elsewhere (e.g. the papers in Crick, 1981) that in periods of recession those subordinate groups which are most vulnerable to unemployment, poverty and various forms of social and economic deprivation tend not to challenge the existing social order in collective and organised ways (that is, in actions which are either directly or indirectly political). Responses tend to be individuated and fragmented. A connection between unemployment and crime (which is widely feared but remains unproven) would be consistent with this, as are many of the acts of 'defiance' performed by young people (see Coffield, 1983, p. 332). It

is possible that such behaviour deflects energies from collective responses, and thus indirectly lends support to the status quo.

6. In describing this concept, Banfield observed: 'One cannot afford the luxury of charity, which is giving others more than their due, or even of justice, which is giving them their due. The world being what it is all those that stand outside of the small circle of the family are at least potential competitors and therefore also potential enemies' (Banfield, 1967, pp. 110–11).

7. An example is Lord Young's speech to The Society of Education Officers on 25 January 1985, in which he argued that one cause of youth unemployment is young people's lack of motivation to work.

8 Polarisation, Unemployment and All Forms of Work[1]

CLAIRE WALLACE AND RAY PAHL

It is frequently asserted that the harsh effects of the overall shift in the pattern of employment from a manufacturing-based to a service-based economy are mitigated by certain social processes of adjustment. The first suggestion is that unemployed people find rewarding and compensating activity in the so-called 'black economy' (Ditton and Brown, 1981; Mathews, 1983; Parker, 1982). As Parker categorically asserts: 'with high unemployment more and more people are getting caught up in the web of the underground economy' (1982, p. 33).

A further suggestion is that it is not so much the 'black' or 'underground' economy which attracts more work from the unemployed but rather the so-called 'domestic economy' (Rose, 1983). Rose states that 'when demand for labour in the Official Economy slackens individuals will spend less time in work, and marginal workers will be counted out of its labour force. But this gives more time and more incentive for individuals to produce goods and services in the Domestic Economy' (1983, p. 33).

A third claim is that, for poor working-class households, there is a kind of social capital in the long-established neighbourhoods and communities, so that those who hit misfortune are aided by those who have more resources whether of time, money or goods and services. This approach, which has long antecedents, is based on assumptions about collectivist tendencies among both kin and non-kin brought about by longstanding social relationships cemented through propinquity. While there may be some discussion about how far such community supports have been eroded by urban renewal and consumerism, many commentators still emphasise this response to adversity. Thus, for example, Lowenthal has said 'although needs may go unmet and thus give rise to problems such as poor health and sub-standard housing . . . many needs are provided for not through money income, but by the social networks and mutual aid systems that people participate in' (1981, p. 91).

These three putative adaptive responses of the unemployed – remunerated activity in the 'black economy', increased productive activity in the 'domestic economy' and, finally, utilising supportive systems of mutual aid in their localities – do not exhaust all possibilities but provide testable hypotheses which form the focus of this paper. How far do they affect the reality of responses to unemployment?

The main body of the argument which follows is drawn from research conducted by the authors on the Isle of Sheppey, in Kent, during 1981. Before turning to that data, however, recent empirical research, which bears directly on the issues under consideration, may be mentioned. Detailed studies have been carried out in Brighton (Miles, 1983), Kidderminster (McKee and Bell, Chapter 9 in this book), South Wales (Lee, Harris and Morris, 1983) and a number of other places. Miles' work in Brighton shows very clearly that the unemployed in practice are deprived of the tools, transport and the social networks based on the place of employment which might enable them to work for cash in the 'black economy'. Furthermore, such unemployed men tend to have rather few formal skills or qualifications. What is more, they are significantly disadvantaged in terms of ownership of household equipment, access to working space and gardens (Miles, 1983, p. 64). He goes on to note that the unemployed are less likely than the employed to own bicycles. His findings in Brighton were supported by a national representative sample survey of 1043 unemployed people, commissioned by the Economist Intelligence Unit in 1982. This showed that, whilst 23 per cent had done jobs for other people, only 4 per cent of these had received payment in cash, most of these being in the groups which had received further education (EIU, 1982a), a finding which casts serious doubts on claims that the unemployed are attracted to the 'black economy'. Further evidence provided by Bell and McKee (this volume) showing that unemployed people felt inhibited in engaging in activities outside the home because they believed that they were under constant scrutiny by neighbours so that infraction of Social Security rules would lead to punitive action. Such a breakdown of what has often been seen as a traditional solidaristic community into a prison of jealous eyes has been described with depressing verve in Seabrook's impressionistic accounts (Seabrook, 1982). Finally, a study of the impact of redundancy in the steel industry in South Wales concludes that, amongst ex-steel workers, there is considerable diversity of responses to unemployment. Whilst some may appear well placed to participate in the 'black economy' (or 'hobble' in the local terminology), gaining a degree of social cohesion thereby, others less well placed in hobble-networks are perhaps prompted by their exclusion to be vindictive informers (Lee, Harris and Morris, 1983).

Such studies have shown that the situation of the unemployed is more complex than was hitherto thought, and have helped to cast serious doubt on claims that the effects of unemployment are mitigated by the development of alternative forms of activity for some, or through community support. Our own research does not invalidate these findings, but attempts to situate the work practices of distinctive categories of the unemployed in a wider framework.

THE SHEPPEY SURVEY

Our data was gathered on the Isle of Sheppey, Kent, in 1981, from a one-in-nine random sample of households, yielding 730 cases with a response rate of 79 per cent. The investigation was concerned with all forms of work done by all households, regardless of the employment status of the occupants and the cell sizes were large enough for detailed comparisons to be made.[1] The survey was specifically designed to avoid gender bias by the random selection of equal numbers of male and female respondents (apart from single person households). All formal social surveys can be criticised, for, as it were, plucking respondents out of context and being insensitive to nuances of meaning. Such criticism might be said to apply a *fortiori* to an investigation of all forms of informal work, since respondents might be particularly wary of admitting to doing certain activities which may be illegal. Nevertheless, our study revealed that, insofar as the activities of all households outside registered employment is concerned, four types of work can be distinguished:

1. Work done by members of a household with their own tools and in their own time for themselves. This provides a range of goods and services – from home grown vegetables to repairs of car

brakes and has been referred to by others as the 'domestic' or 'household economy'. We prefer the term *self-provisioning*.

2. Work outside formal employment for others, outside the household, which is remunerated. This is generally known as 'working on the side'.

3. Work done for others outside the home that is not paid for in money but is repaid in favours or in kind. This may or may not be calculative – as when reciprocities are, as it were, converted into cash terms. Sometimes such work is simply part of an affective involvement with others.

4. Work outside the household to obtain food or materials without involving anyone else, or without it necessarily being illegal. Such activity would include fishing, ferreting, 'totting' and scavenging-type activities.

Information was gathered about the present occupation of all members of the household and the job histories of respondents, and a main concern of the study was to explore the divisions of labour by gender in the forms of work we have mentioned, an area not much explored in recent research.

In the case of self-provisioning, much the most substantial form of informal work, whilst men and women have their distinctive spheres (men fix cars, women knit and sew), there was an increasing tendency for certain decorating and home improvement tasks to be shared by both partners (Polycell, 1981; Pahl, 1984). Both partners may be heavily involved in this kind of work and it cannot be understood in relation to one partner's activity alone. 'Work on the side', which may or may not be illegal, was also undertaken by both men and women. Men may fix cars for cash; women scrub pub floors or work in the fields picking fruit and vegetables. There appears to be an informal segmented labour market as a parallel or shadow of the formal labour market between men and women – and indeed between young and old (Wallace, 1985). Little research has been done on the relative monetary rewards of 'men's informal work' and 'women's informal work' but we do know that much of the work women do is very poorly paid. In the third category – unremunerated supportive reciprocity – there was again a division of labour by gender. Women were more likely to provide emotional and social support – caring for other children, shopping for the elderly, lending food and similar assistance in resolving day to day crises in the community. For men, on the other hand, 'favours' were provided on an aperiodic basis such as helping to mend a fence, lay a path or lending tools. In short, women were most likely to do caring work and men to do practical, manual work. Finally, the work we termed 'scavenging' was almost entirely done by men.

Taking all these forms of work together, and including engagement in the formal economy, it was found that rather than one form of work being a substitute for another (eg work on the side substituting for formal employment), there appeared to be a process of polarisation, which resulted in those in formal employment being *more* likely to do more self-provisioning and informal 'black' work as well. This cumulation of certain forms of work resulted in some very busy productive households at one pole and at the other pole households able to engage in little more than communal reciprocity and scavenging – indeed, some households could not even engage in these forms of work (Pahl and Wallace, 1985a; 1985b; Pahl, 1984).

Previous publications reporting the main findings of our research have not given particular prominence to the unemployed. Rather, they have focused on the way all forms of work have become concentrated in the more affluent households with multiple-earners. For instance, a high proportion of working-class households with multiple earners earn more than those middle-class households with only one earner: these are the working-class households most likely to be engaged in buying their own dwelling from the local authority or in making all kinds of interior improvements if they already own it (Pahl, 1984). This increasing divergence between households with multiple earners and high income undertaking many forms of work and those households with no earners and low income we have terms *social polarisation*.

In this process of polarisation, quite evidently, the loss of employment has implications for the degrees of involvement of household members in other forms of work. It is now clear that there is no direct substitution of various forms of informal work for the loss of employment. Indeed, as O'Higgins has demonstrated, there is a positive relationship between the 'black economy' and the strength of the formal economy and not the other way round (O'Higgins, 1984a; 1984b; Pahl, 1984).

Through a more detailed presentation of the Sheppey sample survey, and a more qualitative analysis of selected Sheppey households in order to describe the actual patterns of work of the unemployed,[2] these general statements about the interrelation between various forms of work can now be explored in more detail.

Self-Provisioning

To measure more precisely the range and scope of self-provisioning of the Sheppey sample, a scale, ranging from 1–6, was devised. This scale[3] included different categories of work which households could perform for themselves, rather than purchase such goods and services formally (Pahl, 1984, ch. 9). In households where the male partner was in full-time employment, the proportion scoring 'high', (i.e. 5–6) was 60 per cent. This dropped to 44 per cent when the male partner was unemployed. Thus, the implication is that, even though unemployed people have the time, and presumably the need, for self-provisioning, they do not have the money or possibly the inclination. This is illustrated most poignantly by Mrs Eades:[4]

> *Did you do more decorating and things around the house then?*
> You just don't have the money to buy paint and the paper. It's all very well saying 'Oh, you've got the time to do it' but unless you can afford the materials you can't do many of the jobs. Every penny was spent before it came in the house really. But to go out and buy a pot of paint, or screws or something like that, you just couldn't do it because that was money that should have been spent on something else.
> *But surely you could have afforded a pot of paint?*
> Well, no, because if you had the money to buy that, then that money was coming off something else, something you had to go without. All that you had was needed. There just wasn't any money for luxuries. It's a day-to-day business, being on the dole, you know.

Mr Sarsby, now unemployed, put the problem like this:

> I got more done when I was employed than when I was unemployed. It's partly financial restrictions, of course. When you're employed you make use of all your time. You come home from work, have a quick bite to eat, a cup of tea, and get stuck into some job you've got to do. You know you've only got a set time. But when you're unemployed you've got all the time in the world and you think, ah, I won't do that today, I'll do that tomorrow. You take a slap-dash attitude, which is wrong. I suppose all your standards slip. You're depressed because of the situation and you

allow your standards to slip. You feel ashamed by it, you know. I did more work then than I do now.

Of course, once this situation is understood, it becomes easy to see why the unemployed are unable to do the self-provisioning many academic and political commentators who are in employment wish upon them. Many of our unemployed respondents made similar points to those of Mrs Eades and Mr Sarsby.

In order to investigate precisely the difference between households in which the male was in employment and those in which he was unemployed, an index of the domestic division of labour was constructed (Pahl and Missiakoulis in Pahl, 1984). Taking into account the characteristics of potentially 41 tasks, the frequency with which they were done by male and female and conventional social judgements about who would generally do each task on the Island, a scale was devised in which the more positive the score, the greater burden of the division of domestic tasks falling on the female partner (i.e. the 'traditional' pattern). Analysis demonstrated that the score for households where the male partner was unemployed was higher than in those where the male was in full-time employment. Paradoxically then, when men are unemployed they do less work in and around the home: the tasks that *are* done are more likely to be done by the female partner, and this is reflected in the moving towards the more 'traditional' pole (see also McKee and Bell, Chapter 9 this book).

Work on the Side

In the full sample survey, respondents were asked 'Do you do any own account work for extra money?' and 4 per cent of the sample replied in the affirmative; a further 1 per cent acknowledged that they did other work for an employer for which they got paid (presumably in cash or in some other informal way). When the 27 respondents who acknowledged that they got extra money informally were analysed some striking contrasts emerged. Of the 11 men, 10 were in full-time employment. Only one was unemployed. Furthermore, of the 10 male full-time workers, 5 were in households which were designated as having a 'high' income. By contrast, of the 16 women, 8 were full-time housewives and 10 were in 'low' income households. This suggests that the relationship between economic circumstances and work on the side may be sharply differentiated by gender, and provides some evidence of a segmented labour marked in the 'black economy'.

It may be objected that we have been misled by our respondents who prudently avoided being explicit about activity they may know is not quite straight. However, the survey also documented the sources of labour for a whole range of tasks connected with maintaining the dwelling and the car – spheres in which households might be expected to draw on the labour of other people working on the side. It was striking that the proportion of households who did pay others to do informal work was also exactly 4 per cent – the same proportion as admitted doing work for others. This exact match of supply and demand makes it extremely doubtful that there was a huge and systematic attempt at deception. It is more plausible to accept this proportion as broadly accurate. It is equally striking that the EIU Report quoted a similar proportion (EIU, 1982).

The overall proportion of those who work on the side is small enough but, when it is recalled that within that proportion there was only one unemployed male, considerable doubt is cast upon claims that this is a major sphere of activity for the unemployed. Mrs Eades, recognised that, even if the will was there, the work was not necessarily:

But did Jerry have any other ways of getting money?
Well, no. It's like, there are so many people out of work. They get the choice of who they have and who they don't have. If they have someone qualified and someone not qualified fo the same money then, obviously, they choose qualified ones.
What you do feel about other people doing jobs on the side then?
Good luck to them, I'd say. If Jerry could have got work on the side, then he'd have done it. But there again you see, it's just so that you can get by.

If the unemployed are able to get a bit of work on the side, it is generally a rare and low-paid activity which they do in great fear of being reported by jealous neighbours.

The most common way of earning extra money on the side on the Island is by doing home-work for an electrical components firm. Whilst, indeed, some of this work is officially declared, all kinds of strategies were devised so that money could circulate informally to those who needed it and who were prepared to work on a subcontracted basis from those officially on the firms' books. This was widely perceived to be a form of 'slave labour' which, for many, produced 60p an hour or less in 1981, but many women were driven to this work by desperation. Officially, the company concerned employed 600 out-workers to assemble electrical components in their homes. Any criticism of the low wage rates paid met with the reply that the company has a turnover of only one in six of its out-workers a year and has never had a problem of recruitment. The waiting list of those wanting to become home-workers is as long as those who actually do it. Mrs Sarsby described how she does this very demanding and time-consuming work:

> I do some work for other people as well and my husband helps me as well and the kids do it. I'm not allowed to earn much you see, that's why I do it for other people and they give me cash, otherwise I'd never get by. If I earned more, I'd get it deducted. I'm only allowed to earn £4 a week. When we was on the dole, I was allowed to earn £15. People just bring the work around and they give me a couple of bob extra for what I do for them. If they say can you do more than a thousand, I do them. They give me the full whack. Oh yes, they can't do me because I do down there and I check up on the price. But it's a help. Some of the kids are a bit expert now. They do the screwing for me. Even the little five year old and the three year old, he puts them together. I gave them money to start with, but when it got a bit tight I explained to them and they just accepted it. They do it for me now. They do it just to help us out a bit, they're pretty good. Myself, I had 200 this week and my pal she had 400 of the sort which she could do and she asked me if I'd just do them for her because she was moving house, she couldn't do them. You sit here all day doing them sometimes. We start at 6 o'clock in the evening and go on till midnight. Usually, if you're not interrupted by neighbours knocking, we can do a thousand of them in an evening. It works out at 75p an hour. You do get done because you have to pay your bus fare to get out there and that's 65p.

Mrs Sarsby illustrates a point that has been commented on elsewhere that home-workers are invariably low-paid and female (Hakim, 1984a; 1984b; Huws, 1984; Kay, 1984). The Sheppey data shows that women in the 'low' income households were the most likely to do extra work on the side, often work of a very tiring and demanding nature.

Unremunerated Work in the Neighbourhood

The Sheppey survey provides information relating to supportive reciprocities for both the supply and the demand side of such work. It was possible to ascertain the proportion of the given range of household tasks performed by friends and neighbours without charge. Considering all the cases where households had jobs done by others (for example, painting the house, getting shopping done, fixing the car, etc), 2 per cent of the complete range of tasks were carried out within the community. The limitation of this finding is that it was not possible to ask about every conceivable task that members of one household could do for another (although the 41 items which were asked about were carefully chosen to represent the actual tasks most likely to be done on the Island). Furthermore, given inevitable limitations of time, it was not possible to sub-divide this communal work according to whether it was done in each case by a man or a woman.

A further scale measuring the amount of informal work received by the household was devised,[5] in order to explore more thoroughly the socioeconomic characteristics of the households most likely to use this form of labour (Pahl, 1984). The conclusions were somewhat paradoxical. Those who used the most informal unpaid labour were either those who could not afford to pay, either formally or informally, but had to get given tasks done – these were most likely to be single-parent families and retired people (particularly when single) – or those who were well-placed to reciprocate informal work – namely women under 35 with growing children. Clearly, reciprocal child-care arrangements fall into this category (Pahl, 1984). These conclusions demonstrate that the range of domestic tasks that most households need to have done depends on the division of labour by gender in the home. Where one partner is missing, the necessary labour has to come from outside the household.

Turning to the supply side of this form of work, the data is much richer. Table 8.1 shows unpaid informal work done for others by the alternate male and female respondents and their economic activity.

TABLE 8.1 *Economic activity of respondent, by whether he/she engages in unpaid informal work outside the household**

Formal economic activity of respondent		Whether respondent engages in informal activity outside the Household						Total
		Men			Women			Total
		Yes %	No %	Total N	Yes %	No %	Total N	N
Full-time work		31	69	206	21	79	81	287
Part-time work		40	60	5	21	79	76	81
Unemployed		19	81	26	38	63	16	42
Retired		21	79	63	22	78	85	148
Full-time housework		–	100	1	23	77	168	169
Other/did not answer		–	–	1	–	–	–	1
	%	28	72		23	77		
ALL	N	84	218	302	96	330	426	728**

SOURCE *Sheppey Survey*, 1981

NOTES
* The question on the interview schedule was: 'Are there any jobs that you do *outside* your home, for other people?'
** Two respondents failed to give information.

From this will be seen that the unemployed men are the *least* likely to engage in such work and the unemployed women are the most likely.

One possible explanation for this finding has already been mentioned, namely the nature of the gender-linked tasks that are done for others. Table 8.2 shows the types of work that are done by respondents.

It will be seen that men are more likely to do home improvements such as minor repairs, carpentry, decorating and gardening – all fixed tasks which *could* have a price and could, therefore, be interpreted as illegal work which could be reported. This was widely understood. Mrs Colclough, wife of an unemployed man, remarked sourly 'You can't even cut someone's lawn. No, if you are seen cutting someone's lawn and you get paid for it, that's it.' Mr Box was particularly grieved about this: 'If they come up here and they saw me doing this, they'd have a go at me, even though it's my own car. They don't ask if it is your own car. They say We saw you working on

TABLE 8.2   *Type of informal labour for others by gender*

Type of informal labour	Men		Women		Totals	
	N	%	N	%	N	%
Routine domestic work	11	18	49	82	60	22
Social support	6	18	28	82	34	13
Personal services	1	8	11	92	12	4
Home improvement	72	87	11	13	83	31
Formal community work	11	35	20	65	31	12
Transport	4	44	5	56	9	3
Other help	19	48	21	53	40	15
TOTAL	124	46	145	54	269	100

SOURCE   *Sheppey Survey*, 1981.

that car.' Whilst there is a market for the activities mainly undertaken by women – domestic work and children, it is not so readily identifiable, and does not attract the same kind of scrutiny.

During more qualitative fieldwork,[6] it also emerged that men typically exchanged a specific task for another: the pattern of doing favours for others was highly ritualised: Mr Knapp put it like this:

Now, if a bloke wanted a favour and I could do it, I would do it. I've no qualms about asking for favours. One time I would have done, before I was out of work, but now I have been out of work for so long you know. I was more independent then, when I was at work.

This norm of reciprocity becomes a burden when it is not possible to reciprocate without fear of the consequences.

Considering the actual tasks women do for others without payment, there is a clear contrast with those done by men. Women overwhelmingly do routine domestic work such as shopping, babysitting and housework, and other caring work in the locality. This work is typically seen to be women's work and, although highly visible, is recognised to be generally unpaid, reflecting the wider social evaluation of different tasks: men's work in and around the house, whether for themselves or for others, is seen to be more 'productive'. Women's work, such as shopping, on the other hand, is not evaluated as 'productive' work but is seen as an extension of women's 'natural' unpaid labour in the home. This unequal evaluation of various tasks is to men's advantage when they are in employment but is held against them if they become unemployed.

The survey probably heavily underestimated the amount of supportive and reciprocal work done by women in the locality. Whether or not women were unemployed, they were embedded in extensive mutual aid networks which could be mobilised to resolve various day-to-day crises. Sally reported on her extensive neighbourly contacts on whom she could rely, even to borrow her Sunday lunch:

> Yes, a few are helpful. I know, yes, a few I know can be rather relied on. Next door, Jennifer, a couple of others, say at the most about a dozen or so. My next door, this side, I find that most things that they've got I can borrow – a lawn mower, sugar, and on the other side from rawplugs to ladders. And even just talking over the fence, hanging the washing out. Sometimes I am out there three or four times a day, saying 'Oh, I've forgotten so-an-so, can I borrow this.' And the other side, they tend to give us vegetables. They grow vegetables. Lettuces in summer, cabbages in winter, but I don't tend to go in and out there.
>
> There was an occasion when I forgot to buy the Sunday lunch, and I shot up the road and borrowed a chicken from someone. They had it frozen, so they had something I could borrow.

The frequent involvement of women in such networks of mutual support and care helps to explain the findings reported in Table 8.1, that unemployed women are most likely to take part in unpaid work in the community. Some unemployed men did, however, begin to do more for others, without the expectation of immediate reward: by, as it were, 'banking' reciprocal goodwill, they are able then to draw on it in the future. However, only a very small minority of the unemployed adopted such a strategy. An alternative coping response was to become more reclusive. For example when Lorna was asked 'Do you turn to neighbours more when times are hard?'

> Well, no, not really. We really keep to ourselves a little more when times are hard, we're more self-reliant actually. When my husband was unemployed we saw the neighbours less. Work contacts have always been more important. Bob was worse off than I was because he didn't know anyone at all around here. No, in fact you lose contact because you can't afford to go down

the pub. He's quite sociable really, he likes playing darts and snooker, he does that all the time at college. But you see, you couldn't afford to do that. I can think of other people in the road who do the opposite. They try harder to make friends. They go in and out of each other's houses and that, but he became very morose. Mind you, you have to remember that he did get sacked. He was pretty devastated about it.

'Scavenging'-Type Work Outside the Home

This final form of work is not very widespread, even on the Isle of Sheppey where opportunities are still relatively good. However, from the more qualitative part of the fieldwork it was apparent that for some households, it was a distinctive work strategy when unemployed. One such scavenger was Sam:

> My boys call me a right old rogue. But this is the way you've got to live, isn't it, eh? A bit of fishing, I go off here and I get a few winkles, mussels, cockles, whelks, stuff like that. Get hold of anything like that, but it all supplements our living.

Sam is in his fifties and is registered as disabled with a life-time's experience in getting by. Another household using this strategy lived for many years without regular employment but refused to accept social security. Clearly, as Mrs Weeks illustrates, scavenging is close to a gipsy lifestyle and is certainly not a realistic alternative for many. Mrs Weeks described her life in South-East England in the 'affluent' 1960s:

> We've lived off dog biscuits sometimes – yes, Bonjos. The dog would sit there watery eyed while we ate his biscuits. Well, not so much the children, the children didn't have to put up with that, because they stopped with my husband's mother, down by Rye, down by Hastings, that way. We went down there that time, and we used to live in the back of a little van, and you had to start it up in the morning when it was parked on the side, start the engine up to get the radiator going so that you had some hot water for shaving with. We lived like Pikies. And then we used to have them (the children) at weekends, and they used to like picking. All the week they stayed with their Nan while we were out working, and then you get paid on the Friday. Well, by Wedn-

esday we were running a bit short, so we used to make sure that there was enough food for the dog, but sometimes we had nothing to eat but sugarbeet, yeah, cut up sugar beet. That's what we used to do and that's what we used to eat as well, or depending on what we were picking, we ate that, cherries, plums, potatoes, but down at Rye it was sugarbeet. But he wouldn't give in you know. However poor we were, he wouldn't give in.

CONCLUSION

Whilst our study of the Isle of Sheppey has collected data relating to all forms of work in all households (indeed, this is its great strength), we have not hitherto considered the specific work patterns of the unemployed. This paper has concentrated upon four distinct categories of informal work and has shown that, contrary to the claims of some academic commentators, the loss of formal work by the unemployed is not generally compensated for by an expansion of informal work. Rather, different kinds of informal work have different rules, codes and procedures, distinctive divisions of labour by gender, and each kind of work expands or contracts under different circumstances. Just as the category of 'the unemployed' must be disaggregated by age, class, gender and other variables if we are to fully understand unemployment, so too must the category of 'informal work'.

When this was done, it was found that work on the 'black economy' and self provisioning is most readily engaged in by those in employment. The informal work of the unemployed is, in general, much more marginal, less rewarding and is extremely limited in its potential for expansion. It is certainly no compensation for work in the formal economy. We have demonstrated in our more extensive work on social polarisation (Pahl and Wallace, 1985) that the unemployed are poor, isolated and unable to engage in any more than marginal informal activities. There is no substitute for more money legally obtained: in Britain in the 1980s, the Mathew effect rules – 'To him that hath, more shall be given'.

NOTES

1. The main part of the research was funded by ESRC Grant No. G/00/ 23/0036. We are grateful to the Council and its officers for considerable

help and support. More detailed information on the survey is available from SCPR, 35 Northampton Square, London EC1V 0AX (please quote P631). The main data set has been deposited in the ESRC Survey Archive at the University of Essex. (For further discussion of the fieldwork and some of the results see R. E. Pahl, 1984; and Pahl and Wallace, 1985(a); 1985(b)). This present paper was written after the project was completed with the support of the Joseph Rowntree Memorial Trust.

2. The analysis began by selecting those men from the Sheppey sample survey who were unemployed in 1981. These were compared with other groups, including those we termed 'affluent workers', based on qualitative, in-depth interviews of each category. A considerable amount of data was gathered on six selected households but their experiences and life-styles were inevitably very diverse and the results at this stage were inconclusive. This attempt to study a 'representative' group of the unemployed by controlling for previous employment, age, tenure, and social class, proved to be counter-productive. Six very different accounts were presented, and even though the households could be selected easily from our computerised data, the interviews were intensely time-consuming. Faced with such inconsistencies, a new wave of interviews were embarked upon in the summer of 1983, in order to place households more fully in their local contexts. This time a different strategy was adopted; two contrasting 'communities' on the Isle of Sheppey were chosen. The first was a private estate of neo-Georgian houses built in the mid-1970s, which contained occupationally and geographically mobile households whose chief earners commuted out of the area for work, and seldom remained on the estate for more than a few years. These were mainly 'affluent' and skilled manual workers and white-collar workers. The second was an older council estate on which many households had lived for 20 years or more. The more affluent households had bought their homes. Most families knew at least 40 people in the near vicinity, having grown up and gone to school with them. These householders were mainly employed in the local factories in rough and heavy manual work. Both areas were generally recognised by their residents as being distinct communities. The analysis began by contrasting selected households from the original random sample, who were known from the previous fieldwork. Both partners in the household were interviewed, where possible, and we then followed up other families mentioned in the interviews, in a 'snowball pattern'. Thirteen households were interviewed in this way – six in the 'traditional' working-class community, and seven in the 'privatised' one (Wallace, 1984).

3. Households were placed on the scale by the number of categories in which they did at least one of the following activities:

1. vegetable growing at any time;
2. either painting or plastering or mending a broken window in the last year;
3. either checking the oil level or tuning the engine or doing work on the brakes of a car at any time;

4. either putting in an RSJ or double glazing or central heating or building a bathroom or an extension or converting an attic at any time;
5. making either jam or beer or wine fortnightly or regularly;
6. making clothes or knitting at any time.

4. The individual respondents are described in more detail as follows:

1. Mrs Eades was in her 20s, married to an unemployed manual worker, with 2 young children. The Eades are owner-occupiers.
2. The Sarsbys were interviewed as part of the neighbourhood study (see note 2). They are in their 30s, and have 5 children. Mr Sarsby is an unemployed steel worker. They live in a council house.
3. Sam lives in the 'traditional' community in a council house and his 5 sons have now left home.
4. Mr Knapp is a lorry driver in the 'privatised' estate, who has been unemployed for four years. The Knapps are in their 40s and live in a privately-owned house with two teenage children, one of whom is also unemployed.
5. Sally lives with a self-employed taxi driver in a council house. She is caring for a son of her husband's and her own new baby. Sally is in her early 20s.
6. Lorna lives in the 'privatised' estate with her 4 year old daughter. She and her husband worked at the local hospital (he as a technician and she as a clerical worker). Her husband was unemployed for some time after being dismissed, but later went to University leaving Lorna to care for the daughter in Sheppey.
7. Mrs Weekes is married to a self-employed business man. Before setting up the business she spent some years being 'self employed' with her husband by doing odd jobs. The Weekes are in their 40s.

5. The informal Labour Scale related to tasks done by friends, neighbours and relatives who were *not* living in the household. This informal labour might be paid or unpaid and no distinction is made on the scale. Although information was gathered about payment, in practice the distinction was very hard to draw and it seemed to make better sense to put all sources of informal labour in the same category. The tasks making up the scale are as follows:

1. either getting painting or plastering or a broken window mended in the last year;
2. either getting the car oil level checked or the car engine tuned or work done on the brakes at any time;
3. either getting an RSJ put in or double glazing or central heating or building a bathroom or an extension or converting an attic at any time;
4. getting clothes repaired or knitted or a dress made;
5. getting the outside windows cleaned;
6. getting a child's hair cut.

6. One of us lived on the Island with an unemployed household for a period of 9 months. In this way, we accumulated extensive knowledge of the survival strategies of the unemployed.

9 His Unemployment, Her Problem: the Domestic and Marital Consequences of Male Unemployment[1]

LORNA MCKEE AND COLIN BELL

We, sociologists that is, have been criticised for not being where the action is. We have been seen as failing to exercise our sociological imaginations. The vital Millsian link between private troubles and public issues (Mills, 1959), never very strong in British Sociology, has been notably tenuous in recent years. Until recently, remarkably little sociological attention has been given to the large number of unemployed people (is it three or four million?) in contemporary Britain. Detailed work to understand their private troubles has hardly begun. There has though been *some* response from the sociological community and at the same time an understandable impatience to know precisely 'how unemployment affects people' (Harris, 1984). Harris asked that question with increasing irritability and exasperation as he discovered that we – sociologists that is – don't really know. He asked, 'what has been the effect of unemployment on family life, on divorce, on child abuse? No one seemed to know exactly. What was the effect of parental unemployment on children's work at school and on truancy? Has unemployment encouraged many people to move or emigrate? Where were the definitive figures on delinquency and crime, race and religion? An embarrassing silence' (Harris, 1984, p. 88).

In fact the reality is different. Perhaps sociologists were not as quick into the field as they might have been, nor as quick to publish

134

results as a *New Society* journalist might wish. However great the concern, there might be good reasons for this. Catherine Hakim, in her well known paper on 'The Social Consequences of High Unemployment', makes the point that one of the reasons that the evidence is patchy and incomplete is 'a tendency to regard unemployment as a problem only for those most directly involved; a tendency to personalize unemployment as an experience affecting only the unemployed rather than the wider society, and it reflects also the dominance of the interview survey of the unemployed' (Hakim, 1982, p. 459). Harris in his article, critical of sociologists, wonders too whether what he calls the 'curious passivity' of many of the unemployed has allowed them to avoid our attention. He also notes the remoteness of the unemployed, in terms of both geography and class, from the centres of power and learning. And he asks whether 'the social science establishment has actually collapsed under the steady sniping from the Keith Joseph quarter and lacks the self confidence to tackle the major social issues of the day' (Harris, 1984, p. 90; see also Bell, 1984). Whilst this isn't entirely without foundation, neither is it quite fair. A number of studies of unemployment – both funded and unfunded – have been carried out and their findings are beginning to see the light of day. And, because of the pervasiveness of unemployment in contemporary Britain, virtually every empirical study in every area has to take it seriously. Few areas of social life are unaffected by the spread of unemployment and the employed are stalked by its omnipresence. Indeed everyone working in the field knows that it is not always easy to sharply distinguish the employed from the unemployed. They also know that much previous 'wisdom' has been called into question. Caution is now advocated in a too ready acceptance that something called 'the informal economy' will expand to fill up the 'space' left by the retreat of the formal economy (Pahl and Wallace, 1983 and this volume). Pahl and Wallace concluded from their study of the Isle of Sheppey that

> 'beyond employment' most likely means poverty, isolation, little opportunity for informal work, involuntary home-centredness, with deteriorating dwellings and capital goods. Multiple earners bring prosperity, however short-lived; no earner brings a downward spiral of economic and social detachment. We find no way of disguising the fact that, in present circumstances, the self-provisioning households (as they call them) on Sheppey would

face a very bleak future 'beyond employment'. (Pahl and Wallace, 1983, p. 44)

This increasing *social polarisation* of the households they studied results from the fact that 'employment status is the key to participation in *all* forms of work, not simply in the formal economy' (Pahl and Wallace, 1983, p. 36).

The focus of this (partial) report of our study in Kidderminster is the gender specific consequences of unemployment. We build on two seemingly contradictory observations: that recognition should be paid to the impact of unemployment on the *family* rather than on the unemployed as individuals; and that the household as a unit of analysis can obscure individual degrees of disadvantage, suffering and inequality.

Kidderminster had a population of just over 50 000 at the 1981 Census and an unemployment rate of just under 12 per cent in the same year. It is a small industrial town in the West Midlands – the region that is currently experiencing the highest rate of increase in unemployment, and where traditionally (i.e. before the mid-1970s) unemployment was well below the national average. Whether because of deindustrialisation or the 'spatial consequences of the restructuring of capital', Kidderminster is suffering (McKee and Bell, 1984 contains a fuller account of Kidderminster's labour market). Our respondents reiterated themes of the town's decline. Images of empty factories; poor amenities; burgeoning consumerism in the growth of supermarkets, and new dual carriageways being built to lead out and away from the town made a vivid impression on us when we surveyed our respondents' experiences. Typical of their comments were such forceful assertions as:

> As far as I can see there's nothing in Kiddy (Kidderminster) for us or the kids, there's nothing, although there's plenty of factories. They started building all these new places, and you think you'd get work but you just can't get hold of one. . . . All the work's gone in Kiddy. There's nothing you can do.
>
> . . . there's half the town lay empty.
>
> They're closin' down factories every day.
>
> Kiddy's a ghost town ain't it? At one time every one of my mates was at work. I bet you I can't even name one that's at work now.

. . . round Kidderminster . . . all they're concerned about is how many cars can we park in so and so car park. They've built an enormous ring road, they don't think about the small shops they've cut off. Multi-storey car parks and one-way streets that's all they're interested in. There's a carpet warehouse and a picture house and tobacconists next to it, they've closed them off to build a bloody supermarket – Asda Superstores – and all the jobs have gone. All the jobs have gone and they haven't even cleared the site yet.

The general objective of our study was to draw conclusions about the impact of unemployment on family and marital relations. We rely on couples' perceptions of their relationships and have talked in depth and at length to them in order to catch the different meanings men and women attach to the experiences of unemployment and to their marriages and family lives. We give as much attention to the man's family relationships as to the more usual economic model of the man as 'ex-worker'. The questions we originally wished to explore concern the implications for families when men's attachment to the labour market is broken. Does the loss of the economic provider role result in changes in the domestic division of labour? Are men freed to become more participative fathers and more active home makers? How are the lives of women and children affected by male unemployment? What is the relationship between economic provision and power and authority within households? Does increased male unemployment herald a breakdown in patriarchal structures and enhance wives' spheres of authority? Whilst these questions provide a general orientation, we now find some of them inappropriate, even simplistic, when faced with the complexity of experiences in households where the male breadwinner is unemployed.

We set out to find a small number of families where the male was unemployed and which had at least one dependent child aged ten or under (McKee and Bell, 1985). Wives' employment status, duration of employment, religion, family size and occupational status varied and could not be held constant. Our intention was to capture the range of problems faced by unemployed families, to detail the processes by which they cope and to describe the variations in life experience.

Whilst determined to draw the families from a single locality, we did not have the resources for anything like a full community study.

We conducted our study *in* a place rather than *of* a place, and we therefore do not have the kind of detailed information that Pahl and Wallace have of the Isle of Sheppey.

Unemployed men were directly approached outside the town's Unemployment Benefit Office, the study was outlined to them and their cooperation was invited. A leaflet describing the aims of the project was distributed at this stage and it was explained that the emphasis was to be on both their own and their partners' experiences of unemployment. The leaflet was to serve as a letter of introduction to partners who were frequently absent at this first point of contact. Confidentiality was assured and no financial incentives were offered.

Out of a total of fifty names and addresses drawn from the street sample, forty-one interviews have been conducted with husbands and partners in their own homes. A further four families drawn from local maternity hospital records have also been included and similarly interviewed.

The characteristics of the families which comprise this study are as follows. Briefly, they are *young* families and a high proportion have pre-school age children. Thirteen (29 per cent) fathers and sixteen (35 per cent) mothers are under twenty-five years of age; thirty-four (75 per cent) fathers and thirty-seven (82 per cent) mothers are under thirty-five years of age. Some seventeen (38 per cent) families have a baby of one year or under and thirty-one (69 per cent) families have at least one pre-school age child. Most parents are at early stage in their marriages. Most of the fathers, thirty-eight (84 per cent), had been formerly employed in manual occupations and nineteen (42 per cent) held unskilled jobs ranging from construction work, labouring through to general agricultural work. Five had previously held managerial positions and nineteen skilled workers were included. This occupational profile is like the national one which shows that unemployment is not a social leveller and the 'burden' continues to fall heaviest on 'particular groups, mainly unskilled manual workers' (Hakim, 1982). Other national trends are mirrored, with very few wives in this sample employed, two full-time and three part-time, and a higher than to be expected number of men with four or more children (nine). In terms of duration of unemployment, nineteen (32 per cent) of the fathers in this study had been out of work for less than twelve months and twenty-six (58 per cent) had been unemployed continuously for more than twelve months at the first point of contact. The families were predominantly local people and white, twenty-six (58 per cent) husbands and twenty-seven (60 per cent) of their partners were born in the town itself. A further ten husbands and twelve partners were born within the West Midlands area. Only four men and three women were born outside the United Kingdom. Nine (25 per cent) couples were not legally married. In what follows, we use the term 'wife' loosely to indicate women living in 'marriage-like' situations. At a later stage of analysis we shall distinguish this group of women and men to see if the position of the women is in any way more or less secure than those legally married. It is important to emphasise that our results relate to a very *specific* study. Whilst the group of families we investigated may reflect some wider patterns, small scale case studies do not permit widespread generalisation and inferences must be made with great caution. Their strengths come from the ability to capture the complete variation of phenomena and to detail social processes and meanings for individuals and particular groups. The questions raised by this study need to be asked in other regions and of other groups before an aggregate picture of unemployment and family life can be drawn.

UNEMPLOYMENT: HIS OR HER PROBLEM?

When we first conceived of this study we identified male unemployment as a circumstance potentially heralding the convergence of the social worlds of men and women, of public and private spheres. Our original postulation was that adjustments might occur in the spheres of domesticity, childcare and productive work. Through our imaginative viewfinder we supposed we might see moving pictures of unwaged men collecting the children from school, preparing family meals while their responsive and adaptable partners sought and secured paid work in the labour market. We were not really so naive! But somewhere at the bottom of our research questions lay hopes concerning social change, a pluralism of lifestyles and the ability of people to choose.

The reality of unemployment and its effects on the majority of the life styles we observed diverges markedly from those suppositions. Indeed, many of the findings suggest that questions about change and choice were inappropriate and stultifying. It is at least *as* useful to look for continuities in the lives of unemployed families, and to focus on constraints against change. We have also found it *as* useful to pinpoint episodes of conflict as opposed to consensus. For example, we have argued in earlier papers that male unemployment can serve to *polarise* the experiences of men and women even more sharply than labour market activity (McKee, 1983; McKee and Bell, 1985). Instead of necessarily creating a unified set of problems for couples to be tackled through joint strategies, unemployment of husbands could have particularistic and negative effects on their partners. It could perpetuate and enhance female inequalities in the labour market. Women with young children could not compete equally with men for scarce jobs, nor were the jobs available to them in any way equal in status or pay (Wallace and Pahl, Chapter 8 in this book). The structure of social security payments, where men are treated as primary claimants, often denied women the chance of earning an independent and adequate income (Buckland and MacGregor, Chapter 11 in this book). A straightforward cost accounting of low wages, childcare costs, travel costs and consequent total benefit deductions kept many women at home. The only women able to contest the status quo were those in well-paid or well-established jobs and these were a small minority in the present study. The women in our sample, instead of taking up jobs, were more likely to be unemployed themselves – and even to give up part-time work or to postpone the return to work, as the following vividly illustrate:

No, no I can't sign on, 'im bein' out of work. It's a waste of time. I won't get nothin' see.

(I was working) . . . part-time so I packed that in 'cause it wasn't worth me working now. They'd have taken it off what he was getting. (worked as barmaid part-time)

That's the problem. You try to build yourself up and they all stop it right away. I think I was allowed to earn £4. I mean, by the time I had me bus fare out of that it didn't add up to nothing, you know, we just couldn't manage. (worked as cleaner part-time)

Any job I get, even part-time, Derek's social security would be cut to the equivalent so therefore I think I'm not going to do anything that I don't like . . . to do a grotty job and have our money cut, I think well what the hell! (former tax officer)

In many cases the traditional attitudes towards men's and women's roles seemed to harden and be reinforced in relation to breadwinning. The loss of the male economic provider role struck deep chords among both wives and husbands and a passionate defence of men's right to provide was invariably raised. The views might read as extreme or atypical but were in fact widespread and did not relate easily to either occupational grade, age or other beliefs about gender roles. Fundamental emotions concerning self-esteem, self-image, pride, views of masculinity, respectability and authority resounded in the expressions of both men and women. The constraining effects of these postures and beliefs in the face of structural change should not be underestimated. A wife commented: 'That would kill Bill', adding

> . . . the man he is, is like a he-man. 'I'll keep my family and nobody else.' That's Bill's attitude anyway. Nobody else keeps his family, he's very old-fashioned that way. He don't believe in this Women's Lib or nothing like that. He says women are equal to men in some ways, but he says men will always be the breadwinners. He says he's been the breadwinner for years and he'll be the breadwinner for another few years.

One husband commented:

> That would be degrading.

And another said:

> I'd have the feeling as if people would be staring behind my back, my missus keeping me, she's paying for all the food, the clothes, the roof over our heads, paying for me to go out and have a drink. . . . If she just worked alone I'd probably go round the bend.

And yet another said:

> I couldn't live off a woman . . . I think I'd leave before I'd live off her. That is the way I am.

It was not just men who supported the status quo. One wife announced:

> I'm not going to slave myself to death while he sits at home all day on his backside doing nothing.

Furthermore, male unemployment could heighten other 'gendered' marital activities, especially in relation to the allocation and control of money, social life and domestic and maternal routines (see McKee, 1983; Morris, 1983). Wives could and often did – especially where the 'whole wage' system was operative – find themselves expected to perform identical account responsibilities and financial management activities on much reduced incomes (Land, 1983; Pahl, 1983). Making the 'money stretch was a recurrent theme reiterated by many wives but it was not a new phenomenon, just more burdensome and extreme in the face of unemployment. One wife identifies the polarisation of the social context of men and women for us:

> I think there's two different situations. As Roy says, he likes to be the breadwinner and that's hard on a man, but the hardest bit on a woman is like *managing on unemployment* . . . that's the biggest problem. 'Cause, to me, being unemployed, I know it sounds daft, but you've got to work at being unemployed if you want to survive.

In view of these attitudes, it is not surprising that conflicts were common throughout the sample over the origin, ownership, usage and control of money. Some of the most vituperative rows reported to us concerned such disagreements. Indeed, management of money did not bring control for many women, with husbands insisting on their own personal spending money without any equivalent allocation to wives. Some felt they had to 'check' their husbands' spending – one explained 'Him and money's soon parted.' Wives' and families' needs were often viewed as coterminous by husbands but they put in a stake for money for themselves, arguing:

> It is supposed to be a bloke's privilege to be able to go out for a chat with the lads and have a drink and play cards or something.

Wives fought back, as this discussion shows:

> *Husband* (unemployed bricklayer): There's been lots of times we've had £150 come in . . . and I've ended up with about £10 or £15 and you've had the rest.
> *Wife* (former secretary): But it's like I keep telling you it's not *me* who has it. He thinks when he got £150 he'd want a bit of it and I have the rest. And he seems to think it's me who's having

it, but it's not me. I spend it on paying the bills, buying food, clothes things like that. But he seems to get the idea that it's me who's having it. Whereas with him, when he has his cut, it's *him* who's having it, it's being spent on him!

The collision between, rather than the harmonisation of, male and female social worlds was a constant theme raised by our respondents. Women could find their social contacts controlled and observed by their menfolk while the men themselves often found the private domain unwelcoming and confining. The restricted social world of unemployed individuals has been well-documented by many studies of the unemployed (Marsden and Duff, 1975; Bunker and Dewberry, 1983). The unique contribution made by our research is to highlight the differential impact this can exact on members of the family unit. We found evidence of *double isolation* with the contacts and social ties of women being dramatically curtailed in response to husbands' job loss (McKee, 1983). Our findings suggest that it was not just unemployed men who had to respond to a reduction of social contacts. So too did their partners. This has the effect not just of dividing off the unemployed from the employed but it separated a wide range of those associated with the employed (wives, children, even parents) from those associated with the unemployed.

Our respondents often explained this increasing privatisation of 'wives' lives either as a consequence of husbands directly or indirectly discouraging women's outside links *or* because of withdrawal of contacts by others. The privacy of homes was stressed by the male's presence and often marital primacy was alluded to. One woman reported 'Mind you I don't like going anywhere where husbands are.' The theme of some husbands having *control over wives social lives* could be detected in the language used. Wives talked about being 'allowed' to keep in touch with friends, to go out socially, and permissive husbands were praised: 'He's very good like that.' In a few cases the impression was also given that husbands *control use of domestic space*, visitors come only with *his* approval even if they are *her* friends. Friends who stay away may just be respectful of marital privacy *or* may be deferring to perceptions of the husband's 'mastery' of his home.

We are far from understanding the full meaning and processes that influence female and male friendship patterns, both of which are affected by marriage and childbearing as well as employment status (Komarovsky, 1962). In dividing up domestic tasks, there was slightly more evidence of change amongst our unemployed couples. However points of tension again surface. The degree of male involvement in domestic routines was very varied (also see Morris, 1983). Two men with full-time working wives provided a fullish range of domestic and childcare services, although one had a housekeeper/ nanny to assist, while other men made no contribution to the running of the home or caring for the children at all. Unemployment had no uniform effect and the extent of male participation in the domestic sphere was something privately negotiated and executed.

We are not so much interested here with 'who does what' or how much, but rather with what sorts of public scripts define and constrain acceptable levels of male involvement and change. From our own sample we were able to identify two different forms of 'rationale', which could be used to explain this phenomenon. Within *female-based rationales* low levels of male participation in housework and childcare were related to themes of *female* nature, skill and expertise and to the *private* competence of mothers, wives. Women were described as doing (or claimed to perform) domestic tasks quicker, better, more thoroughly. Indeed where reduced income led to an enlargement of the domestic role, the expansion of tasks usually fell to women. It was she who shopped around, dealt with creditors, planned meals, and budgeted (McKee, 1983).

Male-based rationales for an unchanging division of domestic labour drew attention to the *public* arena. The legitimacy of the men's preoccupations outside the domestic sphere were held to be primary, rather than their motivation or disposition. Men did not contribute in the home as they were often engaged in the search for work or absent due to job interviews or informal labour market activities. In other words many couples felt that despite a severance from the labour market, unemployed men still had a *public* profile and purpose. Many women seemed to do little to challenge this. They accepted these public credentials for low male involvement, while willingly taking on more and more domestic work and responsibility themselves. In a time of uncertainty, change and volatility it is not surprising to see such retrenchment and protection of feelings, traditions and boundaries. Few of the women in our study had real bargaining power, either the power of the hand or the power of the purse. Decisions by 'wives' to support and protect their men in their outward, public activities can be seen as a rational response to a crisis. It is unusual for women to be able to find jobs for their unemployed spouses. They can only contribute to the conditions which encourage this search. There was considerable evidence that many took this task seriously, circling job advertisements in papers, telephoning endless companies, asking friends, mobilising family resources, and maintaining morale. Any substantial readjustments in the domestic order might have detracted from these efforts and suggested a resignation to continuing male unemployment. Few men or women in our study ever reached this point.

UNEMPLOYMENT: THE KIDDERMINSTER UNEMPLOYED AND THE REST

Our study has indicated how unemployment affects members of family units, and has identified important points of continuity and change, conflict and consensus within families. It has emphasised the gender-specific meanings and reactions which can be mobilised within family units to the experience of unemployment. Though the experiences of gender served to unite responses within the families in our sample, they have very different experiences and histories, which served to differentiate them. Factors such as the circumstances of job loss, size of previous income and past occupational history were significant, as were things like the level and nature of benefits received, support from wider kinship networks and the duration of unemployment. A host of such factors, related to gender and the family, but nonetheless with a wider set of references, served to demarcate groups of more vulnerable and deprived unemployed families from others.

Kidderminster families typically had very young children (69 per cent had at least one pre-school age child) and were in the early stages of setting up homes and consolidating relationships (McKee, 1984). Some 38 per cent of families had a baby of under one year. For these families, the opportunities for '*component*' wages from other family members were highly restricted – since there were few in which either women or adolescent children were economically active. The examples of casual or (in)formal work among women were scarcely well enough renumerated or sufficiently regular/secure to lift their standard of living.

Morris, with reference to redundant steel workers, notes that role reversal is very uncommon and occurs in households where there were no young children (Morris, 1983). Research from Gavron onwards on families with young children identifies this period as a time of stress and potential crisis, incurring both financial and interpersonal costs and adjustments (Gavron, 1966; McKee, 1980). The Kidderminster families have to be seen in this context and it was impossible to determine whether we were witnessing manifestations of 'life-cycle' effects, unemployment effects or poverty effects.

Over half of the Kidderminster families (58 per cent) had experienced male unemployment continuously for 12 months or more. Consequently, the majority were living on social security benefits alone, having either exhausted their unemployment benefit entitlement or never having gained such an entitlement (not having enough work credits). One male respondent had never had a job (he had been on a TOPS scheme for three months), another had only worked for six months since leaving school. Five of the women had never had jobs. Five men had been out of work for three years or more, and one for a total of seven years. A considerable number of families therefore had been living on very limited incomes for considerable periods of time. Even though they had relatively low wages when in employment, this was described as having at least the potential for variability, for example, through overtime or perks. The striking feature of living off state benefits in their constancy at unremittingly low levels. Furthermore, comparisons between states of employment and unemployment were meaningless in some cases, since the latter was the norm. Where relationships were founded in the time of unemployment, questions about changed routines were irrelevant.

The circumstances in which men lost their jobs were varied (taking here their last full-time employment). Redundancy or firm closure only accounted for 40 per cent, while the rest gave a variety of reasons including dismissal, voluntary quitting, ill health, prison sentences, and the cessation of temporary or seasonal work. Any general statements about the 'impact' of job loss is therefore difficult. The evidence suggests that some of the men more personally 'wounded' by unemployment (for instance, men who reported a direct deterioration in their health and well-being) were those who were made selectively redundant in organisations where close personal as well as business ties had been established. Examples include the manager of an off-licence, a middle manager in a steel stocktaking firm and a company director. These men had strong personal attachments to the job and the particular company and its personnel. The shock reaction and emotional cycle described by

Jahoda and colleagues seems to best capture this range of unemployment experiences (Jahoda *et al.*, 1933).

UNEMPLOYMENT: THE UNEMPLOYED AND THE EMPLOYED – THEM AND US

As well as highlighting how the unemployed differ from one another our study revealed the deep divide between the employed and the unemployed. Obvious differences in income levels, use of time, states of physical and psychological well-being, social and occupational background came as no surprise and have been successfully and repeatedly demonstrated by numerous studies (e.g. Hakim, 1982; Marsden and Duff, 1975). What is less well documented and to us more surprising is how the employed and unemployed are differentiated in their maintenance of and access to public and private lives. Male unemployment critically challenges the intersection of public and private realms. Unemployed men are squeezed out of the public realm – but their retreat into the private realm becomes public business. As the boundaries of the market-place close up on the unemployed and they become recipients of benefit, their private lives are opened up to public scrutiny and observation. This contradiction of increasing privatisation and increasing official public attention is something that affects many unemployed deeply and is hard for the permanently employed to appreciate. Social security investigators are a reality for many unemployed people, and are the key to this polarisation of employed and unemployed. Even where no fraudulent or illegal activity takes place, the 'private' acts of the unemployed can be misconstrued. Hobbies or routine household chores can be perceived as 'work' or as fiddling.

The role of State surveillance (actual or perceived) of the unemployed and its effects on individuals (and family members) cannot be underestimated (Franey, 1983). The consequent watchfulness and caution of unemployed families affected the research process from beginning to end of this study. It coloured the receptiveness of families to the researcher's visit, determined degrees of self-disclosure, limited marital communication and finally has inhibited the sorts of data selected for publication.

The effect of a 'policing' of the private affairs of the unemployed is to create not just divisions between the unemployed and the employed but between the unemployed themselves. Many of our unemployed respondents were quick to make classifications between the 'respectable' unemployed and the 'scroungers', between the 'genuine' unemployed and the 'idlers'. There were endless recitations of apocryphal tales of men living on fat incomes while drawing the dole. Yet most research suggests the 'illegal' earnings of the unemployed are small scale, short-lived and bring little reward (Henry, 1982). The amount of misery, fear and anxiety borne by families seems extensive and disproportionate to the nature of the 'illegal' activities performed.

The networks of support to which unemployed families have access could also be damaged by this sense of public visibility. Neighbours were often pushed into distrustful positions *vis-à-vis* one another and secrecy was introduced into relationships where previously there was none. A number of respondents cited false allegations of 'fiddling' – which emerged from neighbours. Divisiveness could extend into family associations too with 'wives', parents and others 'covering' for each other. While interviewing in this study we stumbled on these secrets and cover-ups on more than one occasion. The fear of 'being reported' and of facing harmful (true or false) investigations was a feature of the lives of many unemployed and goes a long way to explain much of the 'isolation' and 'privatisation' of life-styles.

The dilemma of unemployed individuals and their associates is not so much whether to engage in work 'on the side', 'to do a foreigner' or to 'hobble' but rather that they feel their private actions are always liable to be held to public account. This creates a rightful and understandable defensiveness among the unemployed and may explain some of the resistance to social research, a fact scarcely grasped by Martyn Harris (1984) in his explanations for why social scientists know so little about unemployment. Perhaps we should properly keep out or keep 'mum'. The ethics of unemployment research and the clash between the world of the researched and researcher, the private and the public, is encapsulated in the following conversation:

Husband: If somebody asked me these questions on the street I wouldn't answer. I'd just be suspicious anyway, but in the security of your own home it's a different story.

Wife: Do you remember when we read it in the *Evening News* about this survey, and he read it, so many families were going to be chosen. And we said, oh

	I hope they don't pick us, we don't want them snooping around into what we're doing.
Interviewer:	I think that's the general and natural reaction isn't it.
Wife:	And then when you called I thought just *my* luck, we've been picked. We were quite apprehensive weren't we?
Interviewer:	Well I hope it hasn't been too arduous for you, you didn't find it too much of an intrusion.
Wife:	No, as we've said, I think it's good that people should become aware of what it's like.
Husband:	The only thing is don't you think if you're going to say a lot of people work on the side and this report is going to come out, then this will make things a bit hotter.
Interviewer:	I don't even know if I am going to say that. Yes there's a great danger of that which is why I don't know whether I'm going to say that or not.
Husband:	But it's missing a lot out if you don't isn't it?
Interviewer:	Yes . . . I'm very much in a dilemma about that. I just don't know what's for the best.

These 'ethical' issues are also deeply political. Their nature is heightened by the fact that not only do the unemployed have no 'universality of experience' (Wallace and Pahl, Chapter 8 in this book) but they are further divided against and amongst themselves. Their potential for collective action remains a fantasy in the minds of those who know what is good for the unemployed – without knowing the unemployed.

NOTE

1. Based on ESRC Grant: G00230004 'Marital and Family Relations in Times of Male Unemployment'. Thanks are offered to all the health authority staff who assisted us in reaching maternity patients for the purpose of this study.

10 Recent Trends in Parasuicide ('Attempted Suicide') and Unemployment among Men in Edinburgh

STEPHEN PLATT

INTRODUCTION

The onset of economic instability and recession in the mid-1970s was marked by a renewal of concern about the possible relationship between morbidity, mortality and economic change. Nevertheless, it has been suggested (Thomann, 1983) that there is still inadequate understanding and discussion of major research findings on this topic and their potential policy implications. At a Symposium on 'The Influence of Economic Instability on Health' sponsored by the World Health Organisation in 1981, participants expressed the view that more conscious efforts should now be made to heighten professional, political and public awareness of the inter-connectedness of economic activity and health (Barnard, 1983). In this chapter I aim to contribute towards this objective by reporting findings from an investigation into the relationship between unemployment and parasuicide ('attempted suicide') in Edinburgh during the years 1968–83.[1] Utilising a unique set of archival data on patients admitted to the Regional Poisoning Treatment Centre (RPTC) in Edinburgh, the ecological (aggregate) association between unemployment rates and parasuicide rates among Edinburgh males are examined, both over

150

time and cross-sectionally. Subsequently, parasuicide rates *among* the employed and unemployed will be presented for each year in the series, together with measures of population risk.

In December 1984 there were over 3.2 million individuals claiming unemployment benefit in the United Kingdom, constituting over 13 per cent of the workforce. More than a third of claimants had been out of work for at least twelve months. Even these alarming statistics understated the full extent of the problem. The true figure for those seeking work was probably close to or even above 4 million.[2] As C. Wright Mills has noted, unemployment on this scale is no longer a personal trouble or private matter whose resolution lies in the hands of the individual or within the scope of his or her immediate milieu (Mills, 1959). On the contrary, mass unemployment is a public issue: its causes are to be sought at the level of government policy and the workings of the international monetary and financial system, not at the level of individual psychopathology. Peter Warr contrasts the present situation, in which the large majority of those without work are clearly employable *and* anxious to find paid employment, with periods of very low unemployment, when differences between employed and unemployed people may have been largely due to their personal characteristics rather than the effects of unemployment itself (Warr, 1985).

The health consequences of high levels of unemployment (particularly long-term) have come under close scrutiny once again in the last decade. There is insufficient space here to review the extensive literature (see Colledge, 1982; Warr, 1984; Hartley and Fryer, 1984). Research findings point unequivocally to a significant deterioration in psychological health caused by unemployment. Most studies are *cross-sectional* (comparing people who are currently unemployed with those who are employed) and thus present problems of causal interpretation. However, there have been a number of longitudinal investigations which permit conclusions about casual priority. A follow-up study of married men a year after the first contact (at which time they all had paid work) found that those who were unemployed at the second interview expressed significantly lower satisfaction with self (Cohn, 1978). Banks and Jackson (1982), using General Health Questionnaire scores, found significant changes across time in two different cohorts as young people moved from employment to unemployment. Unemployment was associated with sharply reduced well-being, and employment with a substantial increase. Similar transitional changes for negative self-esteem, but not for positive self-esteem, have been recorded (Warr and Jackson, 1983). Tiggemann and Winefield (1980) found that Australian school-leavers moving into unemployment became significantly less satisfied with themselves, less happy and more depressed; no such changes were observed among their employed counterparts. Cobb and Kasl (1977) and Kasl (1976) examined psychological well-being just before plant closure and six weeks later. At the follow-up interviews the unemployed reported significantly more depression, anxiety and suspicion about other people (but not more psycho-physiological symptoms) than those in work.

Among the most extreme personal responses to the experience of unemployment is the act or serious contemplation of suicide. The existence and nature of any association between the economic climate and suicidal behaviour has been the subject of debate for more than 150 years. Most of the voluminous empirical research literature (reviewed in Platt, 1984) is concerned with *fatal* rather than *non-fatal* deliberate self-harm, i.e. suicide rather than parasuicide.[3] A common element in both types of behaviour is the presence of a deliberate intention to endanger the biological organism and its future conscious experience. However it is misleading to consider attempted suicide as a sub-type of completed suicide. Over a quarter of a century ago Stengel and Cook (1958) decried the traditional view of attempted suicides as merely 'failed' suicides, identifying motivational and epidemiological features which differentiated attempted suicide from completed suicide populations. With some exceptions (see Koller and Cotgrove, 1976; Lester, 1970), subsequent researchers have maintained the distinction between the two types of behaviour, whilst noting that they are related: two separate, but overlapping, populations. (For useful summaries of characteristic epidemiological, clinical and psychological differences between the populations, see Kreitman, 1983, 1981; Kreitman and Dyer, 1980). Moreover, the incidence of parasuicide in the UK (upwards of 100 000 episodes a year) is considerably more than that of completed suicide (less than 5000 deaths annually). For both conceptual and practical reasons examination and interpretation by sociologists of trends in parasuicide (considered separately from suicide) is long overdue.

Most studies of unemployment and parasuicide have been cross-sectional, demonstrating that significantly more parasuicides are unemployed than would be expected among general population samples (Hawton *et al.*, 1982), and that parasuicide rates among the unemployed are always considerably higher than among the employed (Kessel *et al.*, 1975; Kreitman, 1973; Bancroft *et al.*, 1975) Aggregate cross-sectional studies provide evidence of a significant association between unemployment and parasuicides rates in Edinburgh (Buglass and Duffy, 1978) and in Brighton (Bagley *et al.*, 1973). In a report on the psychological characteristics of 70 unemployed patients admitted to a psychiatric emergency department (Fruensgaard *et al.*, 1983), the main reason for admission of about half was suicidal behaviour. It was estimated that for 41 per cent of the whole sample their unemployment had played an important part in the current psychiatric illness, although for only 11 per cent was it the sole causal factor. Other possible causes were recorded for three-quarters of the sample. Unemployment, while a significant external factor in suicidal behaviour, seemed most often to be interrelated with other factors, in particular interpersonal conflicts, housing problems and economic difficulties, all, of course, heightened by unemployment. In the one relevant aggregate longitudinal analysis, Furness *et al.* (1984) report that, in Hartlepool, whilst the unemployment rate amongst males aged 16–65 quadrupled during the period 1974–82, the level of parasuicide remained broadly constant.

METHODS

Analyses reported in this paper are restricted to males: women are omitted because the reliability of the employment status classification of female parasuicides (particularly, the married) is extremely doubtful. In addition, official data on unemployment are less adequate for women than for men since a large proportion of women who are out of work and looking for jobs do not register, while some women who are registered have been deemed not to be looking for work (Daniel, 1981).

Aggregate Longitudinal Analysis

The numerator used in the calculation of the parasuicide rates is the number of male patients, aged 15 years and over, admitted to the RPTC from an address in Edinburgh, interviewed by a psychiatrist and diagnosed as a parasuicide. (Only the first admission of those who repeat within a single calendar year is included.) Parasuicide is defined as a non-fatal act in which an individual causes self-injury or ingests a substance in excess of any prescribed or generally recognised therapeutic dosage. This includes overdoses resulting from habitual misuse of drugs or experimentation with drugs 'for kicks', but excludes intoxication with alcohol alone (Kreitman, 1977, p. 3).

The Registrar General's mid-year estimate of the male home population of Edinburgh aged 15 and over was used as the denominator in the calculation of all parasuicide rates.

For the period 1968–82 the male unemployment rate is calculated by expressing the number of males registered with local employment and career services offices covering the Edinburgh area in July each year as a percentage of all male employees in employment and those registered as unemployed in the same area in the same year. The changeover in autumn 1982 to the claimant basis for counting the unemployed necessitated an adjustment to the July 1983 total of unemployed, since the new system is known to produce an undercount compared to the old (DoE, 1982a). On the basis of information supplied by the Manpower Services Commission in Edinburgh, the published total of unemployed was increased by 9.45 per cent to produce a total approximately equal to that which would have been given under the old system.

Aggregate Cross-Sectional Analysis

Parasuicide and unemployment rates were calculated for each of the 23 electoral wards (for the period 1970–2) or 31 regional electoral divisions (REDs) (for 1980–82) of Edinburgh. The numerator for the parasuicide rate was the annual number of male parasuicide patients aged 15 and over, averaged over three years (to avoid the instability inherent in yearly counts). The denominator was the number of males aged 15 and over, as given in the 1971 or 1981 Census. The unemployment rate was calculated by dividing the number of males who were defined (in the relevant Census) as 'seeking work' by the number of males who were 'seeking work' *and* those 'working'. The resultant fraction is expressed as a percentage.

Relative Risk Analysis

For each year parasuicide rates among the unemployed and among the employed were calculated. The numerator for each rate was the number of unemployed or employed male parasuicide patients admitted during the year. (Where an individual was admitted more than once during a calendar year, his employment status was taken to be that recorded on his first admission.) The denominator had to be estimated for most years in the series. Taking the economic activity rate for males in Edinburgh from the 1971 and 1981 Censuses and estimating economic activity rates for other years in the series by interpolation or extrapolation, an approximate total of the economically active male population for each year was calculated. When the Edinburgh unemployment rate (see above) was applied to this total, separate estimates of employed and unemployed were obtained.

For the period 1980–82 data are also presented which relate to individuals and which control for social class position. The numerators consist of the average annual number of male parasuicide patients admitted over the three-year period in each employment status and social class category (e.g. unemployed, class IV; employed, class II). Unfortunately, not all parasuicides were assigned a social class position at the time of admission. In particular, 91 out of 1029 patients (8.8 per cent) were coded 'not known'. Further enquiry suggests that these missing cases most resemble class V parasuicides in their social and clinical characteristics. Consequently two parasuicide rates have been computed for class V individuals: a minimal rate, excluding all 'missing cases' and a maximal rate, assigning all missing cases to class V. Both these rates are presented in the text. The denominator consists of those working or seeking work in each social class, as given in the 1981 Census.

Parasuicide rates by duration of unemployment were calculated for 1982 and 1983. Official (unpublished) Manpower Services Commission data were obtained on the percentage of unemployed males in the Edinburgh Travel to Work Area (TTWA) in four duration categories (0–4 weeks, 5–26 weeks, 27–52 weeks, over 52 weeks) in July 1982 and July 1983. These percentages were then applied to the total of unemployed (calculated by the method described above) in order to establish the denominator totals. Each unemployed parasuicide was also assigned to one of the same duration categories.

Population Attributable Risk Analysis

For each year the population attributable risk of parasuicide resulting from unemployment was calculated by subtracting the parasuicide rate among the employed from the parasuicide rate for the whole economically active male population. A percentage estimate of the amount by which the parasuicide rate might be reduced if the exposure to unemployment were removed is obtained by the formula:

$$\frac{Ip - Ie}{Ip} \times 100$$

where *Ip* is the rate for all economically active males, and *Ie* is the rate among the employed.

RESULTS

Trends over time

There was a marked association[4] (r = 0.87, p < 0.001) between the male unemployment rate and the percentage of (economically active) male parasuicides who were unemployed on admission, notably in more recent years. Thus, between 1979 and 1983, the male unemployment rate in the city of Edinburgh increased from 6.8 per cent to 13.6 per cent, while the proportion of male parasuicides who were unemployed rose from 41 per cent to 62.2 per cent.

Male parasuicide and unemployment rates among Edinburgh residents over the years 1968–82 are shown in Figure 10.1. The temporal association was found to be significantly positive overall (r = 0.62, p < 0.02). It should be noted, however, that the relationship between unemployment and parasuicide over the first eight years of the period was strikingly different to that found over the final eight years: *positive* between 1968 and 1975 (r = 0.92, p < 0.01); and *negative* between 1976 and 1983 (r = −0.67, not significant), reflecting in particular the strong contrary trends in 1982 and 1983.

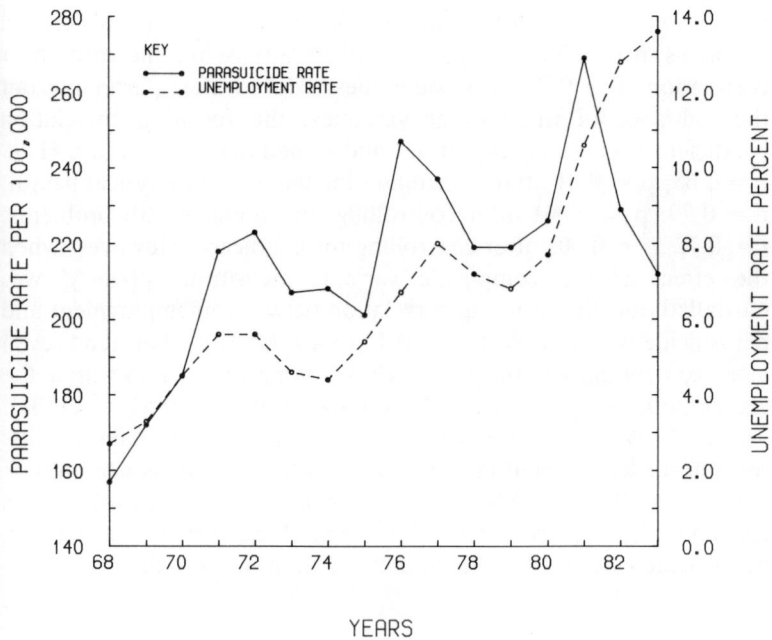

FIGURE 10.1 *Male unemployment and parasuicide in Edinburgh, 1968–83*

Ecological correlations, 1970–72 and 1980–82

The ecological correlations between male unemployment and parasuicide rates across geographical areas of Edinburgh were highly significant in both 1970–72 ($r = 0.76$, $p < 0.001$) and in 1980–82 ($r = 0.95$, $p < 0.001$); the difference between the correlations was also significant. The six Regional Electoral Divisions with the highest parasuicide rates in 1980–82 generated the highest unemployment rates, the rank ordering being identical on each variable: three of these REDS were peripheral working-class council estates, two were central districts, while the sixth was the dockland area. Despite minor modifications of city boundaries and extensive redrawing of geographical divisions within the city between 1970–72 and 1980–82, the highest rates of parasuicide and unemployment tended to be found approximately in the same areas on each occasion.

The ecological relationship between unemployment and parasuicide rates during the period 1970–72 was re-examined after controlling for a number of other variables. These data were collected as part of a project concerned with the distribution of social and medical problems in Edinburgh (Buglass *et al.*, 1980). While the zero-order correlation (r = 0.76) was sometimes reduced after partialling out the influence of these other variables, the resulting correlation coefficient was usually significant and sometimes even higher. (E.g. r = 0.65, p < 0.01 after controlling for the level of physical health; r = 0.79, p < 0.001 after controlling for mental health problems; r = 0.72, p < 0.001 after controlling for handicap.) However, when the effect of the compositie variable measuring 'poverty' was partialled out, the resulting correlation between unemployment and parasuicide was reduced to r = 0.13 (n.s.). On the other hand, even after controlling for the social class composition of the area the correlation, though reduced, was still significant (r = 0.51, p < 0.02). This analysis was repeated with the 1980–2 data, with similar results: the zero-order correlation (r = 0.95, p < 0.001) was reduced to r = 0.81 (p < 0.001). Differences in social class composition thus accounted for approximately 32 per cent of the variation in the area parasuicide rate in 1970–72, and 25 per cent in 1980–82.

Population rates

The parasuicide rate among the unemployed (column A) and among the employed (column B), and the relative risk (column D) for each year during the period are shown in Table 10.1. It can be seen that the parasuicide rate among the unemployed has shown a tendency to fall, especially since 1973, while the rate among the employed generally rose until 1976, thereafter fluctuating and falling steeply in 1982. The relative risk also tended to fall until 1976, since when it has been fairly steady at about 11:1. Over the whole period the unemployment rate was positively but non-significantly correlated with the parasuicide rate among the employed (r = 0.34, n.s.); significantly negatively correlated with the parasuicide rate among the unemployed (r = −0.87, p < 0.001); and significantly negatively associated with the magnitude of the relative risk (r = −0.69, p < 0.01). In other words, a rise in the level of unemployment appears to have been associated with an increase in parasuicide *among* those at work and a decrease *among* the unemployed. A generally upward movement in unemployment has been accompanied by a declining, then fairly static relative risk.

For the period 1980–82 the relationship between unemployment

TABLE 10.1 *Parasuicide rates among employed and unemployed, and measures of individual and population risk, Edinburgh city males, 1968–83*

Parasuicide rate/100 000

Year	Among unemployed (A)	Among employed (B)	Among all economically active (C)	Relative risk (A):(B) (D)	Population attributable risk (C) − (B) (E)	Maximum percent of overall rate attributable to unemployment ((C) − (B)/(C)) × 100 (F)
1968	2824	98	172	29.0	74	43.2
1969	2284	117	188	19.6	71	38.1
1970	1955	122	204	16.1	82	40.4
1971	2302	115	238	20.0	123	51.5
1972	2106	141	252	14.9	111	44.0
1973	2458	134	240	18.3	106	44.2
1974	2374	149	247	15.9	98	39.6
1975	1991	139	239	14.4	100	42.1
1976	2052	173	299	11.8	126	42.0
1977	1779	153	284	11.6	131	45.9
1978	1647	150	257	11.0	107	41.8
1979	1523	160	253	9.5	93	36.6
1980	1663	143	260	11.6	117	45.0
1981*	1730	153	320	11.3	167	52.2
1982*	1344	115	272	11.7	157	57.7
1983	1149	110	251	10.4	141	56.2

NOTES
* Data for these years are based on revised mid-year population estimates and differ marginally from those published in Platt and Kreitman (1984).

and parasuicide among individuals, controlling for social class, has also been examined. As has been well documented (Holding et al, 1977; Bancroft *et al.*, 1975), the parasuicide rate varies inversely with social class. The average yearly patient rate (per 100 000) over the period among males in Edinburgh was 72.3 in classes I and II combined, 179.0 in class IIINM, 269.0 in class IIIM, 536.4 in class IV and 899.1 to 1267.7 (low-high estimates) in class V. Table 10.2 demonstrates that the same pattern was evident among the employed and the unemployed separately. In all social classes the relative risk ratio was at least 8:1, with the highest ratio in classes I and II combined.

TABLE 10.2   *Parasuicide rates among the employed and unemployed, controlling for social class, Edinburgh city males, 1980–82*

Parasuicide rate/100 000			
Social class			*Relative risk*
	Among unemployed	*Among employed*	
I, II	1362	47	29.9
IIINM	1698	129	13.2
IIIM	1697	154	11.0
IV	2505	298	8.4
V (min.)	3274	285	11.5
V (max.)	4990	306	16.3

Analysis of parasuicide rates by duration of unemployment is available for 1982 and 1983 only. Table 10.3 shows that while the relative risk did not increase directly with longer durations of unemployment, the highest rates were nevertheless found among the long-term unemployed. In particular, Edinburgh men without work for over a year ran at least double the risk of parasuicide than those unemployed under a month and nineteen times the risk of those in employment. In 1982, 75 per cent of male parasuicides had been out of work for over six months compared to 56 per cent of the general population of unemployed males in the Edinburgh TTWA; the respective percentages for 1983 were 81 per cent and 57 per cent. The long-term unemployed (over a year) constituted 56 per cent of the unemployed parasuicides in 1982, compared to 35 per cent of the general population unemployed; the respective percentages for 1983 were 68 per cent and 37 per cent. However, the impact of recent job loss should not be underestimated: the relative risk among those unemployed less than four weeks was nearly 9:1 in 1982 and still considerably higher (though less markedly) in 1983. In both years the relative risk was lower among the 5–26 week duration group compared to the recent job loss group, and the overall trends in risk by duration were similar. Whilst the rate among the long-term unemployed was stable, the other duration groups showed a considerable decline in their parasuicide rate. Thus, among those recently losing their jobs the rate fell by 56 per cent (from 1011 to 443); the decline was 45 per cent in the 5–26 week group and 38 per cent in the 27–52 week group.

TABLE 10.3   *Parasuicide rates by duration of unemployment, Edinburgh city males, 1982 and 1983*

Duration of unemployment	1982			1983		
	(N)	*Parasuicide rate/100 000*	*(Relative risk)*	*(N)*	*Parasuicide rate/100 000*	*(Relative risk)*
Less than 4 weeks	(17)	1011	(8.8)	(10)	443	(4.0)
5–26 weeks	(34)	615	(5.3)	(18)	341	(3.1)
27–52 weeks	(42)	1191	(10.4)	(26)	736	(6.7)
Over 52 weeks	(125)	2163	(18.8)	(137)	2119	(19.3)
All unemployed	(222)*	1344	(11.7)	(201)**	1149	(10.4)
All employed	(129)	115		(122)	110	

NOTES
* Includes 4 cases whose duration of unemployment is not known.
** Includes 10 cases whose duration of unemployment is not known.

Attributable Risk

Table 10.1 also presents the data on population attributable risk for parasuicide arising out of unemployment (Column E) and the maximum percent of the parasuicide rate 'attributable' to unemployment in each year (Column F). The trends in the years 1979–83 are particularly noteworthy. The population attributable risk rose from 93 to 141 (peaking in 1982 at 158), while the maximum percent of the parasuicide rate attributable to unemployment increased from 36.6 to 56.2 (57.8 in 1982). Over the whole period a significant positive correlation between changes in the unemployment rate and change in population attributable risk ($r = 0.86$, $p < 0.001$) was found.

DISCUSSION

Methodological Issues

Certain methodological and technical issues require consideration before the substantive findings can be evaluated. The validity of the longitudinal analysis is dependent upon demonstrating that trends in unemployment and parasuicide rates over time are not merely the result of systematic errors in the numerator or denominator. With only the exception necessitated by changing Government procedure in 1982, definitions of both 'parasuicide' and 'unemployment' remained unchanged over the period, and there is no evidence to suggest that the relationship of the achieved samples to their populations varies differentially in coverage or representativeness over the years.

However, it is known that parasuicides admitted to the RPTC do not constitute all the cases in the city (Platt *et al.*, 1983; Kennedy and Kreitman, 1973). Consequently, the parasuicide rates computed from these data will also be less than the true population rates. This underestimation does not give rise to a major problem, provided that the relative reliability of the computed parasuicide rate remains reasonably stable over time, as indirect evidence suggests.

A slightly different problem arises in relation to the individual analysis. Over the period 1968–83 significantly more unemployed patients admitted for the first time to the RPTC reported a previous non-treated episode of parasuicide than did their employed counterparts. Parasuicide among the unemployed may therefore be selectively under-recorded in the RPTC files, with the consequence that the relative risk probably *underestimates* the 'true' difference between the unemployed and the employed in every year. Since the distribution of 'missing' cases by employment status is unlikely to have changed over the period, we can have reasonable confidence in the validity of the findings relating to temporal trends in relative risk.

Substantive Issues

Ecological Findings

The ecological correlations between parasuicide and unemployment comprise the first set of findings of this study. A substantial positive association over time was discovered, although this relationship appears to have been reversed more recently, particularly since 1981. There was also a positive association across geographical areas of the city, both in 1971 and, even more markedly, in 1981. However, while changes in unemployment may have caused the changes in parasuicide, it needs to be considered whether the two variables are both caused by a common third factor, e.g. economic recession, which may lead to high parasuicide *and* high unemployment rates, without the latter being the cause of the former. Such a factor might account for the negative association between parasuicide and unemployment over the years 1976–83. It is also possible that each variable may have been increasing independently over time. However, Figure 10.1 clearly shows that the trend in both parasuicide and unemployment has not been uniformly upwards. What is impressive is the manner in which the two rates have generally followed the same non-uniform pattern over most of the period under review.

The *cross-sectional* or geographical association between the rates of unemployment and of parasuicide raises the problem that the magnitude of both unemployment rates and measures of morbidity and mortality are strongly statistically associated with poverty (Stern, 1981). High ecological correlations between unemployment, parasuicide and poverty in 1970–2 were found and it was noted that the association between parasuicide and unemployment virtually disappeared after controlling for indicators of poverty. This finding is consistent with the hypothesis that unemployment conduces to parasuicide through its impact on living standards and associated psychological trauma. Ecological analysis cannot, however, unravel the complex interrelationship between these variables.

Individual Level Findings

To assume, on the basis of a strong association between unemployment and parasuicide rates, that the two variables are necessarily linked within the same individuals would be an example of the ecological fallacy (Selvin, 1958; Catalano and Dooley, 1983), the unwarranted assumption that what holds true for the collectivity must be true for the individuals who make it up. Similarly, a negative ecological association cannot be assumed to rule out the possibility of a relationship at the individual level. However the relative risk data, presented in column D of Table 10.1, establish the fact that the association between unemployment and parasuicide holds also at the individual level. The rate of parasuicide among the unemployed has always remained dramatically higher than among the employed, and only once in the years 1976–83 has the relative risk been less than tenfold. Nevertheless, inspection of Table 10.1 demonstrates that there has been a generally downward movement in the parasuicide rate among the unemployed to about 40 per cent of its former level (from 2824 per 100 000 in 1968 to 1149 in 1983); in fact trends in this rate were *negatively* correlated with movement in the unemployment rate in the city. Following the earlier discussion, it may be surmised that the high rates in the earlier years reflect a marked degree of psychological and social impairment among those comparatively few individuals who remain unemployed in times of full employment. The decline in their parasuicide rate over subsequent years is interpreted to reflect the dilution of the 'unemployable' group by others whose status is less and less a consequence of personal handicap and more and more the outcome of impersonal, economic factors.

A third set of findings concerns the relationship between parasuicide, unemployment and social class. It has long been known that parasuicide is highest in social class V, which comprises the largest group of unemployed. Consequently, the determining factor could be class rather than unemployment. However, even when social class is held constant the relative risk is never less than 8:1 (Table 10.2). The highest relative risk is to be found in social classes I and II combined, whereas the unemployment rate is actually lowest (and the status of being unemployed most deviant) in these classes.[5]

Trends in population attributable risk constitute the fourth set of findings. The declining rate of parasuicide among the unemployed over the years has been more than offset by the increase in the numbers at risk. In consequence, the absolute numbers of unemployed parasuicides and the proportion they form of all hospitalised parasuicides have increased steadily over the period. It is this trend in population attributable risk which is most relevant in assessing the social and economic cost of unemployment.

The fifth finding concerns the relationship between parasuicide and duration of unemployment. While the impact of short-term joblessness is marked, with at least a fourfold increase in parasuicide among those unemployed less than four week compared to their employed counterparts, the highest rate is found among the chronically unemployed. After one year the risk is more than double (1982) or more than four times (1983) that for the recently unemployed and about nineteen times the risk for the employed.

CONCLUSIONS

The key findings of this study can be briefly summarised. The ecological (aggregate) association between unemployment and para-suicide rates among males in Edinburgh was positive and highly significant over time (although contrary trends were noted in 1982–83) and across geographical areas of the city. More crucially, throughout the period the parasuicide rate among the unemployed was considerably higher than that among the employed, although the relative risk tended to be greater during the 1960s and early 1970s. Controlling for social class did not markedly reduce the strength of the relationship between unemployment and parasuicide, at either the aggregate or individual level of analysis. Data available for 1982 and 1983 revealed that while the highest relative risk was found among the long-term unemployed, those recently losing their jobs were also characterised by a marked increase in their parasuicide rate compared to the employed. Population attributable risk showed a tendency to rise in line with the upward trend in the unemployment rate.

Taken together, those findings are entirely compatible with the hypothesis that unemployment is a cause of parasuicide. However, other interpretations are possible, and explicit recognition is made of the fact that parasuicide almost certainly results from the complex interaction of many factors. Clinical experience suggests that many male parasuicides lead a chronically marginal existence. Their lives are characterised by irregular employment, petty crime, excessive alcohol consumption and loneliness. Being unemployed (particularly over a long period) re-inforces this marginality. Economic recession dramatically alters the threshold at which individuals are likely to become ill or engage in deviant behaviour. Its maximum impact is undoubtedly felt by those who are already vulnerable because of their precarious location within society. Further, the 'knock-on' effect upon the families of the unemployed, and even upon the employed, should not be under-estimated. While this study provides no data upon the former point (but see Madge, 1983; Moen, 1979; Thomas *et al.*, 1980), it has demonstrated the existence of a close geographical and temporal relationship between changes in the para-suicide rate among the employed and changes in the unemployment rate.

The public health implications that arise from this study most undoubtedly cause concern. The high level of risk among the long-term unemployed may be reduced to some extent by allocating more resources to help alleviate the economic, psychological and social impact of prolonged joblessness. But while the provision of counsel-ling services or more generous social security benefits or opportuni-ties for voluntary work might make unemployment more bearable, these measures do not address the underlying problem (Unemploy-ment and Health Study Group, 1984). A consensus is slowly emerging across most of the political spectrum that mass unemploy-ment of increasingly lengthening duration is the major public issue of our day. The unanticipated social consequences of economic policies revealed in this study must occupy the attention of government and its agencies more centrally than they have done in the past.

NOTES

1. A summary of selected findings from this study has already been published (Platt and Kreitman, 1984).
2. In a press release from the Unemployment Unit (dated 3 January 1985), it is calculated that the total would have been 400 000 higher under the old method of counting the unemployed. It is also pointed out that as long ago as 1981 the 'old count' figures omitted around 400 000 'unregistered' unemployed. The Department of Employment also estimate that at the end of December 1984 the direct effect of special employment and training measures was that about 475 000 people were removed from the official unemployment totals.
3. The term 'parasuicide' (coined by Kreitman *et al.*, 1969) refers 'to a behavioural analogue of suicide but without considering a psychological orientation towards death being in any essential to the definition'. It replaces the term 'attempted suicide' which has been extensively criticised on the grounds that it assumes an intention to die is always present in such behaviour (see Kessel, 1965).
4. The ecological association between parasuicide and unemployment is represented throughout by the Pearson product-moment correlation coefficient. Partial-correlation coefficients were also calculated in order to describe the relationship between these two variables while adjusting for ('partialling out') the effects of additional third variables. All p values are two-tailed.
5. According to the Census, the 1981 unemployment rate by social class

among Edinburgh males was as follows: social class I, 1.0%; II, 2.3%; IIINM, 3.2%; IIIM, 7.5%; IV, 10.8%; V, 20.5%.

11 Discipline, Training or Welfare?: the Functions of a Re-establishment Centre[1]

SARAH BUCKLAND AND SUSANNE MACGREGOR

Before it is just to say that a man ought to be an independent labourer, the country ought to be in such a state that a labourer by honest industry can become independent. (William Ackroyd, speaking at a dinner of the Poor Law Guardians of Stourbridge, April 1841)

INTRODUCTION

The above quotation, used by William Beveridge in the preface to his book *Voluntary Action* (1948), indicates a central dilemma of policies on long-term unemployment. How far to 'blame the victims' and introduce remedial treatment to deal with their defects, whether inherent or acquired; or how far to focus action on the labour market, through either increased or reduced government intervention, depending on one's view of political economy.

We do not pretend to have the answers to these grand questions. What this essay more modestly aims to do is to portray the experience of unemployment among men attending a re-establishment centre in South London, and through this to indicate the range of their experience and the complexity of their needs. To argue that is for more sensitive treatment of the long-term unemployed and the recognition of the need for a wider range of service provision. At present, the lack of such a range produces a situation where existing services such as re-establishment centres (RECs) are used in practice in ways rather different from those envisaged by central policy makers. Higher civil servants tend to see RECs as being primarily concerned with training or making men fit for employment. From our study, we argue instead that a combination of functions is at work, one being for training but others focus around principles of discipline and welfare. These three principles interact to produce an experience of unemployment and REC attendance somewhat different from that assumed by central government officials.

Over the last fourteen years, the number of long-term unemployed, that is, claimants unemployed for more than one year, has increased ten-fold. In 1970, about 100 000 people were long-term unemployed. By October 1981, the number had increased to 747 000. By the end of 1982 it stood at one million and in mid-1984 at 1 188 000 with a further 590 000 who were officially known to have been out of work for over six months. Between April 1983 and April 1984 the number of UK long-term unemployed increased by 15 per cent while total unemployment increased by only 2 per cent. In April 1984, among unemployed males, 25 per cent had been unemployed for over two years and a further 19 per cent for between one and two years. The proportion of men who were long-term unemployed increased with age (CSO, 1985).

What has government done to deal with this trend? In 1981–82, the Community Enterprise Programme replaced the Special Temporary Employment Programme and in October 1982 the Community Enterprise Programme was in turn replaced by the Community Programme. The general aim of these schemes was to provide temporary work for those out of work for long periods. In 1983–84, the Community Programme assisted 134 000 people of whom 23 per cent were women. The total number supported by all the government's special measures peaked in the first quarter of 1981 at over 1.1 million and then fell back to 504 000 in the second quarter of 1982 before rising again (CSO, 1985).

In addition, encouragement to workers to 'price themselves into jobs' is a theme found in contemporary discussion of unemployment. The incentive to labour, it is argued, needs to be maintained and some point to the operation of the social security system as one which discourages potential workers caught in what has come to be known as the 'unemployment trap' produced by the interaction of fiscal measures, benefits and the costs of employment. To encourage the incentive to work, training opportunities are the carrot offered by the programmes of the Manpower Services Commission. And DHSS has some sticks to wield. The long-term unemployed receiving supplementary benefit continue to be restricted to the lower short-term rate. Other categories of claimant graduate to a higher, long-term rate after being on supplementary benefit for one year (in 1984 worth £11.05 per week for a couple).

RECs are another part of the institutional response to long-term unemployment. The first state-run REC was set up in the 1950s by the National Assistance Board (forerunner of the Supplementary Benefits Commission, now disbanded and absorbed within DHSS). In 1985, eighteen RECs exist which are the responsibility of the Secretary of State for Social Services. Their formal purpose is to 'help men who, because of long-term unemployment have become unacceptable to potential employers and appear unsuitable for the more sophisticated forms of rehabilitation and vocational training' such as the training schemes provided by the Manpower Services Commission (SBC, 1976, pp. 73–5). The approach adopted is designed 'to revive the will to work; to restore the habit of getting up and going to work and to give men confidence in their ability to hold down a job under normal conditions' (Stern and Burchall, 1984, p. 1).

Men selected to attend RECs are usually referred by unemployment review officers in local DHSS offices. Their job is to review the cases of claimants who are most frequently unemployed 'without good reason' and those unemployed for six months or more. This entails assessing the claimant's capacity for employment both as an individual, including past work experience and current and future work expectations and in relation to the work available in the locality. They also review claimants who 'appear not to be making positive efforts to obtain work'.

When RECs were started in the 1950s it was on the perhaps reasonable assumption that a high proportion of the long-term unemployed and 'repeat unemployed' were different in characteristics and motivation from the majority of manual workers. It was thought that so long as they could turn up for eight hours a day and do some kind of work, there was a good chance there would be a job for them after their REC attendance. Neither of these assumptions holds today, although the concept of a residual 'hard-core' of unemployed remains, as illustrated in the following quotation. In his study, Michael White concluded that explanations of long-term unemployment in terms of personal disadvantage have surprisingly limited value and that characteristics of the labour market are much more useful. But he went on to comment:

> It may still be possible to identify the original type of long-term unemployed person as a sub-group within the new composition of long-term unemployment but their distinguishing characteristics will no longer be of great use in explaining long-term unemployment as a whole. (White, 1983, p. 59)

The exact size and the specific characteristics of the 'hard-core' is a question not answered however even by those who claim its existence. In the 1950s, official policy towards the long-term employed was based on the view that they were a group set apart from the rest of the labour force by reason of age, ill health, poor attitude to work, low intelligence or minority ethnic group membership. The more recent increase in the number of long-term unemployed has drawn in people who are not initially noticeably dissimilar from other workers. However, long-term unemployment produces secondary effects, poverty being only the most obvious. Other effects noted include loss of self-confidence, isolation, loss of financial independence, disorientation and depression (Tyrell and Shanks, 1982; Miles, 1983). Special 'welfare' services might be needed to help here.

An ambiguity of objectives, those of welfare and control, has been present in the REC system from its inception, as it was evident in the work-centres of the thirties (Campling, 1978; Krafchik, 1984). To the tension between these two objectives has been added more recently an increased concern with 'training'. This was indicated in the experimental 'up-grading' of one REC and indeed it was from this REC that our case studies are drawn.

The REC we studied differed from other RECs in that it offered a 'higher standard' of instruction by employing instructors seconded from MSC and had more substantial equipment and machinery than was usually available. It was not, therefore, typical but indicated what might be possible if extra money were to be spent and some of the problems the MSC might encounter if it were to begin to provide training centres for the long-term unemployed.

The research involved the collection and analysis of information from administrative records on all 349 referrals to this REC between November 1981 and July 1983. We have information on 327 men referred in this twenty-one month period of whom 134 attended and

193 did not. Forty-one men attending the course between January and July 1983 were interviewed on two separate occasions in the REC, at the beginning of the course and approximately three months after the end of the course. (One man refused to be interviewed.) Interviews with a group of thirty-two men who were referred but decided not to attend were carried out in their homes.

PERCEPTIONS OF THE LONG-TERM UNEMPLOYED AND THE ROLE OF RECs

The tension between the objectives, discipline, training and welfare, can be illustrated in the views expressed by unemployment review officers in a group discussion on their role. These are here presented as ideal types of the different sets of objectives, using a composite of direction quotation from the discussion. The officers expressed the training and welfare functions thus:

> The more attractive RECs can be valuable to men attending. They can restore their confidence and motivation. Men referred are grateful for the opportunity to attend. Attending is also valuable in giving a man an opportunity to get out of the house. He could convince his wife that he is willing to make the effort. The man who is seeming to sink below the waves can be pulled up before he submerges. People who have missed out on education, not acquiring the basic skills, can benefit, like the man who is basically quite bright but has missed out on CSEs. An REC can possibly act as a back entry to a TOPs course, otherwise they have no chance of getting on to one. An REC could be a positive help in finding work if it built up contacts with local employers. A good unemployment review officer has a welfare function, showing interest in people who are otherwise neglected.

The discipline and training complex of functions was expressed by the officers thus:

> RECs' main concern is remotivation. They should act to separate the genuine from the non-genuine. The way this works is that if they are genuine they will go to the REC. The non-genuine won't. The Unemployment Review Officer is then able to watch the non-

genuine next time they come up for review. Some RECs, in particular, are used to frighten people. These less attractive RECs have a punitive function. Residential RECs are useful for those suspected of fiddling. Some men are suspected of fraud, but where it is difficult to prove, they can be referred to the REC. Referral to an REC acts as a warning shot across the bows. The man knows he is being watched and he has time to think about it before the next review. Many on the Unemployment Review Officers' list disappear at that stage. Those who have difficulty getting up in the morning might be helped by having to attend an REC regularly. One has a way of saying 'you are going to an REC' which can act as a threat, without having to use Section 10. (Section 10 of the *Supplementary Benefits Act* 1976 states that if a man, who has been refusing or neglecting opportunities of employment, declines to attend an REC, he may be directed to attend as a condition of continuing to receive supplementary benefit. In practice, only a very small proportion of men attending RECs do so under this direction)

CHARACTERISTICS OF ATTENDERS AND NON-ATTENDERS AT THIS REC

In our study, the oldest man referred was fifty-eight and the youngest was seventeen with an average age of thirty. About half were married and slightly under half had dependent children. Only 29 per cent had a dependent child under the age of five years. Out of a total of 272, 91 per cent were previously employed as manual workers, most (66 per cent) as unskilled manual workers. Their most recent job had been of relatively short duration, for just less than two-thirds (62 per cent) lasting for six months or less. Even more notable, one quarter (26 per cent) of these had lasted for one month or less. However, for another quarter the length of their most recent job had been over one year. In White's study (1983) 45 per cent of long-term unemployed men had held their last job for less than two years. Among the men referred to the REC, the proportion was much higher, 85 per cent.

The average length of time out of work was twenty-seven months, while the longest time anyone had been unemployed was eight years. These men had thus been out of work for relatively shorter periods than the long-term unemployed as a whole who had been out of work on average for four-and-a-half-years (White, 1983). These REC referrals are also significantly younger than the long-term unemployed as a whole.

The factors which distinguished the men referred to the REC from all long-term unemployed in Britain in the eighties were: age (REC referrals being younger); length of last job (shorter among those referred); level of skill (less skilled men being more likely to be referred); gender (men only referred to RECs); disability (the registered disabled are not normally referred); and length of time unemployed (shorter among those referred, largely linked to their younger age).

Both attenders and non-attenders were mainly British born and Caucasian in appearance. Of those who were married, their wife was in most cases not employed (see McKee and Bell, Chapter 9 and Wallace and Pahl, Chapter 8 in this book). Over a third of both attenders and non-attenders were living at home with their parents; 51 per cent of all non-attenders and 38 per cent of all attenders lived with their wife; while 23 per cent of attenders and only 12 per cent of non-attenders lived alone or in other non-family households. The majority lived in council housing. Most had lived in the area for over ten years and well over three-quarters for over sixteen years. Almost all left school at the minimum school leaving age and many left without gaining any qualifications. Less than one in five had CSEs, O-levels or the equivalent. Most had had no further education but more (about a quarter) had had some form of further training usually 'on the job'. One in five had some degree of difficulty in reading or writing.

Financial problems were evident in a large number of cases. 59 per cent of attenders owed money (as did 32 per cent of non-attenders). The most common debts were for rent or fuel bills. Of all those interviewed, lack of money was cited as the main dislike about being unemployed, but one-third emphasised the boredom. Apart from the obvious cash reward from having a job, a quarter mentioned the positive satisfaction they derived from working and a further quarter said that they would prefer having a job to the boredom of unemployment.

The non-attenders were generally younger than the attenders. Those who were hostile to attending were more likely to have a non-manual or skilled manual background. Those who were most enthusiastic about attending were more likely to have a 'problem' recorded, to be unskilled manual workers, to have been out of work for a shorter period and to be over thirty-five years of age. The attenders seemed more likely than non-attenders to blame themselves rather than external circumstances for being unemployed. They were less likely than the non-attenders to be construction workers and more likely to have worked in transport or personal services. The non-attenders were more likely to be looking for work of a type very different from that practised at the REC, whereas the attenders' hopes for work matched more closely the type of work available there. The non-attenders were in general more dispirited than the attenders and this factor probably influenced their decision not to attend. Those who were least optimistic were likely to be older.

Social isolation, the experience of constraint (especially debt) and a rational assessment of what might be gained from attending the course seemed then to be the main factors influencing the decision whether or not to attend.

Very many men experienced the process of referral as involving pressure to attend. In spite of this, of the 327 referred, 60 per cent did not attend, while of those who did, not all stayed for thirteen weeks. For example, one man had felt under pressure to attend as his unemployment review officer clearly suspected him of working 'on the side' and made him sign on weekly instead of fortnightly. After visiting the centre, he decided not to attend as he felt he 'did not need to get back into the work routine', he 'could go to work tomorrow' if he got a job, 'no problem'. Another said, he had been told to 'go down and see these people or we'll stop your dole'. But as he said, he was not interested 'in working for dole money' so he did not go and nothing seemed to happen. Of those who did attend only one in two said that at that stage they had actually wanted to go on the course. But after visiting the place and talking to the instructors, the majority (seven in ten) felt keen to attend. 'I was going to refuse point blank beforehand. It's a good job I came down because you can do all sorts of things here.' 'It sounded like an open prison to me. I was told that under Section 10 I could be made to go. But speaking to the instructors and the manager they explained that they only wanted people who came freely. They pointed out things I hadn't taken into consideration: being made to get up in the morning and having something to do; maths lessons are available –

that's my weak point; and I could get a reference for a future employer.' Another man commented, 'you don't get a lot of people you can sit down and talk to. He [the instructor] was interesting and not demanding. I think that's the right way to be'.

THE INADEQUACY OF STEREOTYPES

We now present evidence from our case studies to show the diversity of conditions experienced by the long-term unemployed and the inadequacy of stereotypes about the 'hard-core'.

Through presenting three 'typical' case studies of men attending the course, we hope to cast some light on the issue of how far the men attending RECs are a special category among the unemployed. In addition, we hope by setting out how the men themselves describe their situation, to portray something of the conditions experienced by unemployed people in Britain today, in particular their over-whelming sense of isolation, neglect and rejection.

Mr Smith

Mr Smith was thirty-seven, divorced, and living alone in a private rented bedsitter. His last job had been as a cleaner at a sports centre. He had worked there for eighteen months, the last twelve of which had been on night shift. He left because he felt he was being over-worked at low pay. He had since been unemployed for just over three years.

He left school at the age of thirteen, when he was sent to Borstal for two-and-a-half years. He had no educational qualifications. His first job had been as a van boy for a laundry company. He left this after two years to move to an area where he thought his prospects would be better. At the age of twenty-two he was taken on by a company as a coffee roaster and stayed for five years. The company trained him in this work, but this did not give him a formal qualific-ation. The reason he left this job, which he liked so much, was that his wife 'suddenly' left him and he said he 'just couldn't cope'. He had since then lost several jobs because of ill health.

When he first became unemployed, he did not sign on for any benefit for a year. He said that at the time he did not know he was entitled to claim. He got by doing odd jobs, getting just enough to keep going. He did not like claiming benefits, and would have much preferred to be working.

> It's nice to pay your own rent, I feel like a heel taking money I haven't earned. [Working] keeps you sane, stops you getting depressed, makes you look smarter, you wash in the mornings [and so on]. I'm a totally different person when I'm working – I'm happier because I'm independent and I know I can do the job well . . . it cheers me up a lot. . . . 'The social' think I don't want to work, say I've got to get out of my rut, but I've done something by coming here [to the REC].

When he first started the course, Mr Smith felt optimistic: 'now I'm started here, I know I'm all right – it was just that little kick that was needed . . .'. However, he only stayed on the course for nine days, and left because he said he found it difficult standing still in one place for long periods of time. Subsequently, he went on sick benefit for two months.

Mr Smith seemed to have too many problems for the course alone to solve. He was clearly very lonely and sad. Since his marriage break-up, he felt he had gone steadily downhill. He said that he didn't eat properly because he could not afford to, and he spent £5.60 of his £21 a week benefit on feeding his two cats. This payment of £21 was less than he should have been entitled to. Mr Smith felt it was too little but did not know why he received this amount.

He did not like 'to impose on his family', and 'had lost most of his friends through being unemployed'. His accommodation did little to help, as he lived alone in a small room and saw few people. Until recently he had had no television or radio. 'It gets me depressed, my room, just one room and a small window. It gets me down. I'm not happy here at all . . .'.

Mr Jones

Mr Jones was forty-two, married with one son aged eleven and had been unemployed for two years. He left school early at the age of twelve without any qualifications and spent the next four years working on a relative's farm in Ireland. At the age of twenty, he got a job working for a large building company doing concreting. This lasted for eight years until the firm went bankrupt, and he was made redundant. Apart from his current spell of unemployment, Mr Jones had been in almost constant employment, the longest time without work being only one week. The last job that he had was also concreting work for a large company from which he was made redundant after two years.

He was not very keen to attend the course, and was unsure as to why the unemployment review officer had suggested that he should go. The only explanation he could give was: 'Maybe they thought I was on the fiddle or something. They do think that about a lot of people, but I had no guilty conscience.'

Mr Jones attended the course for nine weeks. He was never late in the mornings and the only time he had off was a couple of days when he went job hunting.

He felt that attending the course would take him out of the house a bit but he could not see a lot of point in it as he was not being given any extra money for attending and that at his age he was too old to learn new skills. He had plenty of experience of gardening/ concreting type work so there was little to learn.

> To tell you the truth, I get fed up at times, I don't see myself getting anywhere really . . . Well, they're not doing much for me . . . And, like, they can't learn me anything more than I know already . . . it might be good for the young ones . . . but I'd say for a man of 40 . . .

Despite his doubts about the course, he received glowing reports from the instructors throughout.

> Week 1: He has maintained 100 per cent effort throughout. . . . At the moment he seems totally reliable and keen to prove himself.
> Week 4: Still maintaining a good working routine, and is displaying some initiative on the gardening work.
> Final report: His level of work is at Builders' Labouring Standard and we have no doubt he would make an ideal employee on this type of work. . . . We feel he should have no problems in attaining and holding down employment once building vacancies improve.

The longest time that Mr Jones had given up looking for jobs since he became unemployed was for six weeks over a Christmas period when there were very few jobs around because of the time of year.

In the few weeks prior to attending the course, he had been looking three to four days a week, and throughout the course he was looking every week and applied for five or six jobs. Between leaving the course and the time of the follow-up interview, he had applied for a further thirty jobs but all with no success. He believed that the best chance he had of getting work was by just turning up at the site and asking if any jobs were going. But he felt there was a very poor chance of his gaining work within the next few months because 'I don't think there seems to be much about, all you see is two or three men when there used to be 150, they're cutting the labour down'.

He was nevertheless very keen to find work and was spending a lot of his time looking:

> It's not that I wasn't trying, I'm always trying, if I see a phone number I'm on the phone. . . . I'm only one of the three and a half to four million. I used to look on the boards [Job Centre], but it was from eighteen to twenty-five-year olds they wanted.

Personal contact was very limited as a source of hearing about work. When asked to give three people he mixed with or saw most often, he said there was no one apart from his immediate family. He did not see his friends very often as he could no longer afford to go out with them.

Mr and Mrs Jones had no major debts, they had managed to scrape by, borrowing small amounts from neighbours and delaying payments to the butcher and milkman. Their relatives were in no position to help them as they had problems of their own. Their most recent worry had been trying to buy their son's school uniform as he had just started senior school.

> Things are not *really* bad, because we manage – but only just manage – to keep our heads above water. . . . There is times we have to have cheap dinners, can't have meat everyday. There are things you look at and say, it can last a bit longer; we haven't bought any clothes this year.

Mr Brown

Mr Brown is twenty-six, his wife is twenty and they have been married for three years. Their only son is ten months old. On leaving school at the age of fifteen, without any qualifications, Mr Brown first worked in a supermarket, shelf-filling. This lasted only three days, as he found the work boring. During the next four years, he was unemployed for one year and spent twelve months in borstal, and a couple of months in prison on a charge of Grievous Bodily Harm. In his early twenties, he got a permanent job with the council as a gardener, where he worked for two years, until he decided to leave with plans to work abroad. These never materialised and he was unemployed for several weeks before getting a labouring job on a building site. This lasted for a month. He left because he did not get on with the people he was working with and still had vague hopes of working abroad. Since then, for the last four years, Mr Brown had been unemployed except for a couple of months spent in prison on two or three occasions.

His feelings about attending the course were mixed. When first told about the place, he got the impression that he would receive some sort of training allowance, while during the first week or two of the course he felt it was like being back at school. Nevertheless, he stayed for twelve weeks. He became more involved with the course:

It gives you something to look forward to, you kinda feel a responsibility, you feel you are a part of the system, not just another reject on the dole like. . . .

He only had one day off and was late on just three occasions which enabled him to obtain a favourable final report:

. . . has made a continued effort to discipline himself into a working routine . . . has made a determined effort to gain himself a good grounding for employment. This has mainly been achieved by his excellent time-keeping and attendance, and in his single-mindedness to prove his worth as a worker.

In the three to four weeks before Mr Brown attended the course, he had not looked for work at all. In the previous six months he had been looking less than once a week, by asking friends and relatives if they knew of any jobs going. This he felt was the only way he stood a chance of getting work. The main reason why he was looking so little was that he had got tired of trying.

I was bored, I'd been looking for a job so long, that I just got bored, like I say, I know it ain't up to the government to find me a job, but you know I think they should have more options than just the Job Centre.

He did not apply for any jobs while he was at the REC, and only a couple after he left. When asked how many interviews he had had since becoming unemployed, he replied:

Loads, I lost count after the first year. In the first couple of years I used to go for loads, but [there was] always a catch, have to move, or start on trainee money or something. . . . I always think I haven't got a chance, so that it don't break me up if I don't get it – you got to take a slim view of getting it – with my record, I haven't got a chance.

He felt he had been unable to find work because there simply were not the jobs around and, in addition,

. . . whose going to take me on with my criminal record, it's in my past but they don't forget it – you're branded. It's like having a number tattoed on your head.

He saw a lot less of his friends than he used to, as the majority were working and he could not afford to go to the pub with them.

Mr and Mrs Brown had rent arrears, and owed £200 for electricity. They were paying these debts off weekly and had gas and electricity meters. They also had a carpet on hire purchase and about £400 of goods bought through a catalogue. They said that they had had to reduce the amount they spent on food a lot.

CONCLUSION

These three men differed in the degree to which they engaged with the REC course. Mr Smith hardly got into first gear, leaving after nine days; Mr Jones complied with the demands of the situation to the satisfaction of the instructors but he did not want to be there and did not feel he had gained anything; and Mr Brown after a slow start, accelerated by leaps and bounds, found the course satisfying and received a good final report. Like the other two, however, he remained unemployed afterwards.

Of the 134 men attending the course, on leaving 12 per cent went directly into a job and 7 per cent to attend a TOPS course. Of forty-two attenders followed up three months later, twelve managed to find some employment at some time after leaving. However, only seven were still working at that time. This was slightly better than for the thirty-two non-attenders, only five of whom were employed when interviewed.

The view that poor 'job search' activity contributes to unemployment underlies the rationale for re-establishment centres, together with the assumption that after being out of work for a time, skills and work discipline fade. These explanations now figure more prominently than the earlier stress of the fifties on the distinctive characteristics of the long-term unemployed and the 'repeat unemployed'. At this REC, job search activity saw a marked improvement because of the specific attention devoted to it by the instructors. A few men found jobs as a result. Others who found work, however, did so without attendance playing any obvious part in the process. Being put in touch with a job by a friend or relative was of more importance. Job chances were thought by the men to have been improved as a result of attendance but given the state of the labour market this generally proved a false optimism. Those who benefited most from the course did so for its educational value and because it provided a chance to meet people in similar circumstances and to share experiences.

The discipline function operated principally through the fact of being referred to an REC. Once there, emphasis was placed on the voluntary nature of attendance. However, the 'voluntariness' of attendance was undermined by the remaining fear of compulsion and the men's sense that they had to be seen to be playing the game, observing the rules, since there had been some threat to the safety of their social security payments, clearly a particularly marked constraint on those already heavily in debt.

About half the men were considered to be 'unemployable' at the end of their stay on the course. Now, however seriously these assessments are taken (and the instructors who had long experience of conditions in industry made their judgements in good faith), one must note that for some men the 'test' of employability [working at the REC] was not undertaken wholeheartedly. They did not see it as 'real work' and some were there unwillingly. The lack of any reward for working, or of a goal to work towards, other than the approval of the instructors, reduced considerably the effort they displayed.

However, it is clear that a large proportion of the men seen at this REC were competing under a disadvantage in the job market. Some lacked work experience; some lacked the skills to get on to a TOPS course; others had criminal records. Where employers value reliability and discipline (Blackburn and Mann, 1979) a course which gives men the chance to prove themselves might help in making them more attractive to potential employers. Others had more complex problems. Previous serious illness, depression or family problems might be better dealt with through medical and social services. A proportion, however, especially the sizeable group (about one third) drawn from the building trade, simply required an upturn in industry to improve their chances of re-employment.

One implicit function of RECs seemed to be to maintain the sexual division of labour within the household. In the absence of a real job to go to, it was thought beneficial for a man to pretend to be going out to work to maintain the conventional pattern of relationships in the family and neighbourhood. This was taken for granted as a 'good' by most unemployment review officers we spoke to. The system as a whole upholds this view quite explicitly since women are not referred. And a man who allowed himself to become 'too involved' in domestic labour would be judged as evidencing poor motivation to work or as not being 'available for work'.

Another interesting issue which emerged from our interviews had to do with the way dislike of RECs was expressed as 'like being back at school'. These men are the rejects of the conventional schooling system: the strata whom the educational system has failed and who have emerged with an antipathy to learning which reflects that experience.

Given the likely continuance of high unemployment to the end of the century without a radical change of policy, what are the prospects for the long-term unemployed? The toughening of treatment of the poor and unemployed which has developed in the 1980s (MacGregor, 1985) may increase further following the Fowler reviews of social security, but this reflects more the overriding desire to constrain public expenditure than a return to the much harsher attitudes and measures of the 1930s. At the same time, the development of MSC programmes has brought into focus the issue of the relation between MSC and DHSS provision. The future of re-establishment centres and resettlement centres (for homeless single men) will be under discussion in 1985. Charities may be asked to take over the resettlement centres or provide alternative accommodation. The training facilities provided by RECs may be transferred to MSC.

In a society which devotes relatively little attention to training in general, one may be excused for being less than sanguine about the kind of training that may be provided for the long-term unemployed. The Institute of Manpower Studies report, *Competence and Competition* (1984) records that British industry has not provided money for training and is unwilling to invest in training. In this context, some might look to government to take a lead but at present the Department of Employment is closing training centres and scrapping industrial training boards. The MSC is considering proposals to close twenty-nine Skillcentres involving the possible loss of 450 instructors' jobs. Plans for peripatetic instructors attached to workplaces are of little relevance to the long-term unemployed.

It seems then that for the men and their families trapped within the existing stereotypes of the 'hard core' and the confusion of objectives surrounding provision for the long-term unemployed, the prospect is one of continuing poverty and neglect. Pieces of wood may be thrown to some to keep them temporarily afloat but the lifeboat is not in sight. As one man replied ironically, when asked how he saw his future: 'like a fairy tale – Grimm'.

NOTE

1. This study was financed by a grant from the Department of Health and Social Security (DHSS) to whom we are grateful. The views expressed in this essay are those of the authors, not of DHSS. (An approach to the non-attenders contacted was made first by central office of DHSS providing them with the opportunity to refuse interview before we were allowed access and at this stage six men indicated that they did not wish to be included in the survey. A further six either refused interview when the interviewer called or could not be contacted at that address. Interviews were completed with 32 non-attenders. One man, although agreeing to be interviewed, asked not to have the data recorded on the computer and we complied with this request.)

Bibliography

P. Abrams, *The Origins of British Sociology: 1834–1914* (The University of Chicago Press, 1968).

D. H. Aldcroft, *The Interwar Economy, 1918–1939* (London: Batsford, 1970).

H. E. Aldrich, C. J. Cater, T. P. Jones and D. McEvoy, 'Business Development and Self Segregation: Asian Enterprise in Three British Cities', in C. Peach, V Robinson and S. Smith (eds), *Ethnic Segregation in Cities* (London: Croom Helm, 1981).

P. Allatt, Stereotyping: Familism in the Law', in B. Fryer, A. Hunt, D. McBarnet and B. Moorhouse (eds), *Law, State and Society* (London: Croom Helm, 1981).

P. Allatt, 'Men and War: Status, Class and the Social Reproduction of Maculinity', in E. Gamarnikow, D. Morgan, J. Purvis and D. Taylorson (eds), *The Public and the Private* (London: Heinemann, 1983).

S. Allen, 'Some Theoretical Problems in the Study of Youth', *Sociological Review*, 16 (1968) 319–331

S. Allen, 'Confusing Categories and Neglecting Contradictions' in E. Cashmore and B. Troyna (eds), *Black Youth in Crisis*, (London: Allen & Unwin, 1982a).

S. Allen, 'Continuity and Change in Production and Reproduction', (Paper presented to the World Congress of Sociology, Mexico City, 1982b).

S. Allen, S. Bentley and J Bornat, *Work, Race and Immigration* (University of Bradford School of Studies in Social Sciences, 1977).

S. Allen, K. Purcell, A. Waton and S. Wood (eds), *The Changing Experience of Employment: Restructuring and Recession* (London: Macmillan, 1986).

M. Anwar, *Young People and the Job Market* (London: Commission for Racial Equality, 1982).

D. Ashton and M. Maguire, 'Young Women in the Labour Market: Stability and Change', in R. Deem (ed.), *Schooling for Women's Work* (London: Routledge & Kegan Paul, 1980).

D. Ashton and M. Maguire, *Youth in the labour market*, Research Paper No. 34 (London: Department of Employment, 1982).

D. Ashton and M. Maguire, *The Vanishing Youth Labour Market* (London: Youthaid, 1983).

D. Ashton and M. Maguire, *Young People and the Labour Market* Department of Employment Research Paper (London: Department of Employment, forthcoming).

D. Ashton, M. Maguire and V. Garland, *Youth in the Labour Market*, Research Paper No. 34 (London: Department of Employment, 1982).

K. C. Backett, *Mothers and Fathers* (New York: St. Martin's Press, 1982).

C. Bagley, S. Jacobson, and C. Palmer, 'Social Structure and the Ecological Distribution of Mental Illness, Suicide, and Delinquency', *Psychological Medicine*, 3 (1973) 177–87.

E. W. Bakke, *The Unemployed Man* (London: Nisbet, 1933).

J. Bancroft, A. Skrimshire, F. Reynolds, S. Simkin, and J. Smith, 'Self-Poisoning and Self-Injury in the Oxford Area: Epidemiological Aspects 1969–73, *British Journal of Preventive and Social Medicine*, 29 (1975) 170–7.

E. C. Banfield, *The Moral Basis of a Backward Society* (New York: The Free Press, 1958).

M. H. Banks and P. R. Jackson, 'Unemployment and Risk of Minor Psychiatric Disorder in Young People: Cross-Sectional and Longitudinal Evidence', *Psychological Medicine*, 12 (1982) 789–98

K. Barnard, 'Influence of Economic Instability on Health', in J. John, D. Schwefel and H. Zollner (eds), *Influence of Economic Instability on Health* (Berlin: Springer-Verlag, 1983).

C. Bell, 'The SSRC: Restructured and Defended' in C. Bell and H. Roberts (eds), *Social Researching* (London: Routledge & Kegan Paul, 1984).

D. Bell, N. Fraser, F. Kirwan and E. Tait, *Youth Unemployment: Some Key Questions?* (Scottish Centre of Political Economy, Heriot-Watt University, 1981).

W. H. Beveridge, 'An Analysis of Unemployment', *Economica* 3 (1936) 357–87.

W. H. Beveridge, 'An Analysis of Unemployment II', *Economica*, 4 (1937a) 1–17.

W. H. Beveridge, 'An Analysis of Unemployment III', *Economica*, 5 (1973b) 169–83.

W. H. Beveridge, *Full Employment in a Free Society* (London: Allen & Unwin, 1944).

W. H. Beveridge, *Voluntary Action* (London: Allen & Unwin, 1948).

R. Blackburn and M. Mann, *The Working Class in the Labour Market* (London: Macmillan, 1979).

N. Bosanquet and P. Doeringer, 'Is There a Dual Labour Market in Great Britain?, *Economic Journal*, LXXXIII (1973) 421–35.

A. K. Brah, *Culture and Identity: the Case of South Asians* (Milton Keynes: Open University, Course E354, Units 8–9, 1982).

A. K. Brah and R. Minhas, 'Structural Racism or Cultural Conflict?', in G. Weiner (ed.), *Just a Bunch of Girls: Feminist Approaches to Schooling* (Milton Keynes: Open University, 1985).

A. K. Brah and P. Golding, *The Transition from School to Work among Young Asians in Leicester* (Centre for Mass Communications, University of Leicester, 1983).

H. Bradley, 'Work, Home and the Restructuring of Jobs' in S. Allen, K. Purcell, A. Waton and S. Wood (eds), *The Changing Experience of Employment: Restructuring and Recession* (London: Macmillan, 1986).

N. Branson and M. Heinemann, *Britain in the Nineteen Thirties* (London: Weidenfeld & Nicholson, 1971).

P. Brelsford, G. Smith and A. Rix, *Give Us a Break: Widening Opportunities for Young Women within YOP/YTS*, Manpower Services Commission Research and Development Series No. 11, (Sheffield: Manpower Services Commission, Training Division, 1982).

British Association for the Advancement of Science, *Britain in Recovery* (London: British Association for the Advancement of Science, 1938).

British Youth Council (BYC), *Youth Unemployment: Causes and Cures* (London: British Youth Council, 1977).

D. Brooks, 'Young Blacks and Asians in the Labour Market – a Critical Overview', in *Racism, School and the Labour Market* (London: National Youth Bureau, 1983).

D. Brooks and K. Singh, *Aspirations Versus Opportunities: Asian and White School Leavers in the Midlands* (Walsall Council for Community Relations, Community Relations Council Leicester, Commission for Racial Equality, 1978).

C. Brown, *Black and White Britain* (London: Policy Studies Institute, 1984).

P. Brown, 'Schooling and the Schooling/Post-school Transition: an early assessment' (Paper presented to the British Sociological Association Annual Conference, Bradford, 1984).

I. Bruegel, 'Women as a Reserve Army of Labour: a Note on Recent British Experience', *Feminist Review*, 3 (1979) 12–23.

D. Buglass and J. C. Duffy, 'The Ecological Pattern of Suicide and Parasuicide in Edinburgh', *Social Science and Medicine*, 12 (1978) 241–53.

D. Buglass, J. Duffy and N. Kreitman, *A Register of Social and Medical Indices by Local Government Area in Edinburgh and the Lothians* (2 parts), (Edinburgh: Central Research Unit, Scottish Office, 1980).

N. Bunker and C. Dewberry, 'Unemployment behind Closed Doors', *Journal of Continuing Education*, 2 (1983) 37–45.

P. Burnhill, 'The Ragged Edge of Compulsory Schooling' in D. Raffe (ed.), *Fourteen to Eighteen* (Aberdeen University Press, 1984).

N. K. Buxton and D. H. Aldcroft (eds), *British Society Between the Wars* (London: Scolar Press, 1979).

A. Calder, *The Peoples War* (London: Jonathan Cape, 1968).

B. Campbell, *Wigan Pier Revisited* (London: Virago Press, 1984).

M. Campbell and D. Jones, *Asian Youth in the Labour Market* (Bradford College, 1981).

J. Campling, 'Centres for "layabouts" ', *New Society*, 44 (1978) 196–7.

M. Casson, *Youth Unemployment* (London: Macmillan, 1979).

R. Catalano and D. Dooley, 'Health Effects of Economic Instability: a Test of Economic Stress Hypothesis', *Journal of Health and Social Behavior*, 24, (1983) 46–60.

Cato, *The Guilty Men* (London: Gollancz, 1939).

R. Cavendish, *On the Line* (London: Routledge & Kegan Paul, 1982).

Central Statistical Office (CSO), *Social Trends 15, 1985* (London: HMSO, 1985).

Centre for Contemporary Cultural Studies (CCCS), *The Empire Strikes Back* (London: Hutchinson, 1982).

W. S. Churchill, Speech in the House of Commons, *Hansard*, vol. 4, col. 388, 1909, quoted in Low Pay Unit, *Who Needs Wages Councils?*, Pamphlet No. 24 (London: Low Pay Unit, 1983).

C. Clark, 'The Emerging Consensus . . .?', in A. Seldon (ed.), *Essays on the Interplay between Ideas, Interests and Circumstances in the first 25 years of the I.E.A.*, (London: Institute of Economic Affairs, 1981).

S. Cobb and S. V. Kasl, *Termination: the Consequences of Job Loss* (Cincinnati: National Institute for Occupational Safety and Health, 1977).

F. J. Coffield, C. Borril and S. Marshall, 'How Young People Try to Survive Being Unemployed', *New Society*, 64 (1983) 332–4.

R. M. Cohn, 'The Effect of Employment Status Change on Self Attitudes', *Social Psychology*, 41 (1978) 81–93.

M. Colledge, 'Economic Cycles and Health: Towards a Sociological Understanding of the Impact of the Recession on Health and Illness', *Social Science and Medicine*, 16 (1982) 1919–27.

Commission for Racial Equality (CRE), *Looking for Work: Black and White School Leavers in Lewisham* (London: Commission for Racial Equality, 1978).

P. Corrigan, *Schooling the Smash Street Kids* (London: Macmillan, 1979).

A. Coyle, *Redundant Women* (London: The Women's Press, 1984)

A. Cragg and T. Dawson, *Unemployed Women: a Study of Attitudes and Experience*, Research Paper No. 47 (London: Department of Employment, 1984).

C. Craig, J. Rubery, R. Tarling and F. Wilkinson, *Labour Market Structure, Industrial Organisation and Low Pay* Cambridge University Press, 1982).

B. Crick (ed), *Unemployment* (London: Methuen, 1981).

S. Cusack and J. Roll, *Families Rent Apart: a Study of Young People's Contributions to Their Parents' Housing Costs* (London: Child Poverty Action Group, 1985).

W. W. Daniel, *Racial Discrimination in England* (Harmondsworth: Penguin, 1968).

W. W. Daniel, *The Unemployment Flow Stage 1: Interim Report* (London: Policy Studies Institute, 1981).

R. Davies, 'Problems of Unemployment: Are Women Taking Men's Jobs?', *The Political Quarterly*, March (1931) 126–30.

L. Davidoff, *The Employment of Married Women in England*, unpublished MA thesis, University of London, 1956.

A. Deacon, 'Concession and Coercion: the Politics of Unemployment Insurance in the Twenties', in Saville, J. and Briggs, A. (eds), *Essays in Labour History*, vol. 3 (London: Croom Helm, 1977).

A. Deacon, *Scroungers and Welfare in the 1930s* (London: Greene & Sons, 1980).

A. Deacon, 'Unemployment and Politics since 1945' in B. Showler and A. Sinfield (eds), *Workless State* (Oxford: Martin Robertson, 1981).

R. Deem, 'Leisure, Women and Inequality', *Leisure Studies*, 1 (1982).

Department of Education and Science (DES), *Statistics of Further Education Students in England: 1982–3*, Statistical Bulletin 15/83 (London: Department of Education and Science, 1983).

Department of Employment (DoE), 'Characteristics of the Unemployed: Sample Survey, June 1973', *Employment Gazette*, 82 (March 1974).

Department of Employment (DoE), 'Compilation of the Unemployment Statistics', *Employment Gazette*, 90 (1982a) 389–93.

Department of Employment (DoE), *Time Rates of Wages and Hours of Work, 1982* (London: HMSO, 1982b).

Department of Employment (DoE), *Employment Gazette*, 92 (February 1984a).

Department of Employment (DoE), 'The Unemployed: Survey Estimates for 1983 Compared with the Monthly Count', *Employment Gazette*, 92 (August 1984b) 367–70.

J. Ditton and R. Brown, 'Why Don't They Revolt?', *British Journal of Sociology*, 32 (1981) 521–30.

M. Douglas, *Purity and Danger: an Analysis of the Concepts of Pollution and Taboo*, (London: Routledge & Kegan Paul, 1966).

M. Douglas, *Implicit Meanings: Essays in Anthropology* (London: Routledge & Kegan Paul, 1975).

E. Durkheim, *The Division of Labour in Society* (New York: The Free Press, 1964).

J. Eatwell and R. Green, 'The Economy and Socialism' in B. Pimlott (ed.), *Fabian Essays in Socialist Thought* (London: Heinemann and Gower, 1984).

Economist Intelligence Unit (EIU), *Coping with Unemployment: The Effects on the Unemployed Themselves* (London: Economist Intelligence Unit, 1982a).

Economist Intelligence Unit, *Unemployment in the U.K.* (London: Economist Intelligence Unit, 1982b).

P. Eisenberg and P. F. Lazarsfield, 'The Psychological Effects of Unemployment', *Psychological Bulletin*, 35 (1938) 358–90.

P. Elliot, 'Intellectuals, the Information Society and the Disappearance of the Public Sphere', *Media, Culture and Society*, 4 (1982) 243–78.

Eurobarometer, 'Public Opinion and Poverty in Britain', *Eurobarometer* (1982).

D. Finn, 'The Youth Training Scheme: a New Deal?', *Youth and Policy*, 1 (1983) 16–24.

D. Finn, 'Britain's Misspent Youth', *Marxism Today*, 28 (1984) 20–4.

D. Finn and S. Frith, *Education and the Labour Market* (Milton Keynes: Open University, Course E353, Unit 4, 1981).

R. Franey, *Poor Law* (London: CHAR, 1983).

M. Freedman, *The Process of Work Establishment* (New York: Columbia University Press, 1969).

S. Frith, 'Education, Training and the Labour Process' in M. Cole and R. Skelton (eds) *Blind Alley: Youth in a Crisis of Capital* (Ormskirk: Hesketh, 1980).

F. Frobel, J. Heinrichs and O. Kreye, *The New International Divison of Labour* (Cambridge University Press, 1980).

K. Fruensgaard, S. Benjaminsen, S. Joensen and K. Helstrup, 'Psychosocial Characteristics of a group of Unemployed Patients Consecutively Admitted to a Psychiatric Emergency Department', *Social Psychiatry*, 18 (1983) 137–44.

J. A. Furness, M. C. Kahn and P. T. Pickens, 'Unemployment and Parasuicide in Hartlepool, 1974–82' (Paper presented to Autumn meeting of Royal College of Psychiatrists, London, 1984).

Gallup Poll, 15 December 1984, reported in the *Observer*.

H. Gavron, *Captive Wife* (London: Routledge & Kegan Paul, 1966).

J. Gershuny and R. E. Pahl, 'Britain in the Decade of the Three Economies', *New Society* (1980) 7–9.

M. Glucksmann, 'Women and the "New Industries": Changes in Class Relations in the 1930s' (paper presented to ESRC Symposium on Social Stratification and Gender, University of East Anglia, July 1984).

P. Golding and S. Middleton, *Images of Welfare* (London: Macmillan, 1979).

P. Golding and S. Middleton, 'Making Claims: News Media and the Welfare State', *Media, Culture and Society*, 1 (1980) 1–27.

N. Goldstein, 'The New Training Initiative: a Great Leap Backwards', *Capital and Class*, 23 (1984) 83–106.

J. H. Goldthorpe, 'The Current Inflation: Towards a Sociological Account' in F. Hirsch and J. H. Goldthorpe (eds), *The Political Economy of Inflation* (Oxford: Martin Robertson, 1978).

J. H. Goldthorpe, 'The End of Convergence: Corporatist and Dualist Tendencies in Modern Western Societies' (Paper presented to the SSRC Labour Market Conference, Manchester, 1983; a revised version in J. H. Goldthorpe (ed.), *Order and Conflict in West European Capitalism* Oxford University Press, forthcoming).

L. Gow and A. McPherson, *Tell Them from Me* (Aberdeen University Press, 1980).

A. Green, 'Education and Training: under New Masters' in A. Wolpe and J. Donald, *Is There Anyone Here From Education?* (London: Pluto Press, 1983).

F. Green (ed.), *Time to Spare: What Unemployment Means by Eleven Unemployed* (London: Allen & Unwin, 1935).

Guardian, 25 September 1984.

C. Hakim, *Occupational Segregation*, Research Paper No. 9 (London: Department of Employment, 1979).

C. Hakim, 'The Social Consequences of High Unemployment', *Journal of Social Policy*, 11, (1982) 433–67.

C. Hakim, 'Homework and Outwork', *Employment Gazette*, 92 (January 1984a) 7–13.

C. Hakim, 'Employers Use of Homework, Outwork and Freelance', *Employment Gazette*, 92 (April 1984b) 144–50.

S. Hall and T. Jefferson, *Resistance through Rituals* (London: Hutchinson, 1976).

S. Hall, C. Critcher, T. Jefferson, J. Clarke and B. Robert, *Policing the Crisis* (London: Macmillan, 1978).

L. Hannah, The Rise of the Corporate Economy, 2nd edn (London: Methuen, 1983).

M. Harris, 'How Unemployment Affects People', *New Society*, 68 (1984) 88–90.

J. Hartley and D. Fryer, 'The Psychology of Unemployment: a Critical Appraisal', in G. M. Stephenson and J. H. Davis (eds), *Progress in Applied Social Psychology*, vol. 2 (London: John Wiley, 1984).

K. Hawton, J. O'Grady, M. Osborn and D. Cole, 'Adolescents Who Take

Overdoses: Their Characteristics, Problems and Contact with Helping Agencies', *British Journal of Psychiatry*, 140 (1982) 118–23.

D. Hebdige, *Subcultures* (London: Methuen, 1979).

S. Henry, 'The Working Unemployed', *Sociological Review*, 30 (1982) 460–77.

M. Hill, R. Harrison, A. Sargeant and V. Talbot, *Man Out of Work: a Study of Unemployment in Three English Towns* (Cambridge University Press, 1973).

D. Hirsch, *Youth Unemployment: a Background Paper* (London: Youthaid, 1983).

T. A. Holding, D. Buglass, J. C. Duffy and N. Kreitman, 'Parasuicide in Edinburgh – A Seven Year Review 1968–74', *British Journal of Psychiatry*, 130 (1977) 534–43.

J. Hubbuck and S. Carter, *Half a Chance: a Report on Job Discrimination Against Young blacks in Nottingham* (London: Commission for Racial Equality, 1980).

R. Hughes, *The Best Years* (Aberdeen University Press, 1984).

J. Hunt and P. Small, *Employing Young People: a Study of Employers' Attitudes, Policies and Practices* (Edinburgh: Scottish Council for Research in Education, 1981).

G. Hutchinson, N. Barr and A. Drobny, 'The Employment of Young Males in a Segmented Labour Market: the Case of Great Britain', *Applied Economics*, vol. XVI (1984) 187–204.

U. Huws, 'New Technology Homeworkers', *Employment Gazette*, 92 (January 1984) 13–17.

R. Hyman and B. Price, 'Labour Statistics', in J. Irvine, I. Miles and J. Evans (eds), *Demystifying Social Statistics* (London: Pluto Press, 1979).

Institute of Manpower Studies (IMPS), *Competence and Competition* (Institute of Manpower Studies, University of Sussex, 1984).

J. Irvine, I. Miles and J. Evans, *Demystifying Social Statistics* (London: Pluto Press, 1979).

M. Jahoda, *Employment and Unemployment* (Cambridge University Press, 1982).

M. Jahoda, P. F. Lazarsfeld and H. Zeisal, *Marienthal* (London: Tavistock, 1933).

R. Jenkins, *Lads, Citizens and Ordinary Kids* (London: Routledge & Kegan Paul, 1983).

R. Jenkins, A. Bryman, J. Ford, T. Keil and A. Beardsworth, 'Information in the Labour Market: the Impact of Recession', *Sociology*, 17 (1983) 260–7.

H. Jennings, *Brynmawr: a Study of a Distressed Area* (London: Allenson, 1934).

J. Jolly, S. Creigh and A. Mingay, *Age as a Factor in Employment*, Research Paper No. 11 (London: Department of Employment, 1980).

D. Caradog Jones (ed.), *The Social Survey of Merseyside*, 3 vols (Liverpool University Press, 1934).

P. Jones, *What Opportunities for Youth?: Deteriorating Employment Prospects for School Leavers and the Role of Government Schemes* (London: Youthaid, 1984).

B. Jordan, 'Unemployment and the British Political System', *Parliamentary Affairs*, 4 (1982) 408–20.

S. V. Kasl, 'Changes in Mental Health Status Associated with Job Loss and Retirement', in J. E. Barrett *et al.* (eds), *Stress and Mental Disorder* (New York: Raven Press, 1976).

H. Kay, 'Is Childminding Real Work?', *Employment Gazette*, 92 (November 1984) 483–6.

W. Keegan, *Mrs. Thatcher's Economic Experiment* (London: Allen Cave, 1984).

P. Kennedy and N. Kreitman, 'An Epidemiological Survey of parasuicide ('Attempted Suicide') in General Practice', *British Journal of Psychiatry*, 123 (1973) 23–4.

N. Kessel, 'Self-Poisoning', *British Medical Journal*, 2 (1965) 1265–70 and 1336–40.

A. Kessel, A. Nicholson, G. Graves and J. Krupinski, 'Suicidal Attempts in an Outer Region of Metropolitan Melbourne and in a Provincial Region of Victoria', *Australia and New Zealand Journal of Psychiatry*, 9 (1975) 255–61.

K. M. Koller and R. C. M. Cotgrove, 'Social Geography of Suicidal Behaviour in Hobart', *Australia and New Zealand Journal of Psychiatry*, 10 (1976) 237–42.

M. Komarovsky, *Blue Collar Marriage* (New York: Random House, 1962).

W. Kornhauser, *The Politics of Mass Society* (London: Routledge & Kegan Paul, 1960).

M. Krafchik, 'Long-term Unemployment in the 1930s: the Construction of a Social Category', (paper presented to the British Sociological Association Annual Conference, Bradford, 1984).

N. Kreitman, 'Social and Clinical Aspects of Suicide and Attempted Suicide', in A. Forrest (ed.), *A Companion to Psychiatric Studies*, vol. 1 (Edinburgh: Churchill Livingstone, 1973).

N. Kreitman (ed.), *Parasuicide*, (London: John Wiley, 1977).

N. Kreitman, 'The Epidemiology of Suicide and Parasuicide', *Crisis*, 2 (1981) 1–13.

N. Kreitman, 'Suicide and Parasuicide', in R. E. Kendall and A. K. Zealley (eds), *Companion to Psychiatric Studies*, 3rd edn (Edinburgh: Churchill Livingstone, 1983).

N. Kreitman and J. A. T. Dyer, 'Suicide in Relation to Parasuicide', *Medicine*, 36 (1980) 1827–30.

N. Kreitman, A. E. Philip, S. Creer and C. R. Bagley, 'Parasuicide', (letter), *British Journal of Psychiatry*, 115 (1969) 746–7.

H. Land, 'The Boundaries between the State and the Family', in C. C. Harris (ed.), *The Sociology of the Family: New Directions in Britain*, Sociological Review Monograph No. 28 (University of Keele, 1979).

H. Land, 'Poverty and Gender: the Distribution of Resources within the Family' in M Brown (ed.), *The Structure of Disadvantage* (London: Heineman, 1983).

R. Layard, *Youth Unemployment in Britain and the US compared*, Discussion Paper No. 52 (Centre for Labour Economics, London School of Economics, 1979).

D. Lee, 'Skill, Craft and Class: a Theoretical Critique and a Critical Case', *Sociology*, 15 (1981) 56–78.

G. Lee and J. Wrench, *Skill Seekers* (London: National Youth Bureau, 1983).

R. M. Lee, C. C. Harris and L. Morris, 'Aspects of the Everyday Life of the Redundant: the Place of Informal Relations' (Paper presented to the E.S.R.C. Conference 'Urban Change and Conflict', January 1983).

Leicester City and Leicestershire County Council, *Survey of Leicester 1983* (1984)

D. Leonard, *Sex and Generation: a Study of Courtship and Weddings* (London: Tavistock, 1980).

D. Lester, *Why People Kill Themselves: a Summary of Research Findings on Suicidal Behaviour* (Springfield, Illinois: Charles C. Thomas, 1972).

J. Lewis, 'In Search of Real Equality: Women between the Wars' in F. Gloversmith, *Class, Culture and Social: Change, a New View of the 1930s* (Brighton: Harvester Press, 1980).

R. Lipsey, *An Introduction to Positive Economics*, 5th edn (London: Weidenfeld & Nicolson, 1979).

R. Livock, *Screening in the Recruitment of Young Workers*, Research Paper No. 41 (London: Department of Employment, 1983).

Low Pay Unit, *Who Needs Wages Councils?*, Pamphlet No. 24 (London: Low Pay Unit, 1983).

M. Lowenthal, 'Non-Market Transactions in an Urban Community' in S. Henry (ed.), *Can I Have It in Cash?* (London: Astragal Books, 1981).

S. Lukes, *Power: a Radical View* (London: Macmillan, 1974).

A. J. Lush, *The Young Adult in South Wales* (Cardiff, South Wales and Monmouthshire Council of Social Services, 1941).

L. Lynch and R. Richardson, 'Unemployment of Young Workers in Britain', *British Journal of Industrial Relations*, xx (1982) 362–72.

S. MacGregor, 'Making Sense of Social Security?' in P. Jackson (ed.), *Implementation of a Philosophy: UK Conservative Government Policies 1979–83* (London: RIPA, 1985).

L. McKee, *The First Months of Motherhood*, Research Monograph No. 3 (London: Health Education Council, 1980).

L. McKee, ' "Wives" and the Recession' (Birmingham Health Authority, 1983).

L. McKee, 'Parenthood: a Youth Training Scheme for Some', (Paper presented to National Conference on Health Education and Youth, Southampton, September 1984).

L. McKee and C. Bell, 'Marital and Family Relations in Times of Male Unemployment' in R. Finnegan, D. Gallie and B. Roberts (eds), *New Approaches to Economic Life* (Manchester University Press, 1985).

L. McKee and C. Bell, 'His Unemployment/Her Problem', (original (larger) version of this paper presented at British Sociological Association Annual Conference, April 1984).

A. McRobbie, 'Settling Accounts with Subcultures: a Feminist Critique', in T. Bennett, G. Martin, C. Mercer and J. Woolacott (eds), *Culture, Ideology and Social Process* (Milton Keynes: Open University Press, 1981).

N. Madge, 'Unemployment and Its Effect on Children', *Journal of Child Psychology and Psychiatry*, 24 (1983) 311–19.

P. Makeham, *Youth Unemployment: an Examination of Evidence on Youth Unemployment Using National Statistics*, Research Paper No. 10 (London: Department of Employment, 1980).

Manpower Services Commission (MSC), *The Coventry Report*, Report of the Steering Committee of the Coventry Manpower Services Project (London: Manpower Services Commission, 1977).

Manpower Services Commission (MSC), *Young People and Work*: *Manpower Studies*, No. 19781 (London: HMSO, 1978).

G. Markall and D. Finn, *Young People and the Labour Market: A Case Study*, Inner Cities Research Programme No. 5 (London: Department of the Environment, 1981).

D. Marsden, *Workless: an Exploration of the Social Contract Between Society and the Worker* (London: Croom Helm, 1982).

D. Marsden and E. Duff, *Workless* (Harmondsworth: Penguin, 1975).

G. Marshall, 'On the Sociology of Women's Unemployment, its Neglect and Significance', *Sociological Review*, 32 (1984) 234–59.

J. Martin and C. Roberts, *Women and Employment: a Lifetime Perspective* (London: HMSO, 1984).

R. Martin and J. G. Wallace, *Working Women in Recession: Employment, Redundancy and Unemployment* (Oxford University Press, 1984).

D. Massey, 'The Shape of Things to Come', *Marxism Today*, 27 (1983) 18–27.

K. Mathews, 'National Income and the Black Economy' *Journal of Economic Affairs*, 3 (1983) 261–7.

W. Merriless and R. Wilson, *Disequilibrium in the Labour Market for Young People in Great Britain*, Discussion Paper No. 10 (University of Warwick, Manpower Research Group, 1979).

K. Middlemass and J. Barnes, *Stanley Baldwin: a Biography* (London: Macmillan, 1971).

K. Middlemass *Politics in Industrial Society* (London: Andre Deutsch, 1979).

I. Miles, *Adaptation to Unemployment?*, SPRU occasional paper Series No. 20 (Science Policy Research Unit, University of Sussex, August 1983).

F. M. Miller, 'The Unemployment Policy of the National Government', *Historical Journal*, 12 (1976) 449–67.

C. W. Mills, *The Sociological Imagination* (Oxford University Press, 1959).

Ministry of Labour, 'Characteristics of the Unemployed 1961', *Ministry of Labour Gazette*, 70 (1962) 131–37 and 347–9.

Ministry of Labour, 'Enquiry into the Characteristics of the Unemployed', *Ministry of Labour Gazette*, 73 (1965).

P. Moen, 'Family Impacts of the 1975 Depression: Duration of Unemployment', *Journal of Marriage and the Family*, 41 (1979) 561–72.

B. Moore, Jr., *Injustice: the Social Basis of Obedience and Revolt* (New York: M. E. Sharpe, 1978).

L. Morris, '*Renegotiation of the Domestic Division of Labour in the Context of Male Redundancy* (Paper presented to The British Sociological Association Conference, Cardiff, 1983).

L. Morris, 'Patterns of Social Activity and Post-Redundancy Labour-Market Experience', *Sociology*, 18 (1984) 337–52.

R. Murray, 'New Directions in Municipal Socialism', in B. Pimlott (ed.) *Fabian Essays in Socialist Thought* (London: Heinemann and Gower, 1984).

National Youth Employment Council (NYEC), *Unqualified, Untrained and Unemployed* (London: HMSO, 1974).

Office of Population Censuses and Surveys (OPCS), *Classification of Occupations 1970* (London: HMSO, 1970).

Office of Population Censuses and Surveys (OPCS), *1981 Census of Population* (London: HMSO, 1983).

M. O'Higgins 'The Relationship between the Formal and Hidden Economics: an Explanatory Analysis for Four Countries' in A. Wenig and W. Gaetner (eds), *The Economics of the Shadow Economy* (Berlin: Springer-Verlag, 1984a).

M. O'Higgins 'Assessing the Unobserved Economy in the United Kingdom' in E. Feige (ed.), *The Unobserved Economy* (Cambridge University Press, 1984b).

Organisation for Economic Co-operation and Development (OECD), *Youth Unemployment: the Causes and Consequences* (Paris: OECD, 1980).

G. Orwell, *Down and Out in London and Paris* (London: Gollancz, 1933).

G. Orwell, *The Road to Wigan Pier* (London: Gollancz, 1937).

A. D. K. Owen, *A Report on Unemployment in Sheffield*, Survey Pamphlet No. 4 (Sheffield Social Survey Committee, 1932).

J. Pahl, 'The Allocation of Money and the Structuring of Inequality within Marriage', *Sociological Review*, 31 (1983) 237–62.

R. E. Pahl, *'Divisions of Labour'* (Blackwell, 1984).

R. E. Pahl and C. D. Wallace, 'Household Work Strategies in an Economic Recession' in N. D. Redcliffe and E. Mingione (eds.), *Beyond Employment*, (Blackwell, 1985a).

R. E. Pahl and C. D. Wallace, 'Forms of Work and Privatisation on the Isle of Sheppey' in B. Roberts, R. Finnegan and D. Gallie (eds), *New Approaches to Economic Life: Economic Restructuring, Unemployment and the Social Division of Labour* (Manchester University Press, 1985b).

H. Parker, 'Social Security Foments the Black Economy', *Journal of Economic Affairs*, 3 (1982) 32–5.

T. Parsons and F. R. Bales, *Family, Socialization and Interaction Process* (London: Routledge & Kegan Paul, 1956).

Pilgrim Trust, *Men Without Work* (Cambridge University Press, 1938).

B. Pimlott, *Labour and the Left in the 1930s* (Cambridge University Press, 1977).

B. Pimlott, 'New Politics', in B. Pimlott (ed.), *Fabian Essays in Socialist Thought* (London: Heinemann and Gower, 1984).

S. Platt, Unemployment and Suicidal Behaviour: a Review of the literature', *Social Science and Medicine*, 19 (1984) 93–115.

S. Platt and N. Kreitman, 'Trends in Parasuicide and Unemployment among Men in Edinburgh, 1962–82', *British Medical Journal*, 289 (1984) 1029–32.

S. Platt, J. Foster and N. Kreitman, *Parasuicide in Edinburgh 1982: a Report on Admissions to the Regional Poisoning Treatment Centre* (Edinburgh: MRC Unit for Epidemiological Studies in Psychiatry, 1983).

A. Plummer, *New British Industries in the Twentieth Century* (London: Pitman, 1937).

A. Pollert, *Girls, Wives, Factory Lives* (London: Macmillan, 1981).

Polycell, *The Polycell Report on the DIY Market* (London: Paragon Communications, 1981).

K. Purcell, 'Work, employment and unemployment', in R. Burgess (ed.) *Key Variables in Social Research* (London: Routledge & Kegan Paul, 1985).

D. Raffe, 'Can There Be an Effective Youth Unemployment Policy?', in R. Fiddy (ed.), *In Place of Work: Policy and the Provision for the Young Unemployed*, (Lewes, Sussex: Falmer Press, 1983).

D. Raffe, 'The Effects of Industrial Change on School-Leaver Employment in Scotland: a Quasi-Shift-Share Analysis' (Edinburgh: Centre for Educational Sociology, 1984a).

D. Raffe (ed.), *Fourteen to Eighteen* (Aberdeen University Press, 1984b).

D. Raffe, 'The Transition from School to Work and the Recession: Evidence from the Scottish School Leavers Surveys 1977–1983', *British Journal of Sociology of Education*, v (1984c) 247–65.

D. Reeder, 'A Recurring Debate: Education and Industry', in G. Bernbaum (ed.), *Schooling in Decline* (London: Macmillan, 1979).

T. Rees, 'Boys off the Street and Girls in the Home: Youth Unemployment and State Intervention in Northern Ireland', in R. Fidday (ed.), *In Place of Work* (Lewes, Sussex Falmer Press, 1983).

T. Rees and D. Gregory, 'Youth Employment and Unemployment: A Decade of Decline', *Educational Analysis*, iii (1981) 7–24.

K. Roberts, *School Leavers and their Prospects* (Milton Keynes: Open University Press, 1984).

K. Roberts, J. Duggan and M. Noble, 'Ignoring the Signs; Young, Unemployed, and Unregistered', *Employment Gazette*, 89 (1981) 353–6.

R. Rose, *Getting by in the Three Economies*, CSPP Studies in Public Policy No. 110 (Centre for Study of Public Policy, University of Stratchclyde, 1983).

J. Rubery and R. Tarling, 'Women in the Recession', *Socialist Economic Review* (London: Merlin Press, 1982).

Runnymede Trust, *Employment, Unemployment and the Black Population* (London: Runnymede Trust, 1981).

Runnymede Trust, *Bulletin*, 159 (September 1983).

A. Sawdon and D. Taylor, *Youth Unemployment: a Background Paper* (London: Youthaid, 1980).

A. Sawdon, S. Tucker and J. Pelican, *Study of the Transition from School to Working Life* (London: Youthaid, 1979).

P. Scannel, 'Broadcasting and the Politics of Unemployment', *Media, Culture and Society*, 2 (1980) 1–27.

J. Seabrook, *Unemployment* (London: Quartet Books, 1982).

J. Seabrook, 'Unemployment Now and in the 1930s' in B. Crick (ed.), *Unemployment* (London: Methuen, 1981).

J. Seaton, 'Politics and the Media in Britain', *The Journal of Western European Politics*, 1 (1985).

H. C. Selvin, 'Durkheim's "Suicide" and Problems of Empirical Research', *American Journal of Sociology*, 63 (1958) 607–19.

P. Sherridan, *Career Aspirations and Prospects of Asian and Indigenous Students in Suburban and Inner-City Leicster*, B. Ed. dissertation, Leicester Polytechnic, 1982.

A. Sills, M. Tarpey and P. Golding, *Asians in the Inner City* (Inner Area Research Project Social Survey, Centre for Mass Communication Research, University of Leicester, 1982).

A. Sinfield, *What Unemployment Means* (Oxford: Martin Robertson, 1981).

A. Sivanandan, 'Imperialism and Disorganic Development in the Silicon Age', *Race and Class*, xx1 (1979) 111–26.

R. Skidelsky, *Politicians and the Slump* (Oxford University Press, 1965).

R. Skidelsky, *Maynard Keynes*, vol. I (London: Macmillan, 1983).

D. J. Smith, *Racial Disadvantage in Employment* (London: Political and Economic Planning, 1974).

D. J. Smith, *Unemployment and Racial Minorities* (London: Policy Studies Institute, 1981).

A. Stafford, 'Learning not to Labour', *Capital and Class*, 13 (1981) 55–78.

E. Stengel and H. G. Cook, *Attempted Suicide: Its Social Significance and Effects* (London: Chapman & Hall, 1985).

J. Stern, *Unemployment and its Impact on Morbidity and Mortality*, L S E Discussion Paper No. 93 (London: Centre for Labour Economics, 1981).

J. Stern and A. Burchall, *The Effect of Re-establishment Centres on Subsequent Employment: An Evaluation*, Government Economic Service Working Paper No. 68 (London: Department of Health and Social Security, 1984).

J. Stevenson and C. Cook, *The Slump* (London: Quartet Books, 1979).

J. Stevenson, 'The Making of Unemployment Policy 1931–35' in M. Bentley and J. Stevenson (eds), *High and Low Politics* (Oxford University Press, 1983).

R. Strachey, 'Married Women and Work', *Contemporary Review* 145 (1935) 332–6.

Sunday Times, February 1984.

Supplementary Benefit Commission (SBC), *Annual Report 1975*, Cmnd 6615 (London: HMSO, 1976).

R. Taylor, *Workers and the New Depression* (London: Macmillan, 1982).

K.-D. Thomann, 'The Effects of Unemployment on Health and Public Awareness of this in the Federal Republic of Germany', in J. John, D. Schwefel and H. Zollner (eds), *Influence of Economic Instability on Health* (Berlin: Springer-Verlag, 1983).

L. E. Thomas, E. McCabe and J. E. Berry, 'Unemployment and Family Stress: a Reassessment', *Family Relations*, 29 (1980) 517–24.

M. Tiggemann and A. H. Winefield, 'Some Psychological Effects of Unemployment in School-Leavers', *Australian Journal of Social Issues*, 15 (1980) 269–76.

The Times, 'Unemployment and the Future', *The Times*, 15–20 June 1970.

P. Townsend and N. Davidson, *Inequalities in Health* (Harmondsworth: Penguin Books, 1982).

B. Troyna and D. I. Smith, *Racism, School and the Labour Market* (London: National Youth Bureau, 1983).

R. Tyrrell and M. Shanks, 'Long Term Unemployment: Why It Is a Problem and What We Can Do To Solve It', *Work and Society* (1982).

Unemployment and Health Study Group, *Unemployment, Health and Social Policy* (Nuffield Centre for Health Service Studies, University of Leeds, 1984).

UK Census of England and Wales for 1931, *General Report* (London: HMSO, 1950).

S. Walby, 'Patriarchal Structures: the Case of Unemployment' in E. Gamarnikow, D. H. J. Morgan, J. Purvis and D. E. Taylorson, (eds), *Gender, Class and Work* (London: Heinemann, 1983).

C. Wallace, *Informal Work in Two Neighbourhoods*, Appendix II to E.S.R.C. Final Report Grant No. G/00/23/0036/1 (1984).

C. Wallace, *School, Work and Uemployment: Social and Cultural Reproduction on the Isle of Sheppey*, unpublished PhD thesis, University of Kent at Canterbury, 1985.

P. Warr, 'Economic Recession and Mental Health: a Review of Research', *Tijdschrift voor Social Gezondheidszorg*, 62 (1984) 298–308.

P. Warr, 'Twelve Questions about Unemployment and Health', in B. Roberts, R. Finnegan and D. Gallie (eds), *New Approaches to Economic Life* (Manchester University Press, 1985).

P. Warr and P. R. Jackson, 'Self-Esteem and Unemployment Among Young Workers, *Le Travail Humain*, 46 (1983) 355–66.

A. G. Watts, *Education, Unemployment and the Future of Work* (Milton Keynes: Open University Press, 1983).

W. Wells, *The Relative Pay and Employment of Young People*, Research Paper No. 42 (London: Department of Employment, 1983).

S. Westwood, *All Day Every Day: Factory and family in the making of women's lives* (London: Pluto Press, 1984).

M. White, *Long-Term Unemployment and Labour Markets* (London: Policy Studies Institute, 1983).

B. Williamson, 'The Peripheralisation of Youth in the Labour Market: Problems, Analyses and Opportunities: Britain and the Federal Republic of Germany', in J. Ahier and M. Flude (eds), *Contemporary Educational Policy* (London: Croom Helm, 1983).

P. Willis, '*Learning to Labour*' (London: Saxon House, 1977).

P. Willis, 'Youth Unemployment', *New Society*, 67 (1984) 475–77; 68 (1984) 13–15, 57–9.

S. Winyard, *Fair Remuneration*? Report No. 11 (London: Low Pay Unit, 1982).

S. Wood (ed.), *The Degradation of Work? Skill, Deskilling and the Labour Process* (London: Hutchinson, 1981).

Subject Index

Author Index